new
HUMANISTIC
research

The New Humanistic Research Series will present to the teacher, the general reader, and the scholar the findings of research done in the fields of humane learning with the tools of the present. The humanities have traditionally included literature, art, music, history, and philosophy. Although many worthwhile projects have been pursued in these fields with the traditional tools (index cards, pencil, typewriter, paper clips), the moment has arrived when these ancient studies must shed their isolation and move into the present. To accomplish this, humanistic scholars have at hand the knowledge gained in other fields. They must become inter-disciplinary both in field and in technique.

The study of literature can be made more exact by the application of the techniques of modern stylistics. The definition of literature must be broadened to compass film and even television. Art includes problems involved with the display and storage of artistic objects. Musicology contains at its heart a number of bibliographical problems.

In fact, bibliography, repertory, index, and concordance are the major needs of our educational community and the intellectual world, to sort with sensible order the chaos of accumulation. Electronic machines are expert at this kind of data processing and are being used by some humanists who are unafraid of the tools of their time. This series will attempt to bring forth the results of their work in suitable form for the interested layman, teacher, scholar. New Humanistic Research employs every available tool in the pursuit of the truths that have ever challenged the humanist.

PROSE STYLE AND CRITICAL READING

Robert Cluett

Preface by
JOHN STEDMOND

TEACHERS COLLEGE PRESS
Teachers College, Columbia University
NEW YORK AND LONDON

Copyright©1976 by Teachers College, Columbia University
Library of Congress Catalog Card Number: 75-40035

Library of Congress Cataloging in Publication Data:

Cluett, Robert.
    Prose style and critical reading.

    (New humanistic research)
    Bibliography: p.
    1. English language—Style. 2. English prose
literature—History and criticism. I. Title.
PE1421.C57   426   75-40035
ISBN 0-8077-2491-2

Designed by Gustave Niles

Manufactured in the United States of America

*This book is dedicated
to the memory of*
LEE AHLBORN

SERIES EDITOR'S FOREWORD

THIS book is the third in the New Humanistic Research Series. Like its predecessors, it is based on the labor of a computer processing a large amount of humanistic data. Robert Cluett has attempted to present these results in a factual, detailed, and meaningful account of the characteristics of English prose between Philip Sidney and Anthony Burgess.

English prose style is notoriously difficult to discuss without falling into either subjective impressionism or excessive technicality. By examining samples consisting of some three hundred thousand words produced by eighty writers of prose, he has called our attention to the actual characteristics of these writers' language (with separate chapters devoted to Sidney, Carlyle, and Hemingway) and to the changes in English prose to which they may have contributed. By presenting the facts in a readable and spirited manner, he stimulates the reader's imagination to discover the patterns that lie in the quantities produced by the computer.

Anyone interested in the special harmony of prose will find much that is new here and much that will alter his views. The advanced entrepreneur, eager to conduct his own analysis, will find the present volume an indispensable guidebook on this new frontier.

LOUIS T. MILIC
Editor

PREFACE

DESPITE its increasing use in literary studies, the computer is still anathema to many traditional scholars. In a machine oriented age they cry out with D. H. Lawrence against "weird bright motor-productive mechanism," and would likely recoil with distaste from the idea of a computer inventory of prose style. Yet as the present volume demonstrates the application of quantitative methods to the study of writers as far removed from our technological times as Sidney and Milton can result in much valuable information and in fresh literary insights. Admittedly, quantity is not necessarily related to quality, but the data assembled by Professor Cluett and his associates reveal some of the bases on which value-judgments ultimately rest.

Concentration on the abstract structures to which all users of language must conform can enhance rather than limit appreciation of distinctive and individual manipulation of these structures. This study looks at both constant forms and stylistic types, making clear the problems involved in finding useful typological categories. Studies of individual writers, to which the bulk of the volume is devoted, turn out to be the most rewarding. The "richness" of Sidney's prose, the deceptive "simplicity" of Hemingway's, Carlyle's "awkwardness," all take on new meaning and significance when the linguistic phenomena that such adjectives attempt to characterize are thoroughly analyzed.

The York Project seeks to provide as exact a description as possible of certain syntactic aspects of a range of prose stylists from Ascham to such moderns as Mordecai Richler. As well as shedding light on individual writers, the Inventory also furnishes verifiable information about trends in literary prose over time. Although avoiding the slippery notion of "period styles," the study notes syntactic characteristics shared by writers roughly contemporary and indicates the kinds of "norms" that seem to exist, thus giving points of reference from which at least tentative generalizations can be drawn. However, Professor Cluett concludes that there cannot in fact be a "history of style," "but rather the chronicle of a succession of highly distinct and separate" styles.

The usefulness of the York Inventory will increase as its scope and flexibility are extended. Meanwhile this volume shows its value as a research tool and as an aid to the critical reading and fuller understanding of literary texts.

JOHN STEDMOND
Queen's University

ACKNOWLEDGMENTS

THE labors of many people go into the making of a book, especially when the book is technical in character and involves a research project now in its sixth year. In addition, in this case there has been institutional support for both the project and the book, without which neither would have been possible.

The Canada Council, having given several grants totalling $21,000, has been essential to the enterprise. York University has also given generous support in several ways: the Graduate Faculty has provided a Research Assistant for each of the last four years; the Faculty of Arts provided a summer assistant in 1971 and in 1973; the Master of Winters College has given us work space and an office in which to keep our files and our ever-growing yardage of computer output. The Cartographic Office of the York Department of Geography, under the supervision of Miss H. Guzewska, was unfailingly helpful in the production of the 130 figures that appear in the book. The York Department of Information and Publications and its Director, Michael Ecob, were similarly helpful in the setting of type for the tables.

People have been invaluable, especially the translators, those who parse text and convert it into the York syntactic code. These would include Tom Greenwald, Michael Rehner, Derek Dalton, Louise MacDonald, Eva Epstein, Cynthia Rehner, and Judith Fitzgerald. Our programmer, Professor G. J. Carpenter of the Royal Military College, has given tirelessly of himself and his ingenuity in responding to every whim that we have had about ways to strip a text electronically.

His assistants, Richard Levine and Patricia Mallon, have followed the example of his commitment. The two project managers, Donna MacLachlan in the early going and, more recently, Jan Bartley, have kept track of a task that seems at times to be inhumanly complex. Our three cartographers—Robert P. Ryan, Mrs. Carolyn Gondor, and Mrs. Carol Randall—have been competent and cheerful as they have dealt with our offbeat material; similarly our typist, Mrs. Lorraine MacLeod. Finally, there is our Jill-of-all-trades, Miss Joan Laurence, who has served as translator and bibliographer and in the months before publication as (unenviable task!) reader of the galley and page proofs of this book.

As for scholarly indebtedness to a number of people, it is evident everywhere. It would be redundant to mention here the editor of the series and his influence on this work. It is not so to mention Professors Marjorie Nicolson and Joseph Mazzeo, my mentors in graduate school, for although they do not appear here by citation, their imprint is everywhere.

R.C.

Toronto, Ontario
January 1976

CONTENTS

LIST OF TABLES

LIST OF FIGURES

> But our author respecting nether the subtiltie of thone part, nor the an-
> tiquitie of thother, thinketh it fittest according to the simplicitie of
> common understanding, to begin with Ianuarie . . . So, therefore be-
> ginneth he, and so continueth he throughout.
>
> Edmund Spenser, The Shepheardes Calendar

Chapter 1

INTRODUCTORY: This Book

SCHOLARS in the field of stylistics have been more than once compared to the early Hun tribesmen, who are said to have stood
around for days on end before their battles, boasting to get up their
courage. The comparison is not an idle one: in a recent bibliography
of style and stylistics,[1] the 534 entries between 1950 and 1967 contained 312 pieces dealing with theory and methodology, 222 dealing
with the phenomena of style itself. In the years since that bibliography appeared, there have been many articles published on style,
with no marked change visible to me in the 60–40 balance between
discussions of theory and examples of practice. In view of such cus-
toms, readers might reasonably expect a book with a title like this
one's to be centrally concerned with theory and method. In one
sense, this book *is* about theory and method, but only obliquely and
only to the extent that there is a theoretical and methodological co-
herence to the techniques from which the findings of the book are
derived. But it is the findings that are the real subject here—answers
to questions about the history of English style and about individual
stylists themselves.

Although our manner of proceeding will be largely quantitative,
this book is not *primarily* mathematical or statistical in its orientation. Since the advent of the computer, and with particular intensity
since the studies of Mosteller and Wallace in the early 1960's,[2]
scholars with mathematical or sociological interests have used literature as raw material for quantitative studies. These studies tend in
the Newtonian direction of what has been called "an exact science of
literature."[3] In other words, they tend toward a kind of scholarship

1

in which anyone, given the raw materials, the formulae, and the time
to bring the two together, will produce findings substantially similar
if not identical to anyone else's. Their main points of focus and their
main areas of success have been two: quantifiable differentiae between one literary genre and others,[4] and quantifiable differentiae
between one author and others.[5] Although I have great respect for
this work and for its value to the study of literature, I should make
clear now that my work is different from it in direction and emphasis.

My concerns begin in critical reading—the process whereby one
reader tries to make sense out of a literary text. By "making sense"
one means things well beyond the text's literal meaning; one means
formal features of design, of structure, of vocabulary, of allusion; one
means aspects of conscious control and unconscious habit, and indeed the process itself whereby the text was generated. Traditional
humanists, jealous of the web of words that so often has stood as a
spider's defense between them and the visible world, have been inclined to eschew explicitness in all its forms, especially numbers
and numerical treatments of literature. Their objections include the
fact that what is most obviously susceptible of quantification is often
unimportant in a literary interpretation; they also include the fact
that in submitting a text to quantitative treatment, the investigator
can turn the text into a mathematical or sociological object rather
than a literary one; finally, they include a host of Luddite responses
to definition and concreteness in all their forms, a Beckett-like ab-
horrence of trying to "eff the ineffable." The artifacts of this third
class of objection have been dealt with, indeed demolished, by the
editor of this series.[6] The second class has a certain merit; illiteration
being their favorite figure of speech, social scientists have not always fared well in their encounters with the printed word.[7] There
seems to me to be no *a priori* theological objection to other disci-
plines' using literature as fodder, however, just so long as what
comes of that use is not fobbed off on us as literary criticism. The first
class of objection—that what is enumerated is often inane—has
some basis in experience; it has been put forth convincingly by Brian
Vickers, who introduces his study of Bacon[8] with a lengthy citation
of quantified vacuities, by way of justifying his own method. Such
an exercise, however, can be performed on any kind of criticism,
more easily to be sure with some than with others, and what the exercise demonstrates is only that critical techniques are vehicles. Unless they are as rigidly bound as the techniques of Mosteller and
Wallace, at which point they become something other than criticism, they are dependent for their efficacy on intelligent and tactful
handling.

Both as an article of faith and as an empirical fact, I take it that intelligently handled data derived from objectively chosen samples can illuminate much in literature that is not visible to the naked eye plus much visible to the naked eye that we are too careless to see. It can also confirm or refute intuitions that cannot be tested in any other way. Finally, it can serve as a catalyst in the interaction between intellect and text. It is in these uses of quantitative material that this book interests itself, uses in which statistics augment rather than supplant the act of critical reading.

Once our preliminaries are done—a brief discussion of theoretical matters (Chapter 2) and a short description of the texts and data used (Chapter 3)—we shall concern ourselves entirely with literary style: style itself, stylistic types, individual stylists, aspects of stylistic history. I shall do as much that is particular as I can within the compass of a brief monograph. The chapters following Chapter 3 have as their primary end that discovery of constant form which is both the glory and the greatest reward of the act of reading; in a secondary function they are offered to scholars and students of literature as reassurance that the quest for rigorous demonstration and hard data in the humanities need not end at the gates of the Temple of Mammon.

It cannot without injustice be deny'd that they were men of extraordinary strength of mind: they had a great quickness of imagination, and subtility of distinguishing: they very well understood the consequence of propositions . . . But they lighted on a wrong path at first, and wanted matter to contrive: and so, like the Indians, onely express'd a wonderful Artifice, in the ordering of the same Feathers into a thousand Varities of Figures. I will not insist long on the Barbarousness of their style . . . rather stop a little, to examine the matter itself, and order in which they proceeded.

Thomas Sprat, History of the Royal Society

Chapter 2
THEORETICAL MATTERS

A BOOK about style that immediately leapt to the business of practical analysis would seem like an air journey that began in midflight. It might even seem like a hijacking. For the airline there is no avoiding the filing of flight plans, the instruction of the passengers, or the dispensation of cooing sounds by the stewardesses. Similarly for the stylistician there is no avoiding a preliminary discussion of theory and a disclosure of the practical facts of the materials with which he is dealing. In this chapter I shall briefly sketch the theoretical foundations of this study.

One cannot enter upon such a study without being aware that not all literary scholars understand style in the same way and that indeed not all literary scholars are agreed that such a thing as style exists. Even those who acknowledge its existence are likely to lament at times the impossibility of studying it. The literature of theoretical stylistics is now large, having grown with especial intensity over the last ten years. A wide variety of theoretical positions have been blocked out, and to cover them all thoroughly would require a theoretician of inhuman energy, subtlety, patience, and power. Such coverage is quite beyond my aspirations in this book; I shall limit myself to what seem to me the main questions: form and content, norm and language, appropriate abstractions, and grammar.

FORM AND CONTENT

Rhetoric from the *Ad Herennium* through the early Renaissance considered discourse (written) under three heads: Invention, or what is said, the topics; Disposition, or the ordering and arrangement of what is said; and Elocution, or the tricking out of the properly disposed matter with tropes and figures. Since the advent of Peter Ramus, who extruded the first two parts of rhetoric from their traditional third and placed them under logic,[1] the study of rhetoric—synonymous in many minds with style—has never fully recovered its equilibrium. The present age has seen a considerable range of response to the problem of just where *style* begins and ends: for some people, it has included what the ancients would have called Invention, Disposition, and Elocution; for others (like Ohmann) it would include these three things and still more; for still others (like Croce) it would include none of them, on the ground that such a thing as "style" cannot exist apart from content.

Modern views of what style is and is not must be classified as either variants or amalgams of three basic theories: that of organic form, that which Croce contemptuously called "ornate form," and that of style as personality. Theories of ornate form, deriving from the ancient rhetoricians' threefold separation, postulate that form and content in literature can be detached from one another. Considered another way, theories of ornate form postulate "the concept of choice among synonymous expressions."[2] Although modern versions of these theories tend to eschew the rhetorical categories that Croce so despised, they tend to agree in their acceptance of the possibility of synonymity and in the idea that *style* must be separable from the linguistic *medium* out of which it is produced. With such proponents as Martin Steinmann,[3] James Sledd,[4] and Louis T. Milic,[5] variants of the theory of ornate form have had a considerable following in recent years.

It was not always so. It was not so even as recently as 1950.[6] Organic form dominated stylistic theory beginning early in the present century, when traditional rhetorical theory came under a vigorous and apparently convincing attack from Benedetto Croce, who deplored "the harm done by rhetorical distinctions,"[7] and rejected the ideas both of synonymity and of variant expression by trope, holding that "in the aesthetic fact there are none but proper words; the same intuition can be expressed in one way only, precisely because it is intuition and not concept."[8]

The individualist theory, style as personality, seems to be confined in its expression largely to writers rather than to critics.[9] Even though it is probably "the predominant popular view,"[10] it is not a view that figures prominently in current theoretical discussions of stylistics, and this to me is a surprising fact. There need be no contradiction between the individualist position and either Croceanism or ornate form, for the latter two deal with relations between form and content, the former with writer and writing. Any study of the *style* of an individual writer would seem to me to presume that the writer's style is an aspect of whatever distinctiveness he possesses and therefore an extension of his personality. In his *Swift,* Milic (basically an anti-Crocean) explicitly embraced the individualist view; the same was done implicitly by Wimsatt (basically a Crocean) in his *Johnson,* and by Vickers (basically dead center) in his *Bacon.*

The major contemporary critics who are not proponents of some kind of theory of ornate form tend to be proponents of an amalgam between ornate and organic form. They base their amphisbaenic approach on what seems to me a sound principle: that whereas in fact monistic or organic theories are true, no criticism can take place without the establishment of *some* artificial dichotomies. Included among their number are Rene Wellek, Austin Warren, Brian Vickers, W.K. Wimsatt, and Richard Ohmann, the last two having made distinguished contributions to both the theory and the practice of stylistics.

Of this group, Wimsatt is the most nearly Crocean. Rejecting any notion of synonymity, he holds that "words have a tendency to mean" and that "bad style is not a deviation of words from meaning but of meaning from meaning . . . of the actually conveyed meaning (what a reader receives) from the meaning an author intended." He will concede that "one may say different things about the same topic—or different things which are very much alike," but he does not recognize such a thing as "stylistic options available to the writer."[11] This particular theoretical base lay underneath Wimsatt's pioneer study of Johnson. For the study of less distinctive writers than Johnson it has seemed less satisfactory. Yet, Wimsatt's apparent Croceanism extends only part way into his practice; for his treatment of Johnson he chose to rely on the traditional rhetorical categories (Parallelism, Antithesis, Metaphor, etc.).

Ohmann does accept synonymity, recognizing differences between form and content, and—like Milic and others[12]—he sees a need to separate the *medium* (or the language) from the *form* (or style) of a particular utterance. His basis for the latter view is epistemic[13] (any language biases the perception of its speakers) rather than stylistic (style *must* be a deviation from a norm); it nonetheless places him closer to the theorists of ornate form than Wimsatt is. Where Ohmann differs with the latter is in his apparent willingness to give critical consideration to things beyond what classical rhetoric called invention, disposition, and elocution; he would move stylistics into the area of pre-verbal choices: "In so far as critical theory concerns itself with meaning, it cannot afford to bypass the complex and elegant structures that lie at the inception of all verbal meaning."[14]

It is appropriate at this point to consider some kind of analogue—the first of several—for one of the relationships centering on style, in this case the relationship between form and content. Proponents of theories of ornate form have sometimes offered the model of a professional criminal in support of the form-content dichotomy: the crime (burglary, arson, breaking and entering, or what-have-you) is offered as the "content" and the *modus,* as policemen call it, is offered as the criminal's "style." Milic has exploited a version of this analogue in the discussion that precedes his treatment of Swift's style.[15]

It is an excellent model, worthy of further exploration, for the problems confronting us when we try to develop distinctions out of crime and criminals are parallel to those confronting us in an attempt to find appropriate distinctions among styles and writers. One way of considering the crime and the criminal is that the act is content and the *modus* is style, but it is only one way, and we cannot be at all sure that an economist or psychiatrist would agree. Might not the former say that the content is the thief's need to make a living and that the robbery in all its aspects is his style? Might not the other say that the content is Oedipal frustration, sublimated of course, or hyper-repressed sibling rivalry transference, and that the robbery, again, is an aspect of the man's style of expression? Even a rhetorician might consider the robbery as a *Topos* or topic of invention, in short a rhetorical (i.e., stylistic) aspect of carrying out a larger intent. After all, the fact that he is a burglar (has a penchant for a certain kind of *Topos*) is a major feature of the *style* by which he copes with the phenomena of a challenging existence. Hence, even considered rhetorically, the robbery can as easily be a part of style as of content. Similarly within discourse, there will be many contents and many styles, and equally many ways of deciding exactly where the dichotomous incision is to be made, and the multiplicity of things often presents the stylistic critic with a problem.

But the problem is not insurmountable; at least it does not seem so to me. The exact point of incision is in fact a non-problem; any behavioral abstraction that gives a reasonable prediction of either future or other behavior is a viable *formal* statement, whatever intertwinings the statement might seem to have with the content of that of which it speaks. For example, I once knew a salesman who opened nearly every conversation that he and I had with a farmer's daughter joke. I have not seen the man since 1967, but the statement, made this year, "If I see Joe, the first thing he'll do will be to tell me a farmer's daughter joke," is more a statement about Joe's *style* than about his content. One might protest that the jokes are content, and I might agree with that protest. But I would hasten to point out that Joe's *propensity* for telling them in specified social circumstances can be formally abstracted by an observer and is related to a variety of other formal structures that define the context in which the propensity exercises itself. And to speak of any propensity is to speak about form. Under the conventions of the form-content dichotomy, statements about form by definition are *not* statements about content.

Perhaps my own eclectic vision of what comes under the purview of *style* has been best expressed by Meyer Schapiro:

> By Style is meant the constant form—and sometimes the constant elements, qualities and expression—in the art of an individual or group. The term is also applied in the whole activity of an individual or society, as in speaking of a "life-style" or the "style of a civilization."[16]

In short, literary style is that set of propensities that define an author's voice. The abstractions about constant form that this book makes are primarily in the realm of syntax, which must be discussed, but not before some larger normative questions of language are dealt with.

NORM AND LANGUAGE

Few will argue with the assertion by Spencer and Gregory that "one essential dimension for placing a text must be historical." The two men go on to say:

> The language range of any period can be seen as one of the factors which both restrains the writer's linguistic choices and offers him certain creative opportunities. These . . . are never precisely the same in one period as in another.[17]

The matter of norms is important, and it gets us into two related questions: first, how do we decide which norms to choose and in what way do we ascertain them; second, to what extent can "normal" behavior be an aspect of an individual style. The normative question involves more than the problem of time. Norms can have many sources, and not necessarily purely linguistic ones. For example, certain *sub-genres* like the Sonnet in poetry and the Collect in prose impose fairly clear limitations on the behavior of their practitioners, but these are often as much social or other limitations as they are linguistic ones, as with the mode of address in a love sonnet or in a collectual prayer. Furthermore, the linguistic norms of a period 200 or 300 years in the past can be derived only obliquely, if at all. We have no direct record of the actual language, and of the literary dialect of the language we have only a partial record, the phenomena of which have been only partially catalogued in a systematic normative way. Hence in establishing linguistic norms for any individual writer we are reduced to comparing him in significant aspects[18] to other writers of somewhat similar background, education, interest, and age, but we should not confuse the norms of a specialized group of contemporaries with norms for even the literary language at large.

Against the individual yardsticks and the collective yardstick of other similar writers we shall find a writer "normal" in some respects and idiosyncratic in others; a writer's style consists of his particular syndrome of idiosyncratic and normal traits. Let us take a hypothetical writer, X, and five hypothetical contemporaries, A, B, C, D, and E. X might share one prominent quality with all members of the norm group; another he might share with 60% (writers A, C, and E); still another he will share only with writer E, and a final quality he might possess in solitary splendor. Let us assume that we have listed these qualities in what most educated readers or auditors would agree is their order of force or prominence in the discourse of X. The process of recognition of our single writer will not be based on that single, last idiosyncratic aspect of his style.[19] It will be based instead on a process of narrowing: the experienced reader or auditor will initially recognize our man as one of a group of six at quality one (A, B, C, D, E, and X); at quality two, he will eliminate writers B and D; at quality three he will eliminate A, and so forth.

Such a narrowing process would seem to be the major mode of recognition of anything that can be said to have style; for example, music and wine. Most educated people, on hearing an unfamiliar piece by a composer whose other works they know well, will go through some such process of sorting. Similarly, professional winetasters go through exactly this process in identifying the year and vineyard that produced an important wine the name of which they have not been told; their recognition comes from a narrowing down first of the broad geographic areas, then of the possible kinds of grapes, then of the years, then of the particular patches of soil where the grapes for the wine might have been grown.[20] Each of the constituents—vineyard, grapes, and year—possesses a distinctive syndrome of idiosyncratic and normal traits, and the taster's response is based on a cluster of three syndromes rather than on mere idiosyncrasies. It is in deference to an analogous process that examiners in English courses, on an identification-of-quotations, will give partial credit to the student who identifies a Pope couplet as Dryden (giving plausible reasons for his choice), but will give little or no credit to the student who identifies the couplet as Donne or Skelton.

We encounter a further normative problem when we see that the style of a given piece of writing (*not* a given writer) derives from a more complex intersection than that provided by the relationship between the writer's stylistic syndrome and the norms set by similar contemporaries, for the style of a piece can be subject to conventions arising deep in history from audience and occasion as well as from genre, to the extent that any of these bear formalized conventions.[21] A useful example is collect number 541, written by Jeremy Taylor in 1650, then edited in 1662, then re-edited in 1925. The 1925 version as a collect is:

> O God, whose days are without end and whose mercies cannot be numbered: Make us, we beseech thee, deeply sensible of the shortness and uncertainty of human life, and let thy Holy Spirit lead us in holiness and righteousness, all our days; that, when we shall have served thee in our generation we may be gathered unto our fathers, having the testimony of a good conscience; in the communion of the Catholic Church; in the confidence of a certain faith; in the comfort of a reasonable, religious, and holy hope; in favour with thee our God, and in perfect charity with the world. All which we ask through Jesus Christ our Lord. Amen.[22]

Here is a remarkable instance of the intersection of at least two styles: on the one hand, the prayer is well within the bounds of the conventional collect: the mode of address, with nominative of address; the parallel relative clauses, with parallel sense (infinitude); the second person verb *(make us)*; the moderate tendency to isocolon;[23] the relative brevity (160 words maximum); and the terminal appeal to "Jesus Christ our Lord." All these are either universal (or highly probable) generic elements in a collectual prayer;[24] but *they are not usual at all in the prose of Taylor.* At the same time, Taylor's stylistic personality has continued to assert itself through all the generic restraints and through the successive editings: the preoccupation with the brevity and uncertainty of human life; the tendency to pile up phrases in parallel series, especially prepositional phrases and objects of prepositions; the looseness of structure; and the use of the summarizing linkage in the last sentence *(all which).* The last item is a particularly distinctive feature of Taylor's prose, one he needed to pull his readers through the thickets of syntactic underbrush that lay at the ends of so many of his sentences. The broad-reference *this* and the initial *thus*—together with other retrospective devices of summary—are hallmarks of Taylor's style and way of thinking.

As Spencer and Gregory have said, "Language events do not take place in isolation from other events; rather they operate within a wide framework of human activity."[25] In short, the stylistic critic must be responsive to more than merely idiosyncratic behavior,[26] and the norms within which he must work cannot be rigidly limited either by the language or by a particular segment of time, much as he must respect these things.

THE SYNTACTIC ABSTRACTION

Let us briefly draw some inferences from what has gone before. Style is a set of abstractions arising from the formal properties of a piece of writing or a particular writer. These abstractions, when set against similar abstractions from other similar writers, develop a kind of richness and can inform us about the distinctive structural features in the writing, much as a fluoroscope can inform us about distinctive structural features of the body. The kinds of abstraction related to constant form that can be derived from sophisticated literature are many, ranging from the "inner" and "outer" realities of Auerbach, through structure, metaphor, lexis, and finally syntax.

I say "finally syntax" merely in obedience to convention and in full consciousness of the irony. It is the syntactic area of constant form that concerns us here, the one that has most attracted the linguists and most repelled the belletrists and certain others who ground their diffidence in what they believe to be traditional humanistic values. Ironic in this connection is the fact that the Renaissance humanists to whom we trace the origin of the modern literary curriculum were syntacticians *par excellence* and were utterly unafraid of the laborious grammatical drudgery that humanistic scholarship often entails. The current mode among literary scholars (a mode that is perhaps relaxing its grip) is given lofty expression by Ian Watt, who suggests that the process of stylistic inference "will lead one from the words on the page to matters as *low* as syntax and as *high* as ideas, or the total literary structure."[27] People with a more regular linguistic orientation have not shared this contempt for the structure of our native language.

W. Nelson Francis has justly pointed out that however gifted critics may be "in lexical intelligence, logical perception, and doggedness, they are likely to disregard syntax entirely."[28] In accordance with the hierarchy suggested by Watt, "an explicator faced with a difficult poem or passage almost never uses close syntactic analysis to match the scrupulous attention he gives to lexical matters." Since Francis made these remarks (1962), there have appeared several contributions to the study of style that use, in whole or in part, a syntactic approach. Included among these are Ohmann's study of Shaw and his subsequent brief study of Lawrence, Hemingway, and Faulkner, Milic's study of Swift, Hayes's brief study of Gibbon and Hemingway, my studies of Sprat, Gutwinski's study of Hemingway and James, and Oakman's study of Carlyle;* these constitute only a beginning list. But, taken together with the increasing evidence of the significance of syntax in human linguistic development, they provide in both their findings and their theoretical substructure a sufficient justification for approaching a text with syntactic apparatus in hand.

Having decided on a syntactic approach, one is confronted with the problem of deciding which syntactic convention to use. Beyond the traditional grammar that most people over 30 were taught in school if they were taught grammar at all, there are several models available. These are not so much competing as they are overlapping; they cut into the same body of language in different ways and at different levels, each grammar—in accordance with its own style— propelling a different set of abstractions into our field of vision. The major models currently respected among linguists include the transformational-generative, the semantic-generative, the scale-and-category, the tagmemic, and the stratificational. In addition, currently out of the mainstream, there is Charles C. Fries's variant of the structural model.

Each of the grammatical models has strengths and weaknesses. The transformational model has shown an ability to yield a great deal of information, but it is cumbersome to use and hence does not permit the economical analysis of large bodies or blocks of text. Moreover, it has not yet demonstrated an ability to make close distinctions between writers;[29] important as it is to find those elements of syntax that differentiate Hemingway from Gibbon, it would be hard to imagine a system that could fail to distinguish these polar opposites of style. Neither the tagmemic nor the semantic-generative model has yet, to my knowledge, been used successfully in a stylistic study of *literary* English. Tagmemic grammar has formidable potential, especially for the analysis of connected discourse, but at this writing no successful pilot study exists for large-scale use in literature. Both the scale-and-category and the stratificational grammars possess a demonstrated incisiveness in the handling of literary texts, not only incisiveness but extraordinary minuteness and delicacy. Once again, these latter attributes tend to get in the way of a really large study.

There are many questions that underlie the building of an inventory of prose style. Among others, the following: Are there period styles? Do writers develop? If so, how? Do genres have linguistic as well as other markers, and if so, what are they? Does the language of the uneducated (seamen, etc.) differ consistently through history

---

*See Bibliography for titles and publication data.

from that of the educated? If not, how come? What, in fact, were the properties of the most admired styles—those of Sidney, Bacon, Milton, Browne, Dryden, Johnson, Carlyle, James? For such a sizable project, one needed at least 300 to 400 samples from 100 to 120 writers, and the cuts that comprised the samples had to be big enough to demonstrate literary characteristics.[30] Milic's sample size of 3,500+ words in five to ten cuts had a proven validity;[31] smaller samples and smaller cuts seemed to us at the time to be suspect. So, what one wanted was a grammar sufficiently incisive to provide some hypothetical answers to the questions above, yet sufficiently simple to be applied to 1,000,000 or more words of text within a reasonable time limit.

The Fries grammar[32] has considerable theoretical and practical weaknesses concerning which we are under no illusions. It lacks subtlety; it produces unsatisfactory generalizations about clausal rank shifting; in its most abstract form (text encoded as numbers), it tends to render inaccessible subject-verb, modifier-modified relationships that might be very interesting in the literary study of style. And finally, perhaps most damning of all for the literary scholar, there is something grotesque about approaching Roger Ascham and Lancelot Andrewes with a grammar originally derived from 50 hours of phone conversations of the mid-twentieth century! This is a formidable array of theoretical and aesthetic objections. But none is totally disqualifying. We thought this array was more than counterbalanced by a number of the grammar's obvious virtues in a stylistic application.

The virtues are largely logistical. The grammar allows the kind of bulk processing that we wanted. The techniques for encoding and computerizing it were well established and possessed demonstrated incisiveness in the discrimination of one stylist from others. Computer programs were available, and further programs beyond those available have proven feasible. Several of our particular objections to limitations in the original Fries-Milic taxonomy[33] were eliminated by minor re-classifications. As for the linguistic limitations of the grammar, we felt we could tolerate them for two reasons: (1) some of them could be mitigated, and (2) the studies completed to 1970 within the conventions of the system had provided a radical sharpening of our perception of the authors involved. Somewhat improved, and applied to a large number of writers from a broad range of historical periods, a technique based on the Fries grammar promised a considerable increase in the precision with which we understand the history of literary style, an increase sufficient in both magnitude and accessibility to override the objection that the grammar, for really sophisticated linguistic analysis, is a blunt instrument that is incapable of penetrating far beneath the surface features of language.

* * *

Before approaching actual texts with our syntactic apparatus, we have some practical matters to dispose of with respect to the York Computer Inventory of Prose Style, which is the capital base from which our data are drawn. These include: the exact characteristics of the grammar, the details of the processing through which the York Computer Inventory program puts the encoded text, the logistical details of the Inventory itself. To these we can now move in Chapter 3.

The difference between the products of a well disciplined mind and those of an uncultivated understanding, in relation to that we will now venture to call the Science of Method, is often and admirably exhibited by our great Dramatist. We need scarcely refer our readers to the Clown's evidence, in the first scene of the second act of 'Measure for Measure,' or the Nurse in 'Romeo and Juliet.' . . . The absence of Method, which characterizes the uneducated, is occasioned by an habitual submission of the understanding to events and images as such, and independent of any power in the mind to classify or appropriate them. . . . METHOD, therefore, becomes natural to the mind which has been accustomed to contemplate not things only, or for their own sake alone, but likewise and chiefly the relations of things, either their relations to each other, or to the observer, or to the state and apprehension of the hearers. To enumerate and analyze these relations, with the conditions under which they are discoverable, is to teach the science of Method.

Samuel Taylor Coleridge, The Friend

Chapter 3
LOGISTICAL MATTERS

THE MAIN objectives of the York Computer Inventory of Prose Style are to develop hitherto undiscovered data about the syntactic habits of individual writers, to collect those data and the texts on which they are based in a single, convenient repository, and to maintain both this material and the programs that manipulate it in a form (tape) that permits it to be used by scholars anywhere in the world where there is a large IBM computer. Secondary objectives center on the provision of hypotheses and theories in response to crucial questions about the nature and history of prose style. This chapter describes the logistics of the Inventory—text selection, encoding, and manipulation by the computer.

TEXT SELECTION AND SAMPLING

The selection of authors reflects the judgment of the researchers on the Inventory as to which authors are likely to be interesting or representative. It also reflects from time to time, as in the five Mill samples and the early acquisition of DeQuincey, the research interests of

someone who has wanted to use the materials of the Inventory[1]—
either a graduate student at York or a colleague from another university.

The number of samples to be taken from a given author and the
works to be sampled are governed partly by other research, partly by
our judgment, and again partly by demands made upon the Inventory itself. An attempt is made to maintain a density and variety of
samples sufficient to give an extensive sampling of the careers of major authors who wrote in a variety of genres (Bacon and Sidney, for
example).

Once we decide to sample a work, we choose objectively five to
ten cuts from it, 350 to 700 continuous words apiece. The objective
choosing is usually by random number table, although in unusual
cases[2] we have employed the kind of stratified sample used by census takers (every fourth page, every tenth page, etc.). Usually the
cuts run from the first terminal punctuation on the left-hand page to
last terminal punctuation on the right-hand page; again, in cases of
unusual format, we have taken both single-page and four-page cuts.
In any case, enough cuts are taken to provide a sample of 3,400 to
3,500 words of natural language.

We are always asked three questions about the sampling technique: why "objective" choosing? why the 3,500 word sample size?
and why the 350 to 700 word cuts (i.e., why not cuts of 50 words,
like Barron Brainerd's[3])? The objective choosing is calculated to
eliminate as far as possible the biases of the researchers where such
biases have no place.[4] The 3,500 word sample size is justified on several grounds: first, by the precedents of Milic's successful study of
Swift and of my study of Sprat; second, by the fact that within the
conventions of our grammar the 3,500 word size is the one at which
samples seem to become internally reliable.[5] The 350 to 700 word
cuts are justified both by precedent and by common sense. Milic
used a cut of ten periods, or approximately 350 to 500 words; Gutwinski used a cut of roughly 700 words. From cuts of this size, *literary* judgments can be made, i.e., judgments about anaphora and other devices of cohesion, and judgments (if we ever decided to make
concordances out of our samples) about lexical features of the styles
we were analyzing. Cuts much smaller than these could be of use
mainly to someone with statistical rather than literary ends in mind.

TRANSLATION AND ENCODING

Each sample, after being selected, is photocopied and translated into
a 97-slot version of the Fries-Milic Syntactic Code for computers.
The translation is written out on special grid sheets by the translator.

After this, another translator makes an independent translation, which is checked against the original translation; usually, the two translators will differ on 1.5% to 2.5% of the words. The second translator reconciles these differences and sends the grid sheets to the York Institute for Behavioural Research for keypunching. The keypunching, like the translating, is done once, then is independently verified and corrected. At this point in the process, the 3,500 word random sample has been reduced to a syntactically coded deck of 150 IBM cards: each card has space on it for an eight-digit identifying number and 24 "words" of text. The identifying number has four digits of sample identification (author and work) plus four of card identification; a card whose first eight digits were 90980131 would be the 131st card from Dryden's "Original and Progress of Satire." The remaining 72 columns of the card are filled up with translated text, 3 columns for each word and each major punctuation mark (sentence endings and intrasentence full stops).

The code itself represents a third expansion of Fries's original grammar. The first was Milic's expansion, which enlarged the verb system for his study of Swift by separating the verbs of infinite predication from those of finite. The second was my expansion of his version in which *not* was extruded from the function adverbs and the infinitive signal *to* was separated from the other pattern markers *(there, it)*. It is this second expansion, listed in Table 3.1, that is the basic code used in the York Inventory. This is the abbreviated, or "two-digit," version of the code. The third expansion, elaborated by the addition of a third, descriptor digit to the two digits of the basic code, is given in Table 3.2.

We chose to elaborate with a third digit rather than with a new coding system because we wanted to proceed with a minimum loss of compatibility between our results and those of others working within the conventions of the Fries-Milic system. We say a minimum loss simply because there has to be some. "All grammars leak," as Sapir said, and no slot grammar can be designed to describe (prior to actual use) all the varieties of linguistic configuration that one will encounter in actual practice.

Different research teams are going to approach new situations differently even where there may be general agreement as to basic ground rules. Thus, although it is possible to agree on a formula that says one lexeme equals one code, such a formula will nonetheless encounter problems. For example, it is easy to say that "at first" is a function adverb of time (Class 342) and that "in fact" and "in sum" are sentence-connectors (Class 911), but what does one do with "in private," "in public," "in secret"? We coded these as preposition-noun (511-011), although we could probably also understand a cod-

Table 3.1 THE YORK SYNTACTIC CODE (TWO-DIGIT)

00 Omitted Subordinator

01	Noun	06	Participle
02	Verb	07	Gerund
03	Descriptive Adjective	08	Miscellaneous substantive
04	Descriptive Adverb	09	Quoted Material
05	Infinitive		

Function Words

11	Pronoun	44	Interrogative
21	Auxiliary Verb (plus *be*)	45	Correlative
31	Determiner, limiting adjective	51	True Preposition
32	Postposition	61	Pattern Marker (*there, it*)
33	Intensifier	62	Infinitive Signal
34	Function Adverb (plus *only*)	71	Interjection
35	*Not*	81	Numeral
41	Coordinator		
42	Subordinator		
43	Relative	91	Sentence Connector
		97	Parenthesis
	Punctuation	98	Intrasentence full stop
		99	Terminal punctuation

ing of each whole phrase as a single adverbial lexeme. There are problems as well with names, numbers, and titles. Is "John Doe" a single noun? Our answer is yes. Then, is "Doctor John Doe" or even "Doctor John Doe, Dean of Essex," also a single noun? Our solution to this problem was to code the name—even the name Nicholas Cadwallader Terhune Aston-Smith—as a single noun, with appended titles each encoded as single nouns as well: in the example above, "Doctor," "John Doe," "Dean," and "Essex" would each be coded as a single noun. With numbers, a solution seemed simpler: code any number, no matter how many "words" it takes to say it aloud, as though it were written with numerals. In this way, "One hundred and twenty-five thousand" is simply conceived as 125,000 and encoded as 811. Each such decision about techniques of translation is made jointly by the research team and is logged in a lexicon for future reference.

In addition to differences between our research and others' arising from accidental factors such as those described above, there are those arising from deliberate choice. Even our basic coding system has six more categories than the one that Milic used for his work on Swift. We divided his class 61 (pattern-marker: *there, it, to*) into classes 61 (pattern-markers *it* and *there*) and 62 (infinitive-signal *to*); we divided his class 33 (intensifier and *not*) into classes 33 (intensifier) and 35 *(not).* We also added categories 00 (unsignalled subordinator or relative), 09 (quoted material), 97 (parenthesis), and 98 (intrasentence full stop). Beyond the basic coding system, there are other differences. We encode as subordinators only those subordinators that are followed by a main verb: others we code as prepositions (513). For example, "After leaving the ship" is coded not as a subordinator followed by a participial phrase but as a preposition followed by a gerund phrase:

513   071   311   011
After   leaving   the   ship
(Preposition-gerund-determiner-noun)

513   071   511   311   011
While running down the street

513   214   072   511 312   011
When being charmed by our hostess

The purpose of this change was to maintain a strict separation between main verbs and verbals and to avoid, when counting indices of rank shifting (subordinators + relatives + verbals), the counting of some indices twice. Each of the three phrases above, in a cumulative count of rank shifting, would—by the count of the gerund, class 07—appear as one rank shift. If "after," "while," and "when" were counted as subordinators (class 42), then each of the phrases would count twice, which would throw the count off.

Another change made was in the adverbial system. We took some of Fries's Group D adverbs, the intensifiers,[6] and reclassified them under other headings. In Fries's original grammar, an intensifier is an adverbial modifier of an adjective or another adverb, signalling, as Fries says, "some degree of quantity of the 'quality' for which the [other word] stands."[7] In the York version, we retained as intensifiers only those words with a clearly quantitative thrust, moving others to the function adverb (34), the negative (35), and the true adverb (04) category, some on notional, some on morphological grounds.

Morphological shifts came with words like "really" and "awfully," whose use as intensifiers developed as a gradual disintegration of their use as true adverbs. In the early translating, it was particularly difficult, for example, to deal with problems like these:

Table 3.2 THE YORK SYNTACTIC CODE (THREE-DIGIT)

001 OMITTED SUBORDINATOR
(I thought ^{001} she was
pleasant.)
    002 Omitted Relative (The
man ^{002} you saw me with
was John.)

011 NOUN
    012 Attributive (the *railroad*
car)
    013 Possessive (the *railroad's*
director)
    014 Predicate Noun, all
clauses (1) [a]
    015 Noun-Subject, all
clauses (1)
    016 Subjective or Objective
Complement (1) (We
elected him *president.*)
    017 Appositive (John, the
president was not
there.)

021 VERB
    022 Passive form (1)
    023 Progressive form
    024 Copula   (1)

031 ADJECTIVE
    032 Predicate Adjective (1)
(The man was *tall.*)
    033 Participial Adjective (3)
(The *running* man . . .)
    034 Subjective or Objective
Complement (2) (We
thought him *good.*)
    035 Postmodifying Adjective
(John, *angry* at the
news, left.)

041 ADVERB

051 INFINITIVE
    052 Passive form

061 PARTICIPLE
    062 Passive form
    068 Absolute
    069 Passive Absolute

071 GERUND
    072 Passive form

081 MISCELLANEOUS SUB-
STANTIVE or FOREIGNISM
    082 Foreign language
sentence 8 or more
words

091 QUOTED MATERIAL
    092 Quotation of 8 or more
words

111 PRONOUN
    112 Reflexive Pronoun
    113 Negative Pronoun (1)
    115 Pronoun Subject

211 AUXILIARY (tense)
    212 Modal (except *shall &
will*)
    213 *be* main verb
    214 *be* auxiliary
    215 *be* infinitive
    216 *be* participle
    217 *be* gerund
    218 *be* participial absolute

311 DETERMINER (*the, such,
both, every, this, that, each*)
    312 Possessive Pronoun (*his,
her, its,* etc.)
    313 Indefinite Determiner
(*a, any*)
    314 *all, much, some, many,
most*
    315 *no, neither*
    316 *other*

[a]Numbers in parentheses indicate the priority of a given construction over another in case of conflict—e.g., a passive progressive form or a progressive copula: "John was being addressed" is coded as a passive rather than as a progressive; "She was looking good" is coded as a copula.

Table 3.2 (continued)

---

321 POSTPOSITION (get *up,*
     take *off,* step *out)*

331 INTENSIFIER (*very, much,
     more, most, indeed, even,
     such, less,* and, sometimes,
     still* and *far)*

341 FUNCTION ADVERB —
     possibility *(no doubt, probably,
     etc.)*
     342 time (*at first, at last,
          again,* etc.)
     343 place (*here, there,* etc.)
     344 *only* (*but,* sometimes)
     345 qualification (*quite,
          somewhat, at all,* etc.)
          or extent or degree
     346 *never*

351 *not* (*no/nothing,* sometimes)

411 *and*
     412 *but, yet*   415 *or*
     413 *for*   416 *nor*
     414 *as well as* 417 *rather than*

421 SUBORDINATOR (time)
     422 cause
     423 concession
     424 condition
     425 result
     426 other adverbs
     427 noun-clause subordina-
          tor (*that, how, why,* etc.)

431 RELATIVE adjective
     432 noun-clause relative

441 INTERROGATIVE

451 CORRELATIVE
     452 Negative Correlative

511 PREPOSITION
     512 Parallel Preposition
     513 Subordinating Preposi-
          tion

611 PATTERN MARKER (*it*)
     612 P-M *there*

621 INFINITIVE SIGNAL

711 EXCLAMATION
     712 Nominative of Address

811 NUMBER (cardinal)
     812 Number (ordinal)
     813 *once, twice, thrice*

911 SENTENCE CONNECTOR
     912 S-C Adversative
     913 Block Mark/Argumen-
          tative

971 PARENTHESIS Signal

981 INTRASENTENCE FULL
     STOP
     982 Intrasentence ?
     983 Intrasentence !

991 PERIOD
     992 Question Mark   ⎫
     993 Exclamation Mark   ⎬ Punctuation
     995 Fragment Period   ⎭

Is God *really* interested?   (Does the author mean *very* or does he mean
                                    in a real way?)
She was *awfully* old.   (Descriptive or intensifying?)
He was *substantially* better.   (But not spiritually?)

In deference to problems like these, which abound in prose prior to
1700, we decided simply to take all *ly* adverbs at face value as descriptive adverbs.

Notional shifts consisted of moving the qualifying adverbs into
class 34 as class 345. These adverbs include:

| quite | almost | somewhat |
| rather | just | at all |

These shifts were based on extensive reading (and computerization)
of Macaulay and Sprat, both of whom use quantitative intensifiers
far more extensively than they do the qualifiers above. It was our
hypothesis at the beginning that the notional differences evident in
Macaulay and Sprat would appear in many other writers and that
these adverbs might be some kind of key to discriminating the "stri-
dent" voice from the "diffident" voice in prose. The hypothesis has
not proven to be widely valid, and our handling of these adverbs
may well represent a reduction in precision of the original Fries-Milic system.

Nevertheless, we should remind ourselves that the utility of a taxonomy or a grammar in stylistic studies ·like this one is measured
less by its degree of descriptive "correctness" than by other things:
first, and most important, its susceptibility to consistent application;
second, the efficiency with which it can be used; and third, its ability
to produce abstractions from the text that might be useful in a reading of that text. On the basis of our own experience, we can say that
this taxonomy meets the first and second criteria, and on the basis of
the response to the first studies to come out of the Inventory, we can
say that it seems to be meeting the third.

THE COMPUTERIZED HANDLING OF THE ENCODED TEXT

After the translating, the checking, and the verified punching, the
150-card deck is put through the computer. The material on the
cards is manipulated by a 2200-statement program written in For-
tran IV for the G compiler, which analyzes the data on the cards in
several ways. First it prints out the 150 cards of the deck, giving after
it the number of cards, the number of "tokens" (words and punctuation), and the number of words in the text. Next it gives a frequency-
ordered distribution of all the three-digit classes in the deck, plus
the percentage that each class represents of the total text. For example:

Printout

Occurrences	Class	Percent	Explanation/Interpretation*
630	011	18.0%	*There are 630 miscellaneous nouns, comprising 18% of the total text.*
427	511	12.2%	*There are 427 miscellaneous prepositions, comprising 12.2% of the text.*
364	311	10.4%	*There are 364 definite and demonstrative determiners, comprising 10.4% of the text.*

From this point on, the program reads only the first two digits of each word, ignoring the third (descriptor) digit and reading, in effect, in the code as given in Table 3.1. Its next manipulation is a frequency-ordered distribution of two-digit codes (the first two of each three), e.g.:

Printout

Occurrences	Class	Percent	Explanation/Interpretation
742	01	21.2%	*There are 742 nouns of all kinds, comprising 21.2% of the text.*
458	51	13.1%	*There are 458 prepositions, comprising 13.1% of the text.*
452	31	12.9%	*There are 452 determiners, comprising 12.9% of the text.*

Next the program tabulates the incidence of each of 12 prepositional phrase strings—i.e., sequences in which one prepositional phrase is followed immediately by another. For example:

Printout

Sequence	Occurrences	Explanation/Interpretation
51 01 51	12	*The configuration prep-noun-prep ("by men of") occurs 12 times in the sample.*
51 07 51	2	*The configuration prep-gerund-prep ("in departing from") occurs twice in the sample.*
51 11 51	8	*The configuration prep-pronoun-prep ("with those of") occurs 8 times in the sample.*
51 31 01 51	36	*The configuration prep-determiner-noun-prep ("at a house on") occurs 36 times in the sample.*

*The italicized material does not appear on the printout.

Other phrases counted in this listing are:

51–03–01–51	"in large houses at"
51–07–01–51	"by throwing balls to"
51–31–03–01–51	"to the large house of"
51–31–07–51	"by the brewing of"
51–01–41–01–51	"between boys and girls on"
51–31–03–41–03–01–51	"in the pink and green tree of"
51–07–11–51	"while sending them to"
51–31–07–01–51	"with his building houses on"

The next manipulation is a computation of Milic's "D" Statistic, a quantitive measure of syntactic variety, to a limit of 1,000.[8] The "D" statistic is a computation of all the different sequences of three consecutive word classes in a given body of text. Within our coding system, "D" statistics tend to cluster between 820 and 960. Within Milic's coding system, the numbers were somewhat lower because of the different treatment of the adverbial system and because of the smaller number of classes within his taxonomy. The two different coding systems, however, tend to rank the same authors very consistently,[9] even with different coders, different criteria of sentence boundary, and different computer programs. The "D" statistic and its relevance to text are too complex to embark upon here; they are discussed thoroughly in the next chapter.

After giving "D," the computer counts and lists in frequency order all the different three-class sequences, to the 1,000 limit. For example:

Printout

Occurrences	*Pattern*			*Explanation/Interpretation*
151	51	31	01	*There are 151 simple prepositional phrases: prep-determiner-noun.*
133	31	03	01	*There are 133 clusters of determiner-adjective-noun.*
125	01	51	31	*There are 125 clusters of noun-preposition-determiner.*

Then come, vertically listed in order of occurrence, all the two-class sequences that follow major punctuation. This list is as long as the number of sentences; it usually looks something like this:

Printout	Opening Pattern			Explanation/Interpretation
99 *is the*	99	11	21	*The writer depicted here probably*
signal for				*has monotonous habits of sentence*
terminal	99	31	01	*opening; in the five sentences there*
punctuation.				*are only two openings—pronoun/*
98 *is the*	99	11	21	*auxiliary and determiner/noun—*
signal for				*and sentences 1, 3, and 4 might be*
an intrasentence	99	11	21	*an anaphoric series. Looks like Ma-*
full stop.	99	31	01	*caulay.*

or

	99	41	42	*Indication of great variety and a*
	99	91	11	*high degree of initial syndeton, also*
	99	11	43	*of early subordination. Looks like*
	99	42	51	*Sidney.*
	99	41	31	

The main utility of this listing is the provision of a visual scan for anaphora and other stereotypic patterns of handling sentence openings in series.

After this listing, there are two frequency-ordered lists, one of all the different three-class clusters that open sentences, the other of all the three-class clusters that close sentences. The sentence-opening list will look like the following:

	Printout			
Occurrences	*Pattern*			*Explanation/Interpretation*
14	31	03	01	*14 sentences open with the pattern*
9	11	21	02	*determiner-adjective-noun ("The*
5	51	31	01	*big house," "a kind man"); 9 sen-*
4	11	21	21	*tences open with the pattern pro-*
				noun-auxiliary-verb ("He has
				loved," "They will work"); 5 sen-
				tences open with the pattern
				preposition-determiner-noun ("In
				the beginning," "On the hill"). This
				fragment of a printout seems to be
				mid-eighteenth century or later, be-
				cause of the lack of initial connec-
				tion. This question is explored in
				the next chapter.

The sentence-closing list will look like the following:

Printout Occurrences	Pattern	Explanation/Interpretation
15	51 31 01	*15 sentences end with the pattern*
13	01 51 01	*preposition-determiner-noun;* *13*
12	01 41 01	*sentences end with the pattern*
10	31 03 01	*noun-preposition-noun;* *12 sen-*

tences end with a simple noun pair—noun-coordinator-noun;   10 sentences end with the modified noun cluster determiner-adjective-noun.

The program next gives the number of occurrences of nearly 50 word sequences that are *prima facie* evidence of word parallelism, such sequences as noun-coordinator-noun (01 41 01), noun-coordinator-determiner (01 41 31), and adjective-coordinator-adjective (03 41 03). As with the "D" statistic, it is easier to give a full description of this routine while treating text, which we do in the parallelism section of Chapter 4.

The final manipulation is a computation of the internal reliability of the sample. The sample is split, 1,750 odd words vs. 1,750 even words, and a correlation coefficient, based on the frequency of the various two-digit word classes, is computed by Pearson's formula. Surprisingly, although 1,400-word samples have turned up internal reliabilities as low as .90, we have had no full-size (3,500-word) samples under .987 and nearly all have been .995 to 1.00. ("Reliability" is a statistical concept that is treated at some length in Appendix A.) The point of using reliability is simply to establish that the sample is stable, that there are no wild differences between its two halves. A stable sample is presumed to be more typical of the sampled text than is one with internal inconsistencies.

A final routine in the program lists the sentences of the sample in order, calculates the length of each in words, and indicates at what point (i.e., what word) in the sentence there occurs the first instance of each of the following word classes: 61 (pattern marker), 42 (subordinator), 43 (relative). The routine then gives the mean sentence length in words, with a standard deviation,[10] plus the mean point at which the first 61, the first 42, and the first 43 each occur, again with a standard deviation for each. It also gives a total of the number of non-complex sentences (i.e., those containing neither a 42 nor a 43). Take for example a hypothetical sample of four sentences totaling 118 words. The printout might look like this:

Printout

Sentence	Length	D61	D42	D43	Explanation/Interpretation
1	47	0	10	39	*The first sentence is 47 words long*
2	8	1	0	0	*and has no pattern markers. Its first*
3	39	0	5	0	*subordinator occurs at the 10th*
4	24	16	1	15	*word and its first relative at the*

The second sentence is 8 words long; it opens with a pattern marker and has neither subordinators nor relatives in it.

Mean Length is 29.5   SD 14.2
Mean D61 is   8.5   SD   7.5
Mean D42 is   5.3   SD   3.6
Mean D43 is   27.0   SD 12.0
Sentences with neither 42 nor 43:   1

We intend to enrich the routine described above by adding two columns to give the total number of subordinators (class 42) and the total number of relatives (class 43) in each sentence. In addition we plan a routine to inventory all noun clusters. We already know from our first 200 samples that both attributive adjectives and attributive nouns become dramatically more common in post-Victorian prose than they had been before, and we are convinced that an analysis of the noun clusters in our samples will be very informative.[11] This incidentally points up one of the virtues of this system: once the texts have been sampled, translated, and punched, there is virtually no end to the variety of manipulations that can be performed; much can be found in the encoded texts that one might not have anticipated finding out at the beginning.

Everything from beginning to end of the process is retained on file, against the possibility of subsequent verification or amendment.[12] Within a month or two of being run through the computer, the cards of the sample are transferred to tape for portability and economy. The file jackets are retained at the English Department Offices, York University, and are available there for perusal by interested persons.

* * *

These formalities and grave overtures now done, we can proceed to do what the title of this work promises: attempt to see the relevance of all this abstraction and quantification in the perception of constant form in English prose.

*Critics permit themselves, for this or that purpose, to identify litera-
ture with great books, with imaginative writing, with the non-referen-
tial and non-pragmatic, with beauty in language, with order, with
myth, with structured and formed discourse—the list of definitions is
nearly endless—with verbal play, with uses of language that stress the
medium itself, with the expression of an age, with dogma, with the cri
de coeur, with neurosis. Now of course literature is itself and not
another thing, to paraphrase Bishop Butler; yet analogies and clas-
sifications have merit. For a short space let us think of literature as
sentences.*

Richard Ohmann, "Literature as Sentences"

Chapter 4

THE SENTENCE

WITHIN the conventions of the syntactic system used in the York
Inventory, one can examine several features of sentences to discover patterns of habit and repetition that define style. Most obvious
of these and most extensively treated in previous literature is sentence length.[1] Other features include sentence openings, sentence-
to-sentence connection, complexity, suspension, syntactic variety,
seriation, and closing. These have all been examined in previous
literature,[2] but largely as aspects of the study of an individual writer,
sometimes as aspects of the language process.[3] In this chapter we are
considering them simply as *places* where a writer's deviance from or
adherence to common practice gives a reader clues to the elements
of constant form within one style. And let us not forget that any *style*
includes both deviance and conformity.

Our procedure in this chapter will be to consider 22 York Inventory samples from a total of 16 sources (15 writers plus the King James
Bible), examining the samples for quantitative information related to
the sentence features enumerated in the paragraph above. These
samples were chosen for several reasons, not least of which is that
they are a representative cross-section of the samples processed pri-
or to the end of 1972. Because they have been available since then,
we have had sufficient time to study both the texts and the printouts
so that the general differentiae that are discussed in this chapter
could be developed. The samples are given in Table 4.1.

Table 4.1 SAMPLES FOR CHAPTER 4[a]

Sample Number	Author	Work
9004	Sidney	Defence of Poesie
9012	Bible	Psalms (King James)
9013	Bible	Acts (King James)
9031	Clarendon	History of the Rebellion
9033	Clarendon	History of the Rebellion
9048	Milton	Doctrine & Discipline of Divorce
9049	Milton	Early Tracts
9060	Milton	Areopagitica
9066	Coxere	Adventures by Sea
9067	Sprat	Life of Cowley
9068	Sprat	History of the Royal Society
9078	Newton	Opticks
9087	Tillotson	Sermons
9090	Wilkins	Sermons
9100	Davis	Voyages
9102	Gibbon	Decline & Fall
9106	Johnson	Rambler
9103	Ruskin	Seven Lamps of Architecture
9111	Macaulay	Critical & Historical Essays
9301	Hemingway	Death in the Afternoon
9401	Orwell	Essays
9402	Reich	Greening of America

[a]All references to primary text are by author, sample number, work, and page. A full catalog of the samples is given in Appendix B.

LENGTH

It can be said with assurance that average sentence length in words and the degree of sentence-to-sentence variation around that average are important features of the form of any single piece of discourse. To that extent they are aspects of its style. We can clearly say, for example, that Hemingway's short stories are written in short sentences (roughly 15 words average, vs. a contemporary norm of over 20); with equal certitude we can say that Sidney's Old *Arcadia* is written in long sentences (over 70 words, average, in the York samples, vs. an average of 40.7 in the samples of six other Elizabethan novels). We can also say that Clarendon's *History of the Rebellion* shows, within its tendency toward long sentences (71.5 words), consider-

Table 4.2 SPRAT VS. CLARENDON

	$\overline{X}$	Range	SD	N
Sprat	27.07	8-88	15.36	129
Clarendon, Volume I	76.15	20-142	39.58	47
Clarendon, Volume II	77.02	11-356	49.61	46
Clarendon, Volume III	61.64	18-158	32.54	57

able variety of sentence length, and that Sprat's *Life of Cowley* shows sentences cast in a more uniform mold. Clarendon's *History*, in our samples, shows sentences ranging from 11 to 356 words apiece, with many sentences well up between 100 and 150 words in length. The *Life of Cowley*, by contrast, shows short sentences (27.1 words) within a range in our 129-sentence sample from 8 to 88 words; only three sentences exceed 60; over 100 of the sentences fall between 15 and 40 words. The figures for the two men, expressed as mean ($\overline{X}$) and standard deviation (SD),[4] are given in Table 4.2. The table illustrates numerically what we can intuitively sense in reading a page or two of either work: great length and variation of sentence in *History of the Rebellion*, relative brevity and stability in the Sprat work.

I have thus far been careful to circumscribe both average sentence length and degree of variation as aspects of the style of single works. To what extent are they also aspects of the style of any given writer? This is a complicated question that has provoked more than one scholarly study.[5] Few multisample writers in the York Inventory between 1570 and 1870 failed to produce at least one sample within the 30-to-50 word-per-sentence range, and, of our 100 samples between 1576 and 1720, 71 had an average sentence length within that range. Moreover, sample-to-sample comparisons within individual writers have shown differences as great as 25 words per sentence.[6] In spite of these facts, I think it fair to say that sentence length is an aspect of some writers' distinctiveness and that "long," "average," or "short" sentences, relative to contemporary and generic norms, tend to be characteristic of nearly any given writer.

Let us pause briefly to consider this question of how "personal" sentence length is by looking at specific examples. There are three main problems that surround the question: genre, age, and editing. The first is that sentence length is genre-sensitive: a writer's fiction will probably have shorter sentences than will his discursive work and his plays shorter sentences than his novels; a writer's letters will usually contain shorter sentences than his other work. For example, Table 4.3 shows three writers of the seventeenth century for whom

Table 4.3 AVERAGE SENTENCE LENGTH IN WORDS: LETTERS
VS. OTHER SAMPLES

	Letters sample	Other samples (# of other samples)
Marvell	29	40.5 (2)
Bacon	37	48.2 (5)
Sidney	45	52.3 (5)

we have samples of both letters and other prose. Notice that the rank order is the same in the two columns. In writing letters, Sidney remains a relatively long sentence writer,[7] Bacon a high-medium sentence writer, and Marvell a medium-length sentence writer. The second problem is that writers may unconsciously or even deliberately change their sentence length as they develop; Sidney, for example, produced sentences averaging over 70 words in our two "Old" *Arcadia* samples; in the two revised, or "New," *Arcadia* samples the sentences averaged 45.5 words. Nevertheless, even at this chastened figure Sidney remains a relatively long sentence writer as an Elizabethan novelist, for the 45.5 average is higher than that of either Lodge (38) or Lyly (31.5), and not far below that of Nashe (47.4). Third, the matter of editing and the capriciousness of printers, especially prior to 1800, can introduce a genuine ambiguity: how many commas and semi-colons did the editors and/or printers change to periods and vice versa? No doubt in some cases it was a lot. One must tread carefully. Moreover, one should examine the style of sentences for a wide variety of criteria besides length.

Some writers, however, stand out clearly enough against their contemporaries that we can rest on the belief that their sentence length is a fact (Figure 4.1*). Clarendon is obviously a writer of long sentences, just as Macaulay is obviously a writer of short ones.[8] Let us consider two rather typical Clarendon sentences:

> The Horse had out-march'd the Foot, which, by reason of the excessive Heat, was not able to use great expedition: besides there was some error in the Orders, and some accidents of Night that had retarded them; so that when the Enemy appear'd first in view, the Foot and the Artillery was three or four Miles behind.

> The Covenanters, who very well understood the Weaknesses of the Court, as well as their own Want of Strength, were very reasonably exalted with this Success, and scatter'd their Letters abroad amongst the

*At the end of each chapter is a consolidated table covering all the information given in the Figures for that chapter.

Figure 4.1 SENTENCE LENGTH IN WORDS

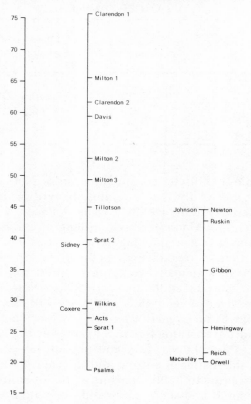

Noblemen at Court, according to the Humours of the men to whom they writ; there being upon the matter an unrestrain'd Intercourse between the King's Camp and Edenborough.

(Clarendon, *History,* 9031, 95)

Much besides length (58, 62 words) could be noted here—their additive development, their disproportioned members—but length is what we have under discussion. Contrast these with Macaulay:

The war was over. Frederic was safe. His glory was beyond the reach of envy. If he had not made conquests as vast as those of Alexander, of Caesar, and of Napoleon, if he had not, on fields of battle, enjoyed the constant success of Marlborough and Wellington, he had yet given an example unrivalled in history of what capacity and resolution can effect against the greatest superiority of power and the utmost spite of fortune.

(Macaulay, *Essays,* 9111, I, 583)

The sentences are 4, 3, 8, and 61 words long, respectively. Their average, at 19 words, is close to that of the sample from which they are picked (20.5). In addition they carry a feature of Macaulay's style that anyone who has read him much will infallibly recognize—the way in which he varies sentence length. The pattern of two, three, or four very short sentences building to a climax in one very long one is common in him.

An interesting comparison with Macaulay's technique is afforded by the Psalms, of which our sample is hardly distinguishable in average sentence length from his. The figures on mean, range, and standard deviation reveal, despite commonness of *average* length, dramatic differences (Table 4.4). The Psalmist seems to have had less reason than Macaulay to be out of breath, more reason to be serene; his sentences, as Table 4.4 suggests, tend to be more uniform:

> Many are the afflictions of the righteous: but the Lord delivereth him out of them all. He keepeth all his bones; not one of them is broken. Evil shall slay the wicked: and they that hate the righteous shall be desolate. The Lord redeemeth the soul of his servants: and none of them that trust in him shall be desolate.
>
> (Bible, 9012, *Psalm* XXXIV, 19–22)

OPENING THE SENTENCE

It has been demonstrated more than once that certain habits of sentence opening will characterize the work of a particular writer.[9] How the writer opens the syntactic box to get his meaning into it is an important feature of his habitual stylistic repertory. We all have at least one acquaintance who has a sentence-opening tic—someone who says "weeell" before answering a question, or someone who every fifth sentence begins, "The problem is . . ." or "Like man . . . ." The sentence-opening tics in the language of recognized writers are likely to be less obvious but are no less present. A convenient starting point for the reader is what the first word of each sentence is and what its grammatical class is.

Until well into the eighteenth century, the most popular way to get into a sentence was with a coordinator, class 41: *and, but, or, for,* plus others. Even in the twentieth century, this class is not utterly despised: its incidence as initial word rises to 10% to 15% in writers as recent as Strachey, Virginia Woolf, and George Orwell. For the

Table 4.4 AVERAGE SENTENCE LENGTH, RANGE, AND STANDARD DEVIATION

	$\bar{X}$	Range	SD
Macaulay	20.5	3-86	12.31
Psalms	19.6	11-41	6.69

analyst of style, the incidence of this class as first word provides an important clue to the degree to which the discourse is syndetic or asyndetic, probably a key symptom of what a writer does and does not use to stitch his sentences one to another. Figure 4.2a gives figures on initial class 41 for our 22 samples. The differences between an initially coordinated style and one relatively free of coordinators can be easily illustrated by contrasting a passage from *Acts* with a passage from Hemingway. In column form beside the passages are translations of the successive sentence-opening words in each.

*Coding of
initial word*

41	*And* certain men which came down from
42	Judaea . . . *When* therefore Paul and Barnabas had no
41	small dissension . . . *And* being brought on their way
41	by the church . . . *And* when they were come to Jeru-
41	salem . . . *But* there rose up certain of the sect of the
41	Pharisees . . . *And* the apostles and elders came toge-
41	ther . . . *And* when they had been much disputing
41	. . . *And* God, which knoweth hearts, bare them wit-
	ness, giving them the Holy Ghost . . .
	(Bible, 9013, *Acts* XV, 1–9)

61	*There* are two things that are necessary for a country
11	to love bullfights. *One* is that the bulls must be raised in
	that country and the other that the people have an inter-
31	est in death. *The* English and the French live for life.
31	*The* French have a cult of respect for the dead, but the
	enjoyment of the daily material things, family, security,
	position, and money, are the things that are most im-
31	portant. *The* English live for this world too and death is
	not a thing to think of, to consider, to mention, to seek,
	or to risk except in the service of the country, or for
	sport, or for adequate reward.
	(Hemingway, 9301, *Death in the Afternoon*, 265)

In addition to offering a (perhaps overdramatic) contrast between a style that is initially coordinated and one that is not, the two examples should dispatch the epithet "biblical" that one sometimes hears applied to Hemingway's style.[10]

Beyond coordinators, yet still within the conventions of our word-class taxonomy, we can consider other things that are initially linking, notably initial subordinators (class 42) and initial conjunctive adverbs or sentence connectors (class 91). By adding the three classes (41, 42, 91) together, as they appear in initial position, we can get a good idea of single-word initial connection within a particular style. Figure 4.2b shows the density of such connection among our 22 samples. It is interesting that, as in previous studies, these statistics combined with those in Figure 4.2a (relating to initial coordinators alone) suggest a strong correlation between initial coordination (class 41 alone) and overall initial syndeton.[11] The rank order of our top eight writers in these two figures is as follows:

FIGURE 4.2a Class 41	FIGURE 4.2b Classes 41+42+91	
		(Rank for Class 41)
Acts	*Acts*	(1)
Milton	Sidney	(4)
Newton	Newton	(3)
Sidney	Milton	(2)
Sprat	Sprat	(5)
Tillotson	Wilkins	(8)
Clarendon	Tillotson	(6)
Wilkins	Clarendon	(7)

Between 4.2a and 4.2b there are only three major changes of rank and two dramatic jumps in percentage, Sidney and Wilkins, both of whose total syndeton figures stand in a ratio of 2:1 to their figures for initial coordination, whereas among the other samples the ratio is between 3:2 (Sprat) and 7:6 (*Acts*). The reason for the exceptions in these two cases is that both men rely heavily on initial sentence connectors: *firstly, moreover, however, furthermore, lastly,* etc. Once again we can offer by way of illustration a contrast between a syndetic style and an asyndetic one, again with translations of the sentence-opening words:

*Coding of
initial word*

41	41	*For* all sense and equity reclaims . . . *And* what his
51		chief end was of creating woman . . . *To* this Fagius, Calvin, Pareus, Rivetus, as willingly and largely assent
41		as can be wished. *And* indeed it is a greater blessing
41		from God . . . *And* with all generous persons married
41	42	thus . . . *And* the solitariness of man . . . *Lest,* therefore,

(Milton, 9048, *Divorce*, 390– 391)

31	01	*The* heavens declare the glory of God . . . *Day* unto
61		day uttereth speech . . . *There* is no speech nor language where their voice is not heard. *Their* line is gone
31		out through all the earth . . . *His* going forth is from
31		the end of the heaven . . . *The* law of the Lord is
31		perfect . . . *The* statutes of the Lord are right . . . *The*
31	31	fear of the Lord is clean . . . *More* are they to be de-
33		sired than gold, yea than much fine gold: sweeter also than honey and the honeycomb.

(Bible, 9012, *Psalm* XIX, 1–10)

Figure 4.2a INITIAL 41 AS % OF SENTENCES

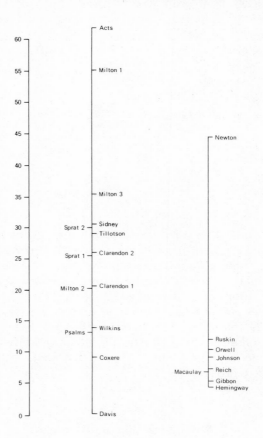

A careful reading of the sentence openings quoted above suggests other ways of binding sentences to one another that are essentially syntactic. For example, Milton's one asyndetic opening, "To this," does some stitching with its predecessor sentence via a prepositional phrase. Similarly, the Psalmist (or his translator), in speaking successively of "The law of the Lord," "The statutes of the Lord," and "The fear of the Lord," clearly intends to achieve not only emphasis but cohesion. Both these techniques deserve attention.

Reconsidering Figure 4.2b, we can see that Gibbon ranks very low in overall initial syndeton, just as he ranks low in initial coordination. Anyone who has read Gibbon, however, knows that he paid careful, professional attention to making his sentences cohere one to another. Not all of this attention was at the lexical level; much was syntactic, consisting of stereotyped, repeated openings, of which we

Figure 4.2b INITIAL SYNDETON AS % OF SENTENCES

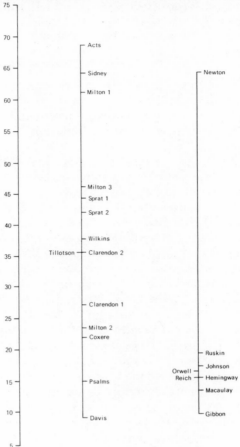

shall speak later, and of opening his sentences with prepositional phrases like the one in the Milton example just above. Thus, although technically not syndetic under our 41–42–91 test, a series of openings like the one below can show considerable attention to cohesion:

> The historian who presumes to analyze [the *Greek-fire*] should suspect his own ignorance and that of his Byzantine guides, so prone to the marvellous, so careless, and, in this instance, so jealous of the truth. From their obscure, and perhaps fallacious hints, it should seem that the principal ingredient of the Greek-fire was the naphtha, or liquid bitumen, a light, tenacious, and inflammable oil, which springs from the earth and catches fire as soon as it comes in contact with the air. The naphtha was mingled, I know not by what methods or in what propor-

tions, with sulphur and with the pitch that is extracted from evergreen firs. From this mixture, which produced a thick smoke and a loud explosion, proceeded a fierce and obstinate fire. . . . For the annoyance of the enemy, it was employed with equal effect by sea and land, in battles or in sieges.

(Gibbon, 9102, *Decline and Fall*, 416–417)

It is easy to see that in addition to the many back references—count the incidence of *their* and *this* with a retrospective noun—a major cohesive factor in the passage is Gibbon's use of initial prepositional phrases, a use in which he is among the highest of our 22 samples, as shown in Figure 4.3a.

The Psalmist's three successive sentences, "The . . . of the Lord," bring us to the last of the syntactic cohesive devices that we shall treat: anaphora. In the narrowest technical sense, anaphora is opening successive clauses with the same word. Pragmatically, it is all but indistinguishable from frontal parallelism, and nearly any lexicon that defines the term will offer an example that not only conforms to the narrow technical definition of anaphora but also is syntactically parallel in its two or three opening words; for example, the often-quoted line from Winston Churchill: "We shall fight on the beaches, we shall fight on the landing-grounds, we shall fight on the fields and in the streets, we shall fight in the hills." Typically, the successive clauses not only begin with the same word but with a cluster of words that are syntactically parallel. In the York Inventory computer program, there is a routine that isolates and lines up vertically the first two words, encoded, from all the sentence and demi-sentence openings from the sample being analyzed in the order in which the openings occur. This vertical listing can be revealing, as we can see by comparing the two passages below. The first is by Sidney, a syndetic writer who seems deliberately to avoid symmetrical parallel forms (of which anaphora is one); the second is by Macaulay.

The Philospher sheweth you the way . . . *But this* is to no man but to him that will read him . . . *Nay truly* learned men have learnedly thought . . . *Now therein* of all Sciences I speak of humane . . . *For he* doth not onely shew the way . . . *He beginneth* not with obscure definitions . . .

(Sidney, 9004, *Defence*, c2)

He called himself a priest . . . *Long before* the war he held curacies in various parts . . . *He was* driven from one place by the scandal . . . *He rode* away from another place on a borrowed horse . . . *He settled* in a third parish . . . *He assured* each of his wives . . . *The only* specimens which remain to us . . . *He compares* himself to David . . . *He declares* that he repents . . .

(Macaulay, 9111, *History*, iv, 196)

Abstracted in the two-digit code, the sentence openings become even more clear in their relationship to one another:

Sidney			Macaulay		
31	01	A	11	02	A
41	11	B	34	51	B
71	04	C	11	21	A
91	34	D	11	02	A
41	11	B	11	02	A
11	02	E	11	02	A
			31	03	C
			11	02	A
			11	02	A

(All finite verbs are considered parallel)

Taking only the coded form, one can obtain a figure for initial anaphora by adding up the number of proximate repeated patterns and deriving the percentage that number represents of the total number of sentences. In such an enumeration, we simply count from the vertical listing the following clusters of types: AA, AAA, ABAA, AABA, plus *any other group of four or more sentences in which the sentence openings fall into no more than two different two-class patterns.*[12] Auxiliaries (21) and main verbs (02) are counted as parallel. Using the Sidney and Macaulay columns above, we can arrive at the possible extremes. Sidney's openings fall into a pattern of ABCDBE: no anaphora, 0% (the two 41–11 openings are not close enough together). Macaulay's openings give a pattern of ABAAAA-CAA: a group of five and a group of four, or nine sentences, or 100.0%. Figure 4.3b offers all our 22 samples, with similar statistics computed for each full sample.

This figure provides some interesting contrasts between highly anaphoric texts (The Bible, Macaulay, and Sprat) and non- or anti-anaphoric texts (Sidney, Milton, and Newton). It is deceptive in two ways, however. First, it makes Gibbon, Coxere, and Davis seem to be more anaphoric than in fact they are. Davis and Coxere, seamen with limited linguistic resources who were just trying to get things down, not writing to be stylish, probably did not even notice that there was little syntactic variety in their openings. Gibbon, undoubtedly by design, made himself a uniquely unvarying writer. In our sample, 59 of his 96 sentences began with 31–01 (determiner-noun), 31–03 (determiner-adjective), or 51–31 (preposition-determiner); hence his encoded openings look more repetitive than they in fact are, as in the following series:[13]

The wealthy Christians	31–03	A
An absolute Monarch	31–03	A
The same messenger	31–03	A

Figure 4.3a INITIAL PREPOSITION AS % OF SENTENCES

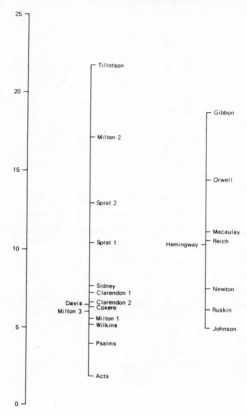

The emperor acquaints	31–01	B
The liberality of Constantine	31–01	B
He assigned	11–02	C
The form of	31–01	B
The timbers were	31–01	B

This offers in the coded tokens eight for eight: a series of three and a series of five. The words, however, show something quite different. Of course, *true* anaphora involves lexical repetition as well as parallel structure—repetition of the kind seen in the Macaulay passage above. And Gibbon, although abundant in parallel forms, was one of the all-time masters of the art of elegant variation of vocabulary. Despite the density of the parallelism, Gibbon is scrupulous to leave it un-reinforced by repeated words.

The second mild deception in Figure 4.3b is that it equates repeated openings in a writer of long sentences with repeated openings in

Figure 4.3b ANAPHORA AS % OF SENTENCES

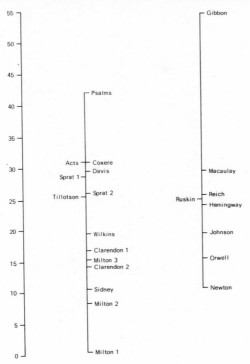

a writer of short ones; hence, Macaulay and Sprat seem close to Tillotson, and anyone who has read them knows they are not. One way of mitigating this is to compute the anaphoras as a percentage of text: take the total number of repeated openings, multiply by two (the number of words in each), and compute the product as a percentage of the entire text. That exercise gives us Figure 4.4. Once again, Gibbon is out of line, but not quite so badly as in Figure 4.3b. The picture given in Figure 4.4 is more nearly accurate.

More discriminating than any of the Figures 4.2 through 4.4 can be a biaxial treatment of anaphora and syndeton. Some writers, like Macaulay, will rely for cohesion on anaphora; others, like Sidney and Milton, will rely on syndeton; others, like Sprat, will rely on both; still others, like Johnson, will eschew both. Figure 4.5 offers such a biaxial treatment of some of our samples. In this figure Johnson and Sprat are the polar writers. It is interesting to look at a few sentence openings from their samples.

> *I naturally* love to talk without much thinking . . . *This, sir,* is sufficiently miserable, but there are still greater calamities behind.

Figure 4.4 ANAPHORA AS % OF TOTAL TEXT

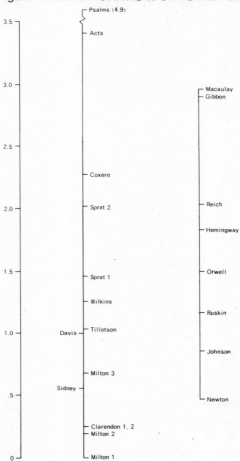

You must have read in Pope and Swift how men of parts have had their closets rifled . . . *These considerations* at first put me on my guard . . . *Others may* be persecuted, but I am haunted . . . *I often* change my wig, and wear my eyes, by which I hope to confound them . . .

(Johnson, 9106, *Rambler*, I, 16)

But to return to my Narration . . . *He now* thought he had sacrificed enough . . . *He had* enjoyed many excellent occasions of observation. *He had* been present in many great revolutions . . . *He had* nearly beheld the splendour of the highest part of mankind . . . *He had* lived in the presence of Princes . . . *He was* now weary . . . *He had* been Perplexed . . . *He was* satiated . . . *These were* the reasons that moved him to forego all Publick Employments . . .

Figure 4.5 ANAPHORA/SYNDETON

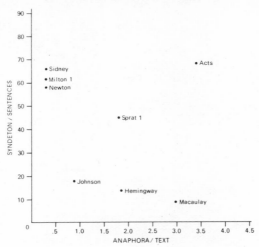

At first he . . . Yet, notwithstanding the narrowness of his Income . . . But upon the settlement of the Peace . . . The last of which . . . Thus he was sufficiently furnished for his retreat. And immediately he gave over . . .

(Sprat, 9067, Cowley, 126–127)

Before leaving the sentence opening as a stylistic feature, we should look again at Gibbon, together with the question (limited range) that we briefly discussed above. It is clear that one aspect of a writer's style is how extensively he uses the range of linguistic resources that his language offers him. Some writers, by design or inadvertence, restrict their options; these would include Gibbon, Macaulay, and Reich among the group tested. Others, primarily by design, exploit the syntactic resources of the language as far as they seem to be able;[14] these would include Sidney and Milton. Such restriction or exploitation usually appears first in the sentence openings. The York Inventory program makes a count of all the different three-class sequences that open sentences in each of its samples; it also tallies them and lists them in frequency order. One revealing statistic is the ratio of different openings to the total number of sentences. This is expressed as a percentage, and is given in Figure 4.6. Notice that although the information given here is similar to that given in some of the other figures,[15] it is not identical. Writers low in anaphora tend to use many different sentence openings and vice versa. Writers of long sentences tend to repeat the same openings less frequently than do writers of short sentences, and writers of short sentences conversely will rank low on any index of sentence-opening variety. But these are only tendencies: Sprat, an anaphoric writer

Figure 4.6 PATTERN VARIETY IN SENTENCE OPENING

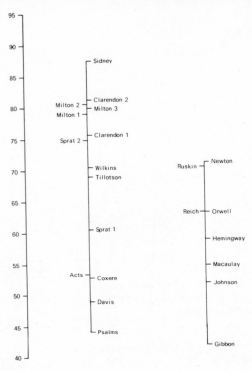

of shortish sentences, ranks high on our index of variety (Figure 4.6). Davis, a writer of long sentences, ranks far lower in opener variety than does Orwell, whose sample showed the shortest sentences of any of the 22 in this chapter.

SENTENCE DESIGN AND ARCHITECTURE

As we noted in Chapters 2 and 3, the word-class taxonomy used in the York Inventory gives us only a surface description of the texts analyzed and does not provide extensive or detailed information about complexity, embedding, inclusion, or rank shifting. Nonetheless, the data provided by the Inventory do permit us to answer some important questions about sentence structure: How many sentences contain no hypotaxis at all (i.e., contain neither a subordinator nor a relative)? In the hypotactic sentences, how far into the sentence (i.e., at what word in the sentence) does the subordination begin? How much hypotaxis is there in the entire sample? How various is the syntax when microscopically examined? How much does the sample show reliance on formulaic word parallelism?

"Biblical in its simplicity" is a staple of amateur stylisticians when they want to say something pregnant-sounding about a style that is relatively unadorned. Usually the expression "Biblical" has little relevance to the style to which it is applied. It does, however, have some application to the style of the King James Version itself. Figure 4.7a presents the number of unsubordinated sentences in each of our samples. As we might expect, the styles of the Bible employ a great number of unsubordinated sentences. After these come Sprat and Wilkins, two prime movers in the reform and simplification of prose style during the latter seventeenth century,[16] men who preferred "the language of Artizans before that of Wits and Scholars,"[17] and with them is Coxere, himself an unlettered "Artizan," a seaman who wrote a chronicle of his voyages. Similarly, the heavily embedded, hypotactic styles of Sidney and Milton eschew simplicity. There are some surprises, however: for example, Hemingway, who is thought by many to have equated subordinated sentences with the wearing of skirts, and Tillotson, like Sprat and Wilkins a reformer of preaching but unlike them not a plain talker in this particular way. Finally there is Davis, like Coxere a seaman. His surprisingly low number of sentences without subordination derives as much from punctuation as from complex syntax; his sentences are among the longest in our 22 samples (Cf. Figure 4.1).

We should not consider the density of unsubordinated sentences without also considering the total amount of subordination in the sample. Figure 4.7b gives the total number of subordinate clause indicators (classes 42 and 43) in each of our samples. Here again there are surprises. So often have we been told that Gibbon's style (like his body) was fat or (like his clothing) lace ruffled that even professionals are likely to think of it as "ornate" and hence as embedded and subordinated. A further confusion derives from the fact that his style is often linked with that of Johnson. "Abstract styles like Gibbon's and Johnson's" or "Elaborate, architectured, eighteenth-century styles like Gibbon's, Swift's, and Johnson's" or "Heavy, nominal styles like Gibbon's and Johnson's," and like phrases ricochet off the walls of my memory from lectures and seminars on the eighteenth century. If one does not go back to the actual texts, it becomes easy to think of Johnson and Gibbon as a sort of stylistic Bobbsey Twins, which of course they were not, least of all in matters of syntax.

Even without going to the extremes of our samples, the Psalms and Sidney, we can contrast an unsubordinated with a hypotactic one:

> And there came a voice to him, Rise, Peter; kill, and eat. But Peter said, Not so, Lord; for I have never eaten any thing that is common or unclean. And the voice spake unto him again the second time, *What God hath cleansed, that call not thou common.* This was done thrice: and the vessel was received up again into heaven.
>
> (Bible, 9013, *Acts*, X, 13–16)

Figure 4.7a UNSUBORDINATED SENTENCES PER SAMPLE

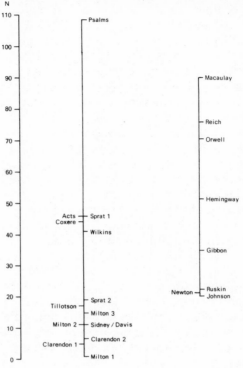

We boast our light; but *if* we look not wisely on the sun itself, it smites us into darkness. Who can discern those planets *that* are oft combust, and those stars of brightest magnitude *that* rise and set with the sun, *until* the opposite motion of their orbs bring them to such a place in the firmament, *where* they may be seen evening or morning. The light *which* we have gained, was given us, not to be ever staring on, but by it to discover onward things more remote from our knowledge. It is not the unfrocking of a priest, the unmitering of a bishop, and the removing him from off the Presbyterian shoulders *that* will make us a happy nation; no, *if* other things as great in the church, and in the rule of life both economical and political, be not looked into and reformed, we have looked so long upon the blaze *that* Zwinglius and Calvin have beaconed up to us, *that* we are stark blind.

(Milton, 9060, *Areo,* 742)

Given a hypotactic style, we might well ask, how and where is it hypotactic? Clearly, some writers are likely to generate a relative clause rather than an adverbial one, given a situation where meanings are roughly equivalent, as in the following case:

(A) The same zeal *which* inspired their songs prompted the more

Figure 4.7b SUBORDINATORS AND RELATIVES PER 3,500 WORDS

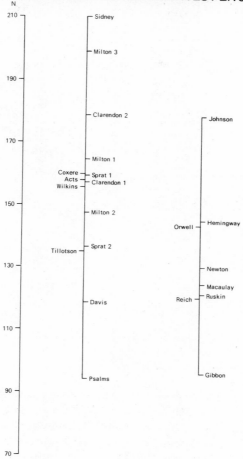

scrupulous members of the orthodox party to form separate as-
semblies . . . (Gibbon)

(B) And *while* they were aflame with song, they also burned with a
     lust for schism . . . (Cluett)

We might infer that, given the choice, Clarendon and Gibbon would
clearly prefer sentence (A), just as Orwell, Hemingway, and Sidney
might prefer (B). Figure 4.8 offers a biaxial treatment of these two
kinds of hypotaxis. In the first 133 samples of the York Computer Inventory, subordinators outnumbered relatives in a ratio of 5:4.[18] As
we can see from Figure 4.8, it is unusual for a writer to use more relatives than subordinators, as Gibbon seems to do; it is almost as unusual for a writer to approach a subordinator-relative ratio of 5:3, as is
done by Hemingway, Orwell, Coxere, and Newton.

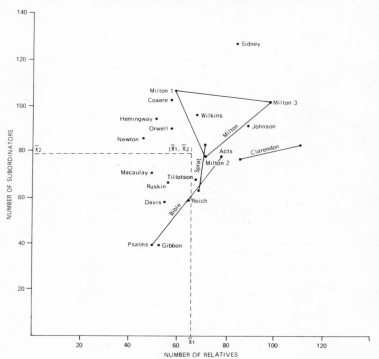

Figure 4.8 SUBORDINATORS AND RELATIVES BIAXIAL

A final aspect of hypotaxis to examine is suspension, a characteristic of what schoolbooks used to call the "periodic" or frontally-subordinated sentence. At what point in a sentence is a writer likely to introduce his first subordinate clause? Figure 4.9 offers a biaxial treatment of sentence length and subordinator (class 42) placement. The vertical axis indicates average length of sentence, the horizontal axis the average word in the sentence at which the first subordinator occurs. It is obvious that, given the scale, the figures *tend* to fall along a 45-degree line; in other words, as a writer's average sentence length increases, he tends on the average to defer his first subordination. This is not, however, an infallible rule: Wilkins, Sprat, and Coxere, all writing "short" sentences for the seventeenth century, tend to subordinate later than does Sidney, with his medium-long sentences. We should recur briefly to Figure 4.7b, to note that Clarendon, Sidney, and Milton all emerge as heavily hypotactic writers, although it is clear from Figure 4.9 that Sidney's tendency is to subordinate much earlier than the length of his sentences would suggest. Indeed, Sidney's (many) subordinations occur very nearly as early as the (few) subordinations in the Psalms, even though his

Figure 4.9 FIRST SUBORDINATION

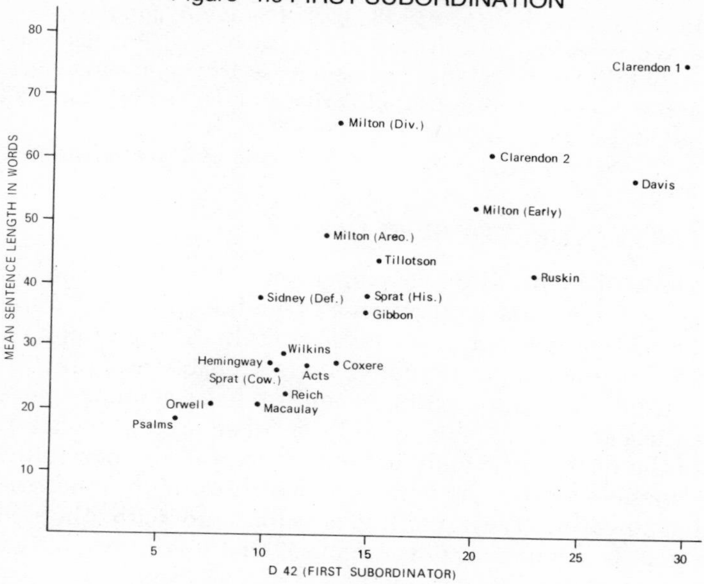

sentences are twice as long. It is instructive, before we move on from initial subordination, to see how different two writers can be who are very nearly equal in total hypotaxis:

> *If* the Poet do his part aright, he will show you in Tantalus, Atreus, and such like, nothing that is not to be shunned . . . And *whereas* a man may say, though in universal consideration of doctrine, the Poet prevaileth, yet that the History . . . The answer is manifest, *that* if he stand upon that was, as if he should argue . . . But *if* he know an example only informs a conjectured likelihood . . . Many times he must tell events, *whereof* he can yield no cause, or if he do, it must be poetically. For *that* a feigned example hath as much force to teach, as a true . . .

> (Sidney, 9004, *Defence*, 7)

The Earl of Stamford, and his Assistants, had departed the Town but few hours before his Majesty's entrance; and had left their Magazine, *which* was indeed the Magazine of the County, in a little Store-House at the end of the Town, guarded by some inferior Officers . . . On the other hand, it was an Act of too great insolence to be suffer'd; and, upon the matter, to leave a Garrison of the Rebels in possession of the Town; and therefore he sent word to the Judge *that* if he took not some legal way to remove such a force . . . In the end, the Gentlemen of the Country, *who* had not otherwise declared themselves on either side, than by waiting on his Majesty, finding that the King would not go from the Town till that Nuisance was removed . . . The other Acci-

dent was, or was like to have proved, more Ridiculous: Some of the
King's Servants, hearing that the Earl of Stamford and the Other Mili-
tia Men were newly gone out of the Town . . . But the Judge be-
sought his Majesty not to put a matter of so great moment, upon *which*
the power of the two Houses of Parliament, and a Parliament sitting,
must be determin'd . . .

(Clarendon, 9033, *History,* III, 40)

SMALLER FEATURES OF SYNTAX

In his study of Swift, Milic developed the "D" statistic, the number
of *different* three-class patterns in a given body of text. To the layman, the "D" statistic may seem mysterious in its origins and elusive
in its implications. Its principal value is probably as an instrument
in the attribution of authorship through stylistic evidence, but it has
other values as well, notably as an index of an author's syntactic variety, of the degree to which he tends to exploit the possibilities of
word arrangement that the language offers him. With some writers it
is such a powerful discriminating tool alone and, with others, such a
strong item in a pair or set of statistics[19] that it is worthwhile for us
to examine how it is derived and how it may be used.

The derivation of "D" is a straightforward process. The computer
starts at the first word of the first sentence in the encoded text and
registers the three-class pattern begun by that word. It then registers
the three-class pattern begun by the second word, followed by the
three-class pattern begun by the third word, and so on until it reaches the pattern begun by the antepenultimate word of the demisen-
tence or the sentence.[20] The process goes as follows:

> The great enemy of clear language is insincerity. (Orwell)
> 31   03   01   51   03   01   21   01   99

The three-class patterns registered by the "D" program from this
sentence would be 31-03-01, 03-01-51, 01-51-03, 51-03-01, 03-01-21,
01-21-01. Notice that the total number of three-word sequences in
the sentence is six, or two less than the total number of words; this is
true of all syntactic units to which the "D" test is applied.

After completing one unit, the program goes on to the next and begins with the first word. Let us assume that the next syntactic unit after the sentence above is a sentence of 31 words, or of 29 *total* three-
word sequences. For each sequence not previously registered as a
pattern, the "D" statistic will rise by one. After the first sentence, we
have a "D" of 6; if the second sentence contains three instances of
51-03-01 and one instance of 31-03-01 plus 25 sequences not in the
first sentence or duplicated in the second, then our "D" will be 31 (6
+ 25) at the end of the second sentence; in the 35 total three-word sequences, there will be 31 different three-class patterns. Usually in

the York Inventory "D" values for full 3,500-word samples are between 820 and 960, although there are many exceptions.[21] What is remarkable about the "D" value is its stability in the cases of most writers. For example, Boyle's "D" exceeded 1,000 between the 3125th and the 3180th word in samples from three different works; Bacon, who possessed a notable degree of control over his syntax and sentence proportions,[22] showed in six widely different samples a "D" that held within the range of 878 to 937, with five of them clustered between 918 and 937. Three Burton samples fell between 980 and 994 on the "D" scale. Six Jeremy Taylor samples fell between 816 and 867. What these and other figures suggest is that in many cases there is a natural range or limit to the degree to which a writer will exploit the syntactic possibilities of the language. Figure 4.10 gives the "D" statistics for our 22 samples.

Despite its immense utility as an attributive instrument, the "D"

Figure 4.10 "D" STATISTIC

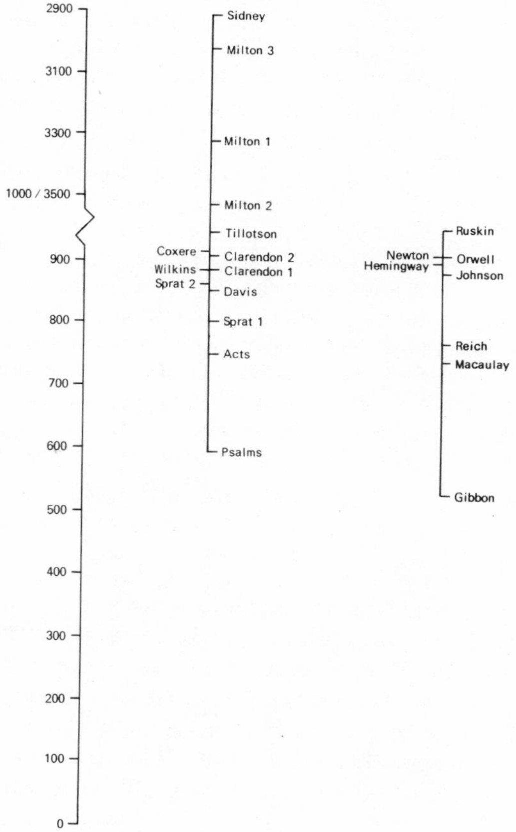

statistic need not be left entirely in the realm of detective work and mathematical abstraction. Both "D" itself and the listing that follows it of all the different patterns in the coded text can give, in an objective form, important information about things which we only vaguely sense in the natural language text, and about which we may be quite inarticulate. By way of illustration, let us consider, to the 51st word, each of two passages, one taken from Gibbon, the other from Sidney. To Gibbon terms like "monotonous" and "unvarying" have been applied; as for Sidney, no one who has read him can have missed the extraordinary richness and variety of texture that his prose presents. Their "D"'s for full samples are 479 and 1000/2975 respectively. Translations are given underneath, to the 51st word:

> One may be a Poet without versing and a versifier without Poetry. But yet presuppose it were inseparable, as indeed it seemeth Scalliger judgeth truly, it were an inseparable commendation. For if Oratio, next to Ratio, Speech next to Reason, be the greatest gift bestowed upon Mortality, that cannot be praiseless, which doth most polish that blessing of speech; which considereth each word not onely as a man may say by his forcible quality, but by his best measured quantity: carrying even in themselves a Harmony, without perchance number, measure, order, proportion, be in our time grown odious.
>
> (Sidney, 9004, *Defence,* 5)

11 21 21 <u>31 01 51</u> 07 41 <u>31 01 51</u> 01 99 41 91 02 00 11 21 03 42 33 61 02 00 01 02 04 11 21 <u>31 03 01</u> 99 41 42 01 <u>03 51 01</u> 01 <u>03 51 01</u> 21 <u>31 03 01</u> 06 51 01 11 21 35 21 03

> The liberality of Constantine increased in a just proportion to his faith and to his vices. He assigned in each city a regular allowance of corn to supply the fund of ecclesiastical charity; and the persons of both sexes who embraced the monastic life became the peculiar favorites of their sovereign. The Christian temples of Antioch, Alexandria, Jerusalem, Constantinople, etc. displayed the ostentatious piety of a prince ambitious in a declining age to equal the perfect labors of antiquity.
>
> (Gibbon, 9102, *Decline and Fall,* II, 466)

31 01 51 01 02 51 31 03 01 51 31 01 41 51 31 01 99 11 02 51 31 01 31 03 01 51 01 62 05 31 01 51 03 01 41 31 01 51 31 01 43 02 31 03 01 02 31 03 01 51 31 01

An interesting quantitative fact is that within 51 words the divergence between these two men is already large: The "D" for 51 words of Sidney is 40, the "D" for exactly the same amount of Gibbon is 32. Other interesting data include the fact that only four of Sidney's patterns (underlined) are repeated: 31-01-51, 03-51-01, 31-03-01, and 01-03-51; in each case there is a single repetition. By contrast, Gibbon gives us five repeated patterns in the following total quantities:

    5   51-31-01
    4   31-03-01
    3   31-01-51
    3   03-01-51
    2   01-51-01

In addition to a quantification of our hunches (everybody's hunches) about syntactic uniformity, the list of Gibbon's repeated phrases offers a preliminary insight into how much of his sentence building was carried out with prepositional phrases. Look again at Figure 4.10 and then return (as we always must) to the text and look again at the building process: the constant avoidance of hypotaxis, the constant reliance on prepositional phrases. We should also return to Sidney, in the light both of his enormously high "D" overall and of the "D" in the passage above. In such a return we can see some of the subtle asymmetry that is so much a part of Sidney's style—the possibly calculated skewing of parallel elements. Notice the asymmetric parallelism between "Poet without versing" (01-51-07) and "versifier without Poetry" (01-51-01), and the similar one between "his forcible quality" (31-03-01) and "best measured quantity" (04-03-01). Similar close reading throughout any piece of Sidney's will reveal his constant avoidance both of exactly symmetrical parallelism and of identical sequences of word classes. Similarly, close reading between the "D" register and the text will repay the reader of Gibbon, Burton, or Stillingfleet. In the case of Burton we have a paradox: enormous range (a "D" value close to 1,000), combined with a very high incidence of his five or six favorite patterns; in short, within an extensive exploitation of the language's resources a heavy dependence on a limited number of stereotyped constructions. In the case of Stillingfleet, we find in the listing of three-class patterns some accounting for that "inability to unbend," that "impression of being in full dress," and that lack of "familiarity of manner" which Mitchell found in him.[23] He is the Inventory's high man in patterns containing the sequences 43-42 ("which if," "who, although"), and 42-42 ("if when," "while unless"), signal marks of a heavily embedded style.

Although it would be possible to infer from the listing of three-class patterns under the "D" statistic the incidence of class clusters that seem to be evidence of parallel forms, it has proven more convenient in the York Inventory to sort them and list them separately. Those we list begin with simple noun-noun-noun (01-01-01) and include noun-noun-noun-noun (01-01-01-01), noun-coordinator-adjective (01-41-03), noun-coordinator-determiner (01-41-31), and pairs of the following joined by coordinator—noun (01), verb (02), adjective (03), adverb (04), infinitive (05), gerund (07)—triplets

Figure 4.11a WORD SERIATION TOTAL

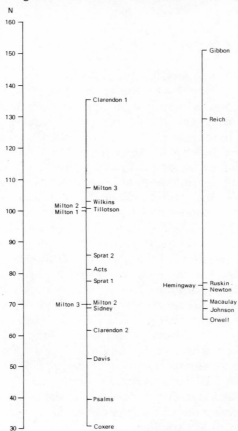

(X-X-41-X) of noun, verb, adjective, adverb, and infinitive, and an additional dozen unusual parallel series such as the polysyndetic tetracolon of infinitives (05-41-05-41-05-41-05). Although the counting of such strings does not give a 100% accurate enumeration of word-parallelism—for instance, sentence compounding often is carried by a sequence 01-41-01 or 01-41-31—the degree of error *tends* to be similar for all samples. Although a hand count of word series will be lower than a machine count because of the effect of sentence compounding, the difference is small, ranging from five in our Gibbon to three in our Macaulay sample. Similarly, attributive nouns, which are the linguistic infantry of Pentagon officials, sociologists, and other social engineers, might inflate the figures for collocations like noun-noun-noun. But fortunately such constructions as "Aircraft lubrication petroleum products," "Negro neighborhood expert," and "repression anxiety syndrome" are relatively uncommon in the writ-

Figure 4.11b WORD SERIATION, DOUBLETS OF NOUNS, VERBS, ADJECTIVES

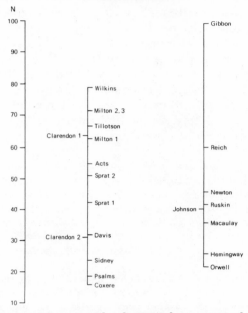

ers under review, except for Charles Reich. A manual count of series in the Reich sample showed a total of 109 vs. 128 counted by machine, the bulk of the error having been interpolated by Reich's noun attribution habit.

The *caveats* deployed, we can turn to Figure 4.11a. This figure confirms a few previously known facts: that the Psalms are written in a "chaste" style (one presumes this means unexpanded), and that Gibbon is among the most fecund seriators in the English Language. Between these two extremes fall some surprises, notably Reich, Sidney, and Johnson. One would think that the seemingly amplified styles of Sidney and Johnson would be rich in word seriation, and one would not expect our contemporary Charles Reich to be seriating more than Milton, Clarendon, and Sprat, even with his attributives factored out. Once again, we are driven back to the texts. One does not have to read far in Reich to find collocations like "furniture and appliances," "see, hear, and meet," "tradition and custom," or "warmth, fondness, affection, and companionship." Reich's fecundity in word series is largely a byproduct of his propensity for tautological and pleonastic redundancy. *His* quantitative mystery is soon unveil'd. The sparseness of word series in Sidney is an aspect partly of his asymmetry and partly of the fact that his amplification, like much of Johnson's, tends to be of more-than-single-word units.

One principal index of stylistic difference used by students of style has been the doublet.[24] It is useful, therefore, in the light of previous stylistic studies, to examine our 22 samples for nothing but pairs of adjectives, nouns, and verbs (X-41-X) (Figure 4.11b). Once again, Gibbon comes in very high, Sidney very low. Like Sidney's, Johnson's low number is surprising, especially in the light of the thoroughly documented treatment of Johnson's tendency to double things.[25] Perhaps some illustration is in order; in the passages by Gibbon and Johnson below, the reason for the difference revealed by Figure 4.11 can be seen; in two writers, both of whom can be said to be "parallelistic," we find the parallelism operating at different levels and on different scales.

> The *discipline and tactics* of the *Greeks and Romans* form an interesting part of their national manners. The attentive study of the military operations of *Xenophon or Caesar or Frederic,* when they are described by the same genius which *conceived and executed* them, may tend to improve (if such improvement can be used) the art of destroying the human species.
>
> (Gibbon, 9102, *Decline and Fall,* III, 576)

> By this procedure, I know not whether the students will find their cause promoted, or the compassion which they expect much increased. Let their conduct be impartially surveyed; let them be allowed no longer to direct attention at their pleasure, by expatiating on their own deserts; let neither the dignity of knowledge over-awe the judgment, nor the graces of elegance seduce it. It will then, perhaps, be found, that they were not able to produce claims to kinder treatment, but provoked the calamities which they suffered, and seldom wanted friends, but when they wanted virtue.
>
> (Johnson, 9106, *Rambler,* I, 87)

In the light of Figure 4.11, the Gibbon paragraph needs no comment beyond the italicizing of the doublets and triplets. The Johnson passage will reward closer scrutiny. Certainly the passage is parallelistic, balanced, and doubled—but primarily at the level of the full predicate or even the complete clause. If we schematize the Johnson passage, perhaps the kind and size of the parallels will be more readily seen:

(1) . . . find their cause promoted
          the compassion . . . much increased

(2) Let their conduct be impartially surveyed;
     let them be allowed no longer to direct attention at their pleasure
     let neither the dignity of knowledge over-awe the judgment
          nor   the graces of elegance   seduce it.

(3) . . . they were not able to produce claims to kinder treatment
          but provoked the calamities which they suffered,

| | and |
| seldom | wanted friends |
| but when they wanted virtue. |

Notice the doubling here specifically of verb units and verbal units: promoted/increased, be surveyed/be allowed, over-awe/seduce, were not able to produce/provoked, wanted/wanted. We shall return to this interesting phenomenon in Johnson's style in Chapter 5. One conclusion that we can draw in the meantime is that in some cases (like Gibbon's and Reich's) the mere data can give us a fairly precise idea of things to look for; in other cases within the conventions we are using, the data—in conjunction with careful reading—can tell us what to look beyond.

SENTENCE CLOSINGS

The most common exit from an English sentence is one of the several varieties of prepositional phrase[26] (as in the clause just concluded); next to that is the pairing of a noun and noun. Third is the nominal cluster (31-03-01). The options open to a writer for ending a sentence are fewer than those for beginning, and for reasons obvious to us if we think a while. Although bound to the context generated in the previous sentence, a writer beginning a sentence has a number of choices; not so when he ends same: he has opened, entered, and occupied the syntactic box, which now he must get out of—out of which he must now get—escape from which is an absolute necessity. Only in rare instances does a writer riffle through the options to find the "right" terminus or work hard to avoid a customary ending.

Both range and predisposition to certain patterns in sentence endings tend to be habitual in a writer, to be in short part of his style, although perhaps less obviously so than some other features because of the prepositional tendency in sentence endings at large in the language. In Figure 4.12, we see different closings (three-class) as a percentage of total sentences, just as we saw different openings in Figure 4.6. Notice that on the average the numbers in this Figure are about 15% lower than in Figure 4.6, Sentence Openings.

Once again, we have a few surprises. For the first time, Sidney falls from being our most varied writer; indeed in this measure he is indicated as less various than Hemingway, who had a harder time achieving variety on this index because he was writing more (and shorter) sentences.[27] Davis's sentences are more various in their closing than in their opening (a real anomaly), and Newton, having given only the eighth most various sample in its openings, has given us a sample the endings of which not only are varied but are distinguished by their high incidence of verbs. A contrast of Newton's endings with those of Gibbon can be revealing:

Figure 4.12 DIFFERENT CLOSINGS AS % OF SENTENCES

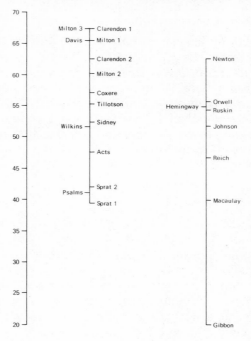

Newton

. . . can pass through both	02-51-11
. . . I have not tried it myself	02-11-11
. . . of very good and full Colours	41-03-01
. . . They do not reflect or transmit	02-41-02
. . . and thereby looks yellow	04-02-03
. . . position of the eye to the light	51-31-01
. . . I cannot yet affirm by experience	02-51-01

(Newton, 9078, *Opticks,* 88)

Gibbon

. . . their various and almost incredible disasters	34-03-01
. . . of the Greek-fire	51-31-01
. . . to that of the emperor	51-31-01
. . . youthful vigor of the Saracens	51-31-01
. . . so jealous of the truth	51-31-01
. . . contact with the air	51-31-01
. . . from evergreen firs	51-03-01

(Gibbon, 9102, *Decline and Fall,* 416)

Gibbon, incidentally, is our high sample in the closing 51-31-01 (preposition-determiner-noun), which accounts for 29% of his sentence endings.

One kind of sentence ending or another *can* be a part of an author's stylistic signature. Sidney is often distinguished by the modified noun cluster 31-03-01 (determiner-adjective-noun), and Macaulay had an inordinate penchant for 01-51-01 (noun-preposition-noun), which is illustrated below:

> *Selected examples:* multitude of adversaries. . . .madness of hunger.
> . . .mind of Addison. . . .summit of power. . . .city of Genoa.
> . . .statements concerning facts. . . .Satires of Juvenal. . . .point
> from Horace. . . .beauty of Lucina. . . .Rape of Proserpine.
>
> (Macaulay, 9111, *Essays*, III, 448-449)

CONCLUSIONS

Perhaps "conclusion" is a misnomer, since except for the chapter's coming to an end there is little to conclude. There has been no argument. We have considered a succession of sentence features that, within the limitations of our word-class taxonomy, can provide clues to constant form. On the basis of what we have seen in the chapter, we can say that Sidney and Milton wrote long, hypotactic sentences characterized by subtle asymmetries—in brief, Ciceronian sentences. This is nothing new. We can also say that there is more to a "Biblical" style than has been suggested, that in syntax Johnson and Gibbon are radically different, and that of all the prose writers of the period 1570–1970 Sidney made the most extensive, perhaps the most daring, exploitation of the riches offered by our mother tongue. These might be in some wise new; they are certainly modest. If, however, an analytic system can provide a chastening of our stereotypes (as this one certainly can), together with a few modest conclusions, then it is worth pursuing further, and having examined constant form in the sentence we can go on to look at the question of stylistic types.

Table 4.5 STATISTICS FOR CHAPTER 4

Category	9004 Sidney	9012 Psalms	9013 Acts	9048 Milton 1	9049 Milton 2	9060 Milton 3	9031 Clarendon 1	9033 Clarendon 2	9090 Wilkins	9067 Sprat 1	9068 Sprat 2
01	19.4	20.4	21.2	19.8	21.8	18.9	21.9	20.2	19.3	19.7	19.1
02	8.2	12.2	11.9	6.5	6.8	7.8	7.0	8.4	6.1	7.2	6.6
03	7.3	3.6	2.8	8.7	8.2	8.5	5.7	5.3	8.3	8.0	8.7
04	1.8	.5	.7	1.7	1.3	1.8	1.1	1.4	1.2	1.6	1.4
05	1.8	.8	.7	2.4	2.1	2.0	2.3	2.0	1.6	1.6	2.3
06	1.4	.3	1.8	1.7	1.5	1.7	1.2	1.0	.7	.6	.8
07	.8	.1	.1	.9	.8	1.2	.7	.6	.8	.6	1.1
11	7.3	10.6	10.4	5.5	.3	5.7	6.0	7.3	6.9	8.6	7.2
21	8.3	8.0	6.0	6.5	6.3	8.3	7.0	8.2	9.8	6.7	7.3
31	11.0	16.7	11.9	12.5	.9	11.6	14.2	.9	11.9	14.1	12.8
33	1.4	2.	.0	1.0	.6	.7	1.0	1.1	1.1	.9	1.1
34	2.4	1.0	1.5	3.2	2.6	2.6	1.7	2.6	1.1	2.8	3.7
35	1.0	1.0	.6	1.1	.9	1.0	.8	.9	.8	.4	.5
41	4.0	4.7	7.6	6.3	5.1	5.7	6.1	5.0	4.8	4.2	5.3
42	3.6	1.2	2.2	3.1	2.2	2.9	2.2	2.4	2.8	1.9	2.3
43	2.4	1.5	2.3	1.7	2.0	2.8	2.4	3.1	1.8	2.1	1.7
44	.1	.6	.3	1.0	.7	.3	.1	.0	.2	.0	.2
45	1.2	.2	.3	1.1	.8	1.0	.5	.3	.6	.8	.5
51	11.1	11.4	12.1	12.3	12.5	10.6	14.0	12.5	12.7	13.6	12.1
61	.8	1.0	.5	.6	.3	.9	.6	.5	1.3	.8	1.0
62	1.8	.4	.7	2.2	1.9	2.1	2.4	2.1	2.1	1.9	2.2
91	1.5	.4	.7	.6	.9	1.1	.5	.4	1.3	.8	.8
Sent L	38.3	19.6	26.8	66.5	53.3	48.7	76.2	61.6	29.7	27.1	39.4
Init 41 N	31	18	76	28	13	26	10	15	15	34	26
Init Syn	61	27	89	32	15	33	12	21	46	50	37
Init 51N	5	6	2	4	11	4	3	4	6	13	12
DSO/N	$\frac{80}{92}$	$\frac{77}{174}$	$\frac{68}{129}$	$\frac{41}{52}$	$\frac{53}{66}$	$\frac{58}{72}$	$\frac{36}{47}$	$\frac{46}{57}$	$\frac{82}{117}$	$\frac{78}{129}$	$\frac{67}{89}$
"D"	$\frac{1000}{2900}$	595	750	$\frac{1000}{3520}$	994	$\frac{1000}{3040}$	899	910	899	800	875
Series	69	39	81	105	100	108	136	62	104	78	85
Doublets	24	18	55	62	71	70	63	31	78	42	51
DSC/N	$\frac{48}{92}$	$\frac{72}{174}$	$\frac{62}{129}$	$\frac{34}{52}$	$\frac{41}{66}$	$\frac{49}{72}$	$\frac{32}{47}$	$\frac{36}{57}$	$\frac{61}{117}$	$\frac{48}{129}$	$\frac{38}{89}$
Strings	58	50	81	74	90	44	144	90	86	136	101
"M"	455	172	171	478	362	398	337	271	402	454	513
Sent (N)	92	174	129	52	66	72	47	57	117	129	89
Unsub Sent (N)	13	109	46	1	15	13	5	5	41	46	19
1st Sub $\overline{X}$	9.8	8.1	12.6	13.8	20.0	14.9	29.3	21.9	11.2	11.9	14.5
Anaphora	10	71	41	0	5	11	8	8	22	33	25

Table 4.5 (continued)

Category	9087 Tillotson	9066 Coxere	9100 Davis	9078 Newton	9106 Johnson	9102 Gibbon	9111 Macaulay	9103 Ruskin	9301 Hemingway	9401 Orwell	9402 Reich
01	19.6	17.5	21.6	21.4	20.3	27.4	24.4	20.6	20.1	20.2	25.7
02	5.8	10.0	8.2	6.2	8.9	7.5	8.7	6.2	8.1	7.1	7.6
03	7.5	4.3	6.2	9.1	6.4	8.4	7.0	9.3	6.7	8.8	9.0
04	1.7	.7	1.1	2.0	1.4	1.1	1.1	1.6	1.5	2.5	1.7
05	2.0	2.2	1.8	1.0	2.3	1.0	1.3	1.1	1.9	1.7	1.5
06	1.0	1.9	2.0	1.5	.8	.1	.7	1.2	2.0	.5	.7
07	1.2	.2	.3	.8	.8	.4	.9	.6	.5	.3	.5
11	8.3	12.6	9.3	5.4	6.5	1.9	5.2	5.6	8.0	7.2	5.3
21'	6.7	7.6	4.0	5.9	7.6	5.4	6.5	7.2	7.5	8.8	7.6
31	12.1	11.6	13.1	14.5	12.4	18.0	13.4	14.2	14.9	12.4	13.3
33	1.0	.6	1.1	1.0	1.1	.4	.6	.8	.9	.6	.2
34	1.8	4.2	1.6	2.1	2.5	1.2	2.0	2.6	2.2	3.3	1.6
35	.7	1.2	.4	.6	.7	.2	.7	.8	.8	1.1	1.0
41	6.1	4.1	4.9	5.6	5.0	6.5	4.2	4.8	4.3	3.9	4.4
42	2.0	3.0	1.6	2.5	2.6	1.2	2.1	1.9	2.7	2.6	1.7
43	2.0	1.7	1.7	1.2	2.4	1.6	1.6	1.6	1.5	1.7	1.8
44	.2	.0	.0	.0	.0	.0	.0	.0	.0	.0	.1
45	.7	.4	1.1	.8	.8	.2	.2	.4	.4	.5	.5
51	13.8	10.5	13.9	13.5	12.9	15.3	14.6	14.4	11.7	11.1	11.9
61	.6	.4	.4	.5	.8	.2	.4	.7	.7	.8	.7
62	2.0	2.4	1.9	.9	2.6	.9	1.6	1.4	1.7	1.9	1.6
91	.4	.4	.7	.9	.3	.0	.3	.4	.1	.4	.3
Sent L	45.0	28.1	58.0	44.1	44.4	36.6	20.5	42.3	26.5	20.4	23.1
Init 41N	20	12	0	34	7	5	12	11	8	18	12
Init Syn	26	26	5	49	13	9	24	18	23	27	25
Init 51N	17	9	4	6	4	18	18	5	14	24	17
DSC/N	54/77	64/123	29/61	58/79	44/81	40/96	92/168	59/82	79/131	105/168	95/151
"D"	944	914	851	911	893	479	740	921	898	913	773
Series	101	31	51	76	68	152	71	77	76	67	129
Doublets	67	16	32	46	40	99	36	42	26	22	60
DSC/N	43/77	72/123	40/61	50/79	42/81	19/96	67/168	44/82	72/131	93/168	71/151
Strings	137	61	84	94	110	133	140	138	81	73	84
"M"	395	338	372	493	402	379	362	498	386	516	428
Sent (N)	77	123	61	79	81	96	168	82	131	168	151
Unsub Sent (N)	18	44	13	21	20	35	90	22	52	72	76
1st Sub $\overline{X}$	16.8	13.5	26.8	10.0	16.0	14.6	9.3	23.3	10.9	8.4	11.2
Anaphora	20	40	19	8	16	52	50	21	31	26	39

It would be endless to run over the several Defects of Style among us: I shall therefore say nothing of the mean *and the* paultry *(which are usually attended by the* fustian,*) much less of the* slovenly *or indecent. Two Things I will just warn you against: The first is, the Frequency of flat, unnecessary Epithets; and the other is, the Folly of using old threadbare Phrases, which will often make you go out of your Way to find and apply them; are nauseous to rational Hearers, and will seldom express your Meaning as well as your own natural Words.*

Jonathan Swift, "Letter to a Young Gentleman"

Chapter 5

STYLISTIC TYPES

T HE LITERATURE of stylistics is saturated with attempts at stylistic typology, attempts to name a supposed set of characteristics that groups of writers all display. We have all heard of those venerable chestnuts Senecan and Ciceronian, the kings of the stylistician's chessboard, flanked by the queens Biblical and Colloquial, the bishops (Attic, Asian, African, and Gorgianic), the knights (dark, obscure, sprightly, and rhythmical), and the rooks (plain, ornate, balanced, and turgid). The pawns are too numerous to name. Indeed, in a single book[1] the eminent scholar George Williamson managed to discover 57 varieties of stylistic type in the seventeenth century alone.

Attempts to develop a typological nomenclature have on the whole been unsuccessful: writers are too individual to be dough for the typologist's cookie cutter, and the typological label often makes confusions between time and style (as in Restoration style) or between the writer's style and his person (Noel Coward's gay style, Gibbon's fat style, King James I's silly style, etc., etc.). Paradigmatic types (Senecan, Ciceronian) are more useful than many, since they refer the reader to specific models, the characteristics of which can be ascertained, but much of the value of such types is negated by human individuality.[2] Of all the types, perhaps the most worthy of preservation are those that direct our attention to particular linguistic facts; literary style, after all, is manifested in linguistic form, and types that direct our attention to language are likelier than others to stand the test of sustained scrutiny. It is with such types that we

shall deal in the present chapter: nominal, verbal, passive, and modifying styles. As in the last chapter, we shall use a limited number of
writers (13) and a limited number of samples (33). The selection of
samples once again reflects the bias of the body of authors included
in the Inventory at the end of 1972; it consists almost exclusively of
people who wrote prior to 1850, preponderantly of people who
wrote prior to 1700. In Table 5.1, the 33 samples are listed.*

NOMINAL STYLES

There are several styles in the period 1580 to 1850 that make extensive use of nouns and nominal constructions. Most of the writers in
this time period of our study used a noun roughly one word in five:[3]
128 of our first 152 samples produced between 19.0% and 22.5%
nouns. It can be said that prior to 1850 a style with 23% nouns is
abnormally nominal. The nominal styles that we first uncovered
were those of Burton,[4] Macaulay, and Gibbon. Figure 5.1 shows the
13 writers for this chapter, with the percentage of nouns for each of
their samples. The percentages of nouns seem straightforward
enough: we can contrast the un-nominal Sprat, Bunyan, Boyle, and
Sidney with our nominal three. In addition, we might make a few assumptions about what other classes of words nouns might carry in
train with them: surely the adjective (which without the noun would
hardly exist); surely also the determiner. Since prepositions are likely to have nouns as their objects, a large number of prepositions
should usually mean a large number of nouns; perhaps the converse
is true, and perhaps the nominal style is rich in both prepositions
and the phrase 51-31-01. All the above assumptions will be tested in
this section.

A look at Gibbon and Burton will show us what nominal styles can
look like:

> To the *west* the Syrian kingdom is bounded by the sea: and the ruin of
> Aradus, a small island or peninsula on the coast, was postponed dur-
> ing ten years. But the hills of Libanus abounded in timber; the trade of
> Phoenicia was populous in mariners: and a fleet of seventeen hundred
> barks was equipped and manned by the natives of the desert.
>   (Gibbon, 9106, *Decline and Fall*, V, 345)

> I will have no bogs, fens, marshes, vast woods, deserts, heaths, com-
> mons, but all enclosed (yet not depopulated, and therefore take heed
> you mistake me not); for that which is common, and every man's, is no

*All references to primary text are by author, sample number, work, and page. A
full catalog of the samples is given in Appendix B. Because of the number of samples
for some authors (e.g., Sidney, Dryden), we have merely marked the high and low
point of each author in each of the Figures.

Table 5.1 SAMPLES FOR CHAPTER 5 [a]

9004	Sidney	Defense of Poesie	1
9005	Sidney	"Old" Arcadia	2
9006	Sidney	"Old" Arcadia	3
9007	Sidney	"New" Arcadia	4
9008	Sidney	"New" Arcadia	5
9009	Sidney	Letters	6
9024	Jonson	Timber	
9028	Burton	Anatomy of Melancholy	1
9029	Burton	Anatomy of Melancholy	2
9030	Burton	Anatomy of Melancholy	3
9031	Clarendon	History of the Rebellion	1
9032	Clarendon	History of the Rebellion	2
9033	Clarendon	History of the Rebellion	3
9064	Bunyan	Pilgrim's Progress	1
9065	Bunyan	Grace Abounding	2
9067	Sprat	Life of Cowley	1
9068	Sprat	History of the Royal Society	2
9069	Sprat	History of the Royal Society	3
9075	Boyle	. . . Style of Holy Scriptures	1
9076	Boyle	. . . Natural Philosophy	2
9077	Boyle	Origin of Forms and Qualities	3
9096	Dryden	Essays	1
9097	Dryden	**Of Dramatick Poesie**	2
9098	Dryden	Original and Progress of Satire	3
9099	Dryden	Essays	4
9106	Johnson	Rambler	
9102	Gibbon	Decline and Fall	
9110	Carlyle	Sartor Resartus	
9111	Macaulay	Essays	
9201	DeQuincey	Confessions	1
9203	DeQuincey	Confessions	2
9205	Coleridge	Biographia Literaria	1
9206	Coleridge	Biographia Literaria	2

[a]All references to primary text are by author, sample number, and work, and pages. A full catalog of the samples is given in the Appendix B. Because of the number of samples for some authors (e.g., Sidney, Dryden), we have merely marked the high and low point of each author in each of the Figures.

Figure 5.1 NOUNS AS % OF TEXT

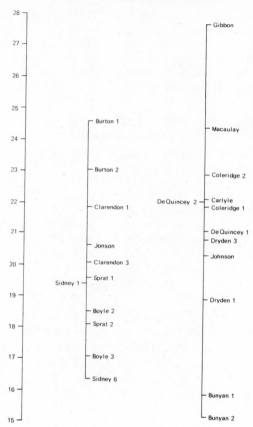

man's; the richest counties are still enclosed, as Essex, Kent, with us, etc., Spain, Italy; and where enclosures are least in quantity, they are best husbanded, as about Florence in Italy, Damascus in Syria, etc., which are liker gardens than fields. I will not have a barren acre in all my territories, not so much as the tops of mountains: where nature fails, it shall be supplied by art: lakes and rivers shall not be left desolate.

(Burton, 9028, *Anatomy,* I, 100)

Of course, we immediately encounter a difficulty. Both styles contain many nouns, but in different ways, for Gibbon seems to be nominalizing all constructions where some option exists, especially in the form of prepositional phrases. For example:

Gibbon	*Possible option*
The hills of *Libanus* abounded in *timber;* the trade of *Phoenicia* was populous in mariners: and a *fleet* of seventeen hundred barks was equipped and manned by the natives of the desert.	The Lebanese hills were well wooded; there were many mariners among the Phoenician merchants; and seventeen hundred barks were equipped and manned by the natives of the desert.

Without egregious distortions or rewording, we have managed to remove four (italicized) nouns from the Gibbon original.[5] Clearly, the nominalizing drive is less strong in Burton, on whom we can perform a similar exercise in reverse:

Burton	*Possible option*
I will have no bogs, fens . . . heaths, commons, but all enclosed (yet not depopulated, and therefore take heed you mistake me not); for that which is common, and every man's, is no man's . . .	I will have no bogs . . . commons, but all within *enclosures* (yet not without *population,* and therefore take heed you make no *mistake*); for *property* in *common,* which is every man's, is no man's . . .

Burton is not generating nominal constructions at every opportunity; there were five or more opportunities in the short passage above that he missed or avoided. What accounts for Burton's great density of nouns is that he tends, like Swift and Rabelais, toward enormously long seriations. Noteworthy in Burton's case is the fact that the series tend to be nouns and are generated almost entirely without determiners:

smiths, forge-men, brewers, bakers, metal-men, etc.

slaughter-houses, chandlers, curriers

druggers, physicians, musicians, etc.

wine, spice, tobacco, silk, velvet, cloth of gold, lace, jewels, etc.

(Burton, 9028, *Anatomy, passim.*)

A look at determiner density in our thirteen writers specifies the observation that we have just made. This is given in Figure 5.2. In short, Burton deviates from an *a priori* assumption about nominal style—that it would be heavy in determiners. And so, we notice in Figure 5.2, does Macaulay. A similar assumption about prepositions[6] shows Macaulay conforming, Burton deviating in Figure 5.3a. Generally, it can be said that nominal styles are high in prepositions, non-nominal styles low.[7] This is particularly true of styles like that of Gibbon, where the nominality of the writing derives from

Figure 5.2 DETERMINERS AS % OF TEXT

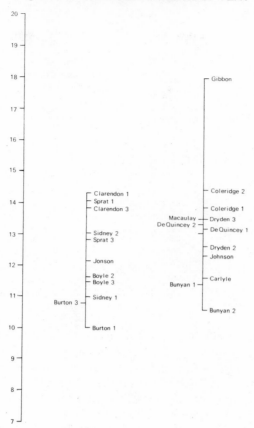

rampant nominalization, especially of predicates, rather than from the mere presence of nouns in abundance. Nominalization, together with suppression of verbs, is likely to produce prepositional sentences like the following sentence from Gibbon, for which I have given a denominalized, deprepositioned translation:

Gibbon	*Translation*
Such formidable emigrations no longer issue *from* the North; and the long repose, which has been imputed *to* the decrease of population, is the happy consequence *of* the progress *of* arts and agriculture. (Gibbon, *Decline and Fall,* IV, 93)	Such formidable emigrations no longer trouble us; the tribes have settled where they are now, not because they are less numerous, but because they have shared *in* the general technological progress *of* Western man.

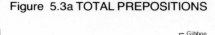

Figure 5.3a TOTAL PREPOSITIONS

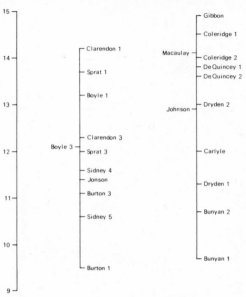

On the other hand, the parallel assumption that nominal styles should be high in the most common pattern in the English language,[8] the preposition-determiner-noun phrase (51-31-01), is refuted by the facts, as shown in Figure 5.3b. Notice that two of our less nominal writers, Sprat and Clarendon, produce three of the four top samples and that our least nominal writer of all, Bunyan, sits in the middle of the group, halfway between the very nominal Gibbon and the nearly-nominal Carlyle. Once again, Macaulay and Burton do not conform to the assumption. Figures 5.2 and 5.3 taken together offer a noteworthy artifact: that density of determiners is more indicative of the pattern 51-31-01 than it is of a large population of nouns.[9] Why this is a fact is difficult to explain. It simply seems to be a property of the language itself that four out of ten determiners are likely to end up in simple prepositional phrases (51-31-01); indeed, this relationship is the strongest that we or any other researchers working with a Fries-based system have thus far been able to discover either within the word classes or between word classes and syntactic clusters. A writer who is to stray far from the 4:10 proportion must be visibly and markedly deviant.

Density of determiners may be indicative, but far less strongly, of density of nouns. The surprisingly small positive correlation between these classes can be readily explained. Some writers write at a level of generalization that fills their discourse with plurals and/or

Figure 5.3b PREPOSITIONAL PHRASES
(51-31-01)

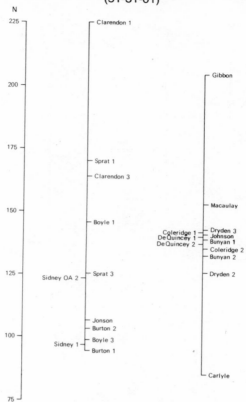

abstractions; despite their density of nouns, they will have fewer determiners than will less nominal writers. One example will suffice:

> Cowley, in *lines* weighty with *thought* and resplendent with *wit,* urged the chosen seed to take *possession* of the promised land flowing with *milk* and *honey,* that land which their great deliverer and lawgiver had seen as from the summit of *Pisgah,* but had not been permitted to enter.
>
> (Macaulay, 9135, *History,* I, 319)

This brings us to the odd case of Macaulay. For Macaulay's curious position as a nominal writer—his lack of determiners and of the phrase 51-31-01—we can look not only at Figures 5.2 and 5.3 together, but at the strung prepositional phrases given after the word-class distributions in the Inventory computer printouts. Macaulay's totals both for strung phrases and for strung phrases *without* determiners are the highest of our three nominal stylists, as we can see in Figures 5.4a and 5.4b. In addition, he is highest among these three for the

Figure 5.4a STRUNG PREPOSITIONAL PHRASES

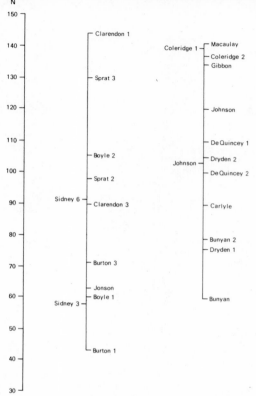

prepositional phrase cluster preposition-adjective-noun ("In green pastures" 51-03-01), as we can see in Figure 5.4b. Notice that in this cluster the determiner is omitted. A glimpse at some more of Macaulay's discourse can give us an example of various ways the determiners get suppressed:

51-03-01	It was *in small circles,* and, above all, in the House
51-01	*of Lords,* that his ascendancy was felt.
01	*Shaftesbury* seems to have troubled himself very
51-01-51-01	little *about theories of government.* Halifax was,
51-01	*in speculation,* a strong republican, and did not conceal
03-01-41-01	it. He often made *hereditary monarchy and aristoc-*
	racy the subjects of his keen pleasantry.

(Macaulay, 9135, *History,* IV, 228)

The italicized noun clusters and prepositional phrases are free of determiners. Another source of this peculiar syndrome in Macaulay's style is the large number of people named, which makes for a high incidence of proper names—"of Marlborough and Wellington," "ob-

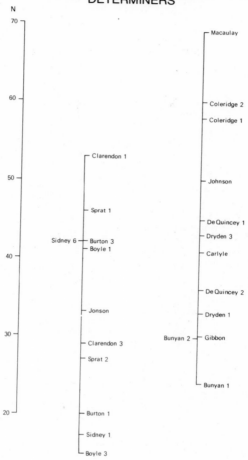

Figure 5.4b TOTAL STRUNG PREPOSITIONAL PHRASES WITHOUT DETERMINERS

jected to Halifax," "give power to Halifax," "the urgency of Lady Temple." This has the effect of sustaining a high level of both nouns and prepositions while suppressing determiners. It could be said of Gibbon, too, that his work is full of people. They do not, however, appear very often as people under their own names; their names, their titles, their functions undergo an unending succession of elegant variations, often through synecdoche and abstract personification. We never hear in Gibbon that "Julian got angry"; instead, we are likely to hear "The wrath of the emperor was stirred. . . ."

Before leaving the nominal style and its implications, we should look at the final class of word that we have associated with nominality—the adjective. Figure 5.5b gives adjective percentages for each of our 33 samples. Of all our criteria of nominality, this one *seems*

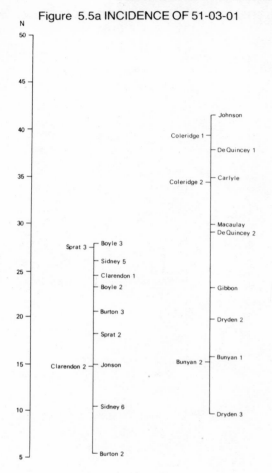

Figure 5.5a INCIDENCE OF 51-03-01

weakest for this group of writers.[10] Our mean figures for all three of our nominal stylists are below not only Carlyle and Coleridge (both "nearly" nominal) but also Boyle and Sprat, two of the least nominal writers in the group.

Perhaps most interesting of all our findings in this section has been that there does not seem to be a single nominal style. Even if we drop our minimum noun criterion to the 22% line (see Figure 5.1), we still have a number of difficulties and ambiguities; indeed, a few more than we had with just three writers; for whereas Coleridge would generally conform with prior expectations, Carlyle most emphatically would not[11] (see Figure 5.3).

The original postulator of a "nominal" *vs.* a "verbal" style, Rulon Wells, suggested as the nominal style's drawbacks its static quality,

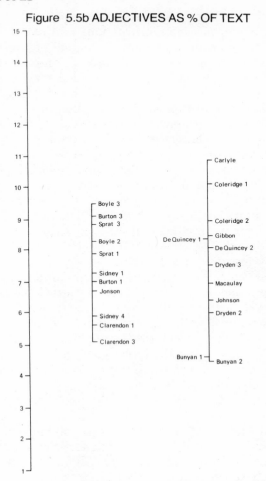

Figure 5.5b ADJECTIVES AS % OF TEXT

its lack of comprehensibility, and its monotony; its advantages are supposedly ease of writing, impersonality, and its distinct difference from conversational style. Staticness it certainly contains and probably the other two properties as well, when the "nominal" vehicle is being driven by a sociologist. It seems, in fact, that something close to the English dialect called Psychosemanto[12] was what Wells had in mind, since all three of the advantages that he offers embody the anti-personal and anti-literary values that Psychosemanto expresses. For example, (1) ease—"it is natural for those who are more concerned with what they say than with how they say it to choose this style"; (2) impersonality—the nominal style is offered as an alternative means to suppress personality, the other being use of the passive voice: and (3) non-conversational marking—"It sets off the writing as esoteric, specialized, technical."

What Wells described is not so much a nominal style as a style that contains many passive constructions and many "philosophic words," one in which anthropomorphic models of human events are suppressed in favor of abstract models. "Nominal" style would change the conversational "Foreman savaged Frazier" to "Aggression took place," or the everyday "I saw the children having their snack" to "Consumption of snack was observed." The second of each of these pairs of sentences carries at least four of the qualities that Wells identifies: staticness, lowered comprehensibility, impersonality, and nonconversational marking; as for monotony and ease, we can leave them to the metaphysicians. Interestingly, however, there are no more nouns in the second sentences of our pairs than in the first, *in spite of the nominalization of the predicate from the first sentence.* Similarly, Johnson, for all his passives and philosophic words, for all his nominalization, writes a style with considerably fewer nouns than do Macaulay and Burton.[13]

Nominal styles are not a guarantee of either staticness, detachment, or impersonality. Macaulay's imagination, with its cast of thousands, was one of the vividest and busiest home movies of the last 200 years, and that vivid activity is everywhere present in his nominal style. Consider the "detachment" of the nearly-nominal Carlyle,[14] whose sociological writings look like early theater of involvement. And finally, take ten intelligent graduate students in English; ask them to read ten pages of the nominal Burton against ten pages of the non-nominal Hobbes. It does not require the imagination of a Macaulay to know which of the two men they would find the more impersonal.

What in the end can be said of a nominal style is what we said at the beginning: it is a style with (comparatively) a high density of nouns. It might acquire those nouns by nominalization, but it might not. It is likely to carry in train with it, or be carried in train with, word classes other than the noun but associated with it: the preposition and the determiner particularly, but possibly not the adjective. Among our three nominal test cases in this section, we have seen—even staying within the boundaries of the nominal syndrome outlined at the beginning—considerable degrees of individuality.

VERBAL STYLES

As with nominal styles, we might say that a verbal style is one in which there are comparatively a lot of verbs. The verb system, however, is a complex thing, containing not only true verbs but auxiliaries, participles, gerunds, infinitives, and the whole "be" system. Which of these "verb items" should be included? Our answer is that all of them should be and that finer discriminations can, indeed must, be made later. Figure 5.6a shows all 33 of our samples with the total percentage of total "verb items" for each.

Using Jonson as our touchstone, we can say that as a style reaches 18.5% in its total of verb items, it tends to become a verbal style.[15] In our group, such a criterion leaves us with Johnson, Clarendon, Sidney, Jonson, Dryden, and Bunyan. It is interesting to explore the verb system to see just to what degree these "verbal" writers are alike.

A natural starting place is the total of main verbs, excluding "be" main verbs.[16] We can see in Figure 5.6b, despite the strong overlap between Sidney and Bunyan for total verb units, that Bunyan is clearly the heaviest user of main verbs. The contrast between our lightest user and our heaviest can be illustrated as follows:[17]

> I was *astonished* to find myself translated by a touch of the pen not only into a Monsieur, but even into a self-multiplied Monsieur; or, speaking algebraically, into the square of Monsieur; having a chance at some future date of being perhaps cubed into Monsieur. From the latter, as I had hastily *torn* it open, out *dropped* a draft upon Smith, Payne & Smith for somewhere about forty guineas.
>
> (DeQuincey 9201, *Confessions*, 59)

> The which when I *began* to do, I *found* their visage changed; for they *looked* not so grimly on me as before I *thought* they did: And first, I *came* to the sixth of the Hebrews, yet trembling for fear it should *strike me, which,* when I had *considered,* I *found* that the falling there intended was *falling* quite away; that is, as I *conceived,* a falling from, and an absolute denial of, the Gospel of Remission of sins by Christ. . . .
>
> (Bunyan, 9065, *Grace Abounding*, 72)

When we try "be" as a main verb by itself, the order changes, as in Figure 5.7a. Bunyan, our original high man (Figure 5.6), has dropped back into the center of the group, with Jonson, Dryden, and the nonfiction of Sidney moving to the top.[18] Dryden's presence there can be ascribed to his tendency to write "exquisitely varied"[19] and distributed sentences, as well as to his tendency to rely on pattern markers in writing them:

> *There is* a sort of merit in delighting the spectators, which *is* a name more proper for them, than that of auditors; or else Horace *is* in the wrong, when he commends Lucilius for it.
>
> (Dryden, 9097, *Essays*, 7)

Jonson's presence also derives in part from pattern markers:

> *It is* a vile and a poor thing to place our happiness on these desires. say we wanted them all: famine ends famine.

> *There is* nothing valiant or solid to be hoped for from such as are always kempt and perfumed and every day smell of the tailor, the ex-

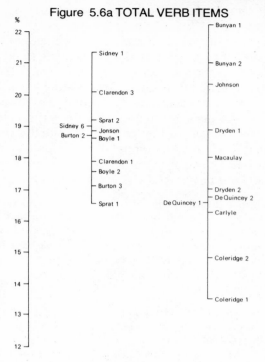

Figure 5.6a TOTAL VERB ITEMS

ceedingly curious, that are wholly in mending such an imperfection in the face, in taking away the morphew in the neck, or bleaching their hands at midnight, gumming and bridling their beards, or making the waist small, binding it with hoops, while the mind runs at waste.

(Jonson, 9024, *Timber*, 32)

It derives in very large part from his affection for aphorism:

He that would have his virtue published *is* not the servant of virtue, but glory.

(Jonson, 9024, *Timber*, 33)

Custom *is* the most certain mistress of language . . .

(Jonson, 9024, *Timber*, 33)

These in their turn are somewhat reminiscent of Dryden's own utterance about Jonson:

He invades authors like a monarch, and what would *be* theft in others *is* only victory in him.

(Dryden, 9097, *Dramatick Poesie*, 466)

No doubt it could be said, of all our examples above, that literary criticism, a magisterial art, must rely on generalization and that high

Figure 5.6b MAIN VERBS EXCLUDING "BE"
(CLASS 02 ALONE)

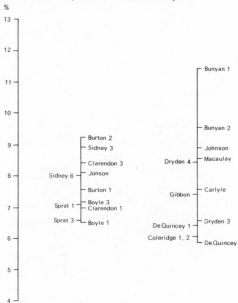

levels of generalization are likely to produce sentences like the following:

> Strong and glowing colours *are* the just resemblances of bold metaphors: but both must be judiciously applied; for there *is* a difference betwixt daring and fool-hardiness.
>
> (Dryden, 9098, *Preface to the Fables,* 327)

It could be said, yes, but it would be undermined by the numbers in Figure 5.7a of Gibbon and Johnson (both of whom wrote at high levels of generalization) as well as by the numbers of Coleridge (a literary critic).

We can turn at this point to another kind of verb item, the auxiliary. In the Inventory's word-class taxonomy, we discriminate three kinds: the tense auxiliaries *(shall, will, have),* the modals *(should, would, can, might, ought),* and auxiliary forms of the verb "be." For our present purposes, they can be lumped together, although in some kinds of author identification it is useful to separate the modals (with Newman, for example, and Mill) or the "be" auxiliaries (with Fitzgerald).[20] Figure 5.7b shows the percentage of auxiliaries among our 33 samples.

Once again, the order is not utterly faithful to what we would expect from Figure 5.6. Sprat and Clarendon, both on the boundary between verbal and non-verbal writers overall, come off rather high in

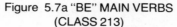

Figure 5.7a "BE" MAIN VERBS
(CLASS 213)

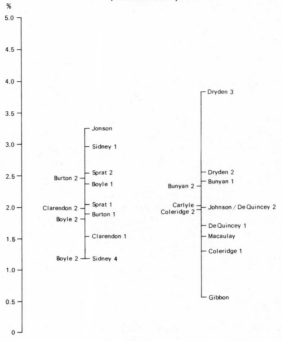

auxiliaries, as does Boyle. Of the general pattern in Figure 5.7b, it might be said that aphorism (which one so often encounters in *Timber*) tends to depress auxiliaries because it tends to make categorical generalizations, which use single, continuing-present verbs. We might also say that history, because of the strength of the temporal element in it, tends to increase them; among our top figures are Sprat's *History*, Clarendon, and Macaulay. Once again, however, a generalization is not so certain as we could wish. Gibbon, despite an enormous number of passive verbs,[21] each of which must take at least one auxiliary, does not in his history even cross the median line of Figure 5.7b. And Bacon, generating 4.7% auxiliaries in our sample from the aphoristic *Novum Organum*, generates fewer than 4% in our sample from the *History of Henry VII*.

Among some of the writers in Figure 5.7b there is a good deal of variation (for example, Burton, Sidney, Sprat). This would seem to indicate that auxiliaries are more context-sensitive than are certain other items in the verb system, notably the verbals and the main verbs. Despite the context sensitivity, there is some tendency for the figures of any one writer to cluster, and some of the writers can be clearly discriminated from all but a few others. Just to see one possi-

Figure 5.7b AUXILIARIES

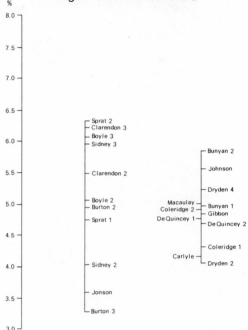

ble kind of difference between a style that uses few auxiliaries and one that uses many, we can look at Jonson and Clarendon:

> Yet we take pleasure in the lie, and are glad we *can* cosen ourselves. Nor is it only in our walls and ceilings, but all that we call happiness is mere painting and gilt, and all for money. What a thin membrane of honour that is! And how *hath* all true reputation fallen since money began to have any! Yet the great herd, the multitude, that in all other things *are* divided, in this alone conspire and agree: to love money.
>
> (Jonson, 9024, *Timber,* 33)

> And then, he *was* not to *be* shaken in his affection to the Government of the Church; tho' it *was* enough known that he *was* in no degree biased to any great inclination to the Person of any Church-man.
>
> (Clarendon, 9031, *History,* I, 332)

Having extruded the auxiliaries from the types of main verb, we can consider main verbs (02) and "be" form main verbs (213) together, as is done graphically in Figure 5.8a. Notice that this procedure is more meaningful than main verbs alone as given in Figure 5.6b. With all predicators taken together, Bunyan and Coleridge become truly isolated from all the others, and Dryden, whom I have always

Figure 5.8a TOTAL PREDICATORS

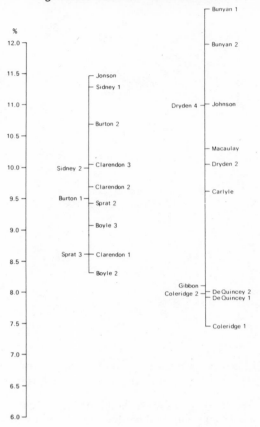

perceived as a more "verbal" writer than either Boyle or Sprat, draws well clear of those two.

Finally, we should look at the verbals: infinitives (05), participles (06), and gerunds (07). I prefer to consider the latter two together, the first separately.[22] We can see in Figure 5.8b that some writers, like Sidney, Jonson, DeQuincey, and Boyle, have a strong tendency to use participles and gerunds, and that others, like Burton, Coleridge, Dryden, and Gibbon, are inclined to stay away from them.

It is useful here to remind ourselves of the difference between a style heavy in gerunds and participles and one that is not:

> Plexirtus, *mingling* forsworn excuses with false-meant promises, glad-ly embraced the offer: and hastily *sending* back for those two Brothers (who at that time were with us *succouring* the gracious Queen Erona) by their virtue chiefly (if not only) obtained the conquest of that good-ly dominion. Which indeed done by them, gave them such an authori-

Figure 5.8b PARTICIPLES AND GERUNDS

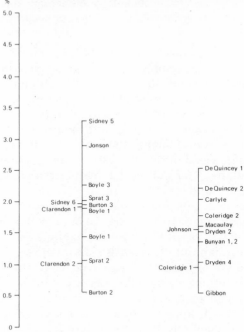

ty, that though he reigned, they in effect ruled, most men *honouring* them, because they only deserved honour; and many, *thinking* therein to please Plexirtus, *considering* how much he was bound unto them: while they likewise (with a certain, sincere boldness, of self-warranting friendship) accepted all openly and plainly, *thinking* nothing should ever by Plexirtus be thought too much in them, since all they were, was his.

(Sidney, 9007, New *Arcadia,* 293)

So that no man almost could conceive hope of *living* but *being left* a-live: and therefore every one was willing to make his self room, by *dispatching* almost any other: so that the great number in the ship was reduced to exceeding few, when of those few the most part weary of those troubles leapt into the boat, which was fast to the ship: but while they that were first, were cutting of the rope that tied it, others came *leaping* in, so disorderly, that they drowned both the boat, and themselves.

(Sidney, 9007, New *Arcadia,* 305)

If our leg or arm offend us, we covet by all means possible to redress it; and if we labour of a bodily disease, we send for a physician; but for the diseases of the mind, we take no notice of them. Lust harrows us on the one side; envy, anger, ambition on the other. We are torn in pieces by our passions, as so many wild horses, one in disposition, another in habit; one is melancholy, another mad; and which of us all seeks for help, doth acknowledge his error, or knows he is sick?

(Burton, 9028, *Anatomy*, 69)

It has been said that heavy use of verbals is "modern,"[23] although the figures on Jonson and Sidney would not seem to bear this theory out. Notice that the gerunds and participles, which I have italicized, in the Sidney illustrations make the sentence both more complex and more elliptical. Many of these verbals serve as verb centers of transformed subordinate clauses, and many of the participial phrases complicate and interrupt the sentence, much as Sidney's adverbial clauses do. Used in this way, the verbals are rather the opposite of "modernizing," assuming that by modern we mean language that is less complex and less interrupted.

In connection with this whole question, it is useful now to look at Figure 5.9, which offers in a biaxial treatment participles and gerunds (vertical axis) *vs.* predicators (horizontal axis). We can note that the intersection point of x-measure and y-measure of the various samples tend to fall along a 45-degree line. DeQuincey is a clear exception; Dryden represents a slight aberration in the opposite direction. A similar effect occurs in a similar plot in Milic's study of Swift, although Swift appears to be a notable exception. What the 45-degree line suggests is that there may be less of an historical trend than we thought; it suggests that, except in highly unusual styles like those of DeQuincey, Dryden, and Swift, writers who use many verbs also tend to use many verbals and that writers who are verb-suppressive are likely to be verbal-suppressive as well.[24] Although Figure 5.9 places some writers together who by traditional humanist prejudices seem to "belong" together (Coleridge and De Quincey, Sprat and Boyle), it also makes some surprising oppositions (Jonson and Johnson, Gibbon and Coleridge), and two of its widest separations (Coleridge and Johnson, Gibbon and Sidney, not to mention Gibbon and Johnson) come utterly unexpected to this writer, simply because not even professional critics habitually think of such "great" and "ornate" prose writers as being polar opposites in *any* measure.

Figure 5.10a gives for our 33 samples the total percentage of *all* verbals (infinitives and gerunds and participles), and Figure 5.10b gives infinitives alone. Notice that the spread between the top and bottom sample of the same writer is greater in both of these than in Figure 5.8b, especially in Burton's case. Notice also that Johnson is not only a positive generator of verbals but the most extensive and comprehensive exploiter of the English verb system that we have seen thus far. Some examples from him are instructive:

Figure 5.9 PARTICIPLES AND GERUNDS/PREDICATORS BIAXIAL

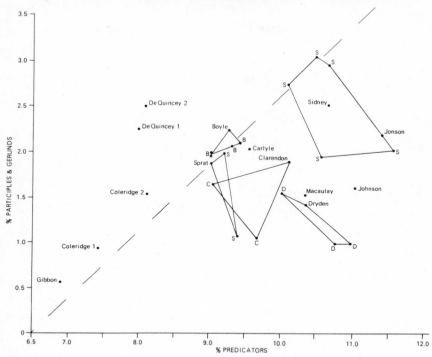

I naturally *love* to *talk* without much *thinking,* to *scatter* my merriment at random, and to *relax* my thoughts with ludicrous remarks and fanciful images . . .

(Johnson, 9106, *Rambler,* I, 90)

I often *change* my wig, and *wear* my hat over my eyes, by which I *hope* somewhat to *confound* them; for you *know* it *is* not fair to *sell* my face, without *admitting* me to *share* the profit.

(Johnson, 9106, *Rambler,* I, 91)

Although a Burton sample has the top percentage of infinitives in Figure 5.10b, Johnson is probably the most extensive user of infinitives among this particular group of writers. Here again, a common-sense return to the texts seems to be in order, so that we might discover what it is that apparently throws Burton's first sample so far out of line with the others. It would not require a ten-man search party to discover that our first Burton sample is thrown off line by its inclusion (through the random number table system) of a large part of one of his more conspicuous tirades, the series of infinitives in "Democritus to the Reader":

Figure 5.10a TOTAL VERBALS
05+06+07

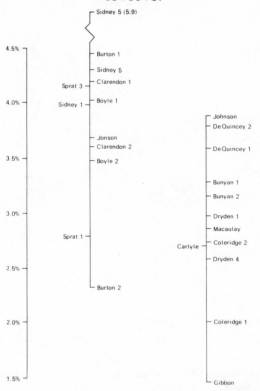

To *see* so much difference betwixt words and deeds . . .
To *see* a man *protest* friendship, *kiss* his hand . . .

(Burton, 9028, *Anatomy,* 69–70).

In the space of 600 words in this passage, Burton cuts loose no fewer than 53 infinitives, this total accounting for almost the entire aberration in his first sample.

As with the "nominal" styles, we have found that verbal styles, even when apparently quite similar in their *overall* usage of the whole verb system (Figure 5.6), can differ drastically in detail. It is probably inaccurate to say that there is a verbal style or even that there are ten verbal styles. The verb system in English (as denominated even by this simple taxonomy) is so complicated as to allow a very extensive set of alternative patterns of habit and choice. It would seem to be more accurate to speak of how individual writers use the verb system: Bunyan mainly in predicators, Johnson all across its range, Sprat most notably in the auxiliaries, DeQuincey in

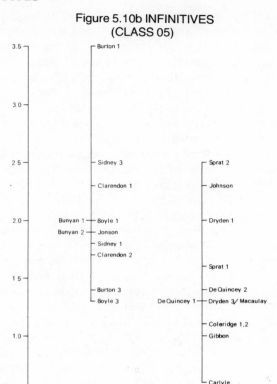

Figure 5.10b INFINITIVES
(CLASS 05)

the verbals while suppressing main verbs, and so forth. Even within the limited range of parameters that we have discussed in this section,[25] each of our writers will be seen to have his own distinctive way of using the system.

PASSIVE STYLES

It is difficult to think of a "passive" style without immediately conjuring up a vision of a social scientist. Such visions have been much reinforced not only by those who advocate Psychosemanto as a proper dialect,[26] but by people fairly neutral about it, such as Rulon Wells, and by its more vehement detractors, such as George Orwell, E.B. White, and James Koerner.[27] Indeed, the visions have both an extensive preceptorial basis and a very sound historical basis as well: The prose of the late Max Weber, as translated by Talcott Parsons, although not extensive in its exploitation of the verb system, could show a density among its main verbs of over 70% neutral ("be" and copula) and passive predication.[28] None of the writers in the York Inventory soars to such Psychosemantic heights, although Edward Gibbon seems to give it an ambitious try, especially in view of the primitive state of the social sciences when he came along.[29]

A combination of Orwell, Strunk-White, humanistic prejudice, and the tendency of our profession toward herd behavior has taught nearly every English teacher in North America that the passive voice is graceless and bad, and should be permitted to be expunged from the available resources of the mother tongue. Many of us have been participants in the movement to extinguish it; that movement has gotten a certain amount of covert (although unintentional) support from the mass marketing of transformational grammar beginning around 1962.[30] Under the conventions of transformationalism, the passive voice is a "transformation" of the active, that is to say, the sentence "Jane was run over by a truck" is a passive transformation of "A truck ran over Jane." Whether rightly or not,[31] this doctrine, when united with a lot of inherited linguistic puritanism, tends to justify the attack to which the passive voice has been submitted. After all, what linguistic puritan could resist preferring "kernel sentences" (suggestions of substance, essence, directness, wheat germ) to "transformed sentences" (suggestions of deviance, unnatural imposition, etc.)? The facts of literary history strongly indicate that the movement has been misguided. Two of the most distinguished, widely praised, and widely studied styles in the language—those of Gibbon and Johnson—turn out to be among the most "passive,"[32] as we can see by looking at the density of passive main verbs in Figure 5.11a.

Surprisingly, although Johnson's style has been noted for its use of pairs and of "philosophic words," it has not been noted for torrents of passive predications such as those below:

> He, by whose writings the heart is *rectified,* the appetites *counteracted,* and the passions *repressed,* may be *considered* as not unprofitable to the great republick of humanity, even though his behaviour should not always exemplify his rules. His intructions may diffuse their influence to regions, in which it will not be *inquired,* whether the author be albus an ater, good or bad; to times, when all his faults and all his follies shall be *lost* in forgetfulness, among things of no concern or importance to the world; and he may kindle in thousands and ten thousands that flame which burnt but dimly in himself, through the fumes of passion, or the damps of cowardice. The vicious moralist may be *considered* as a taper, by which we are *lighted* through the labyrinth of complicated passions; he extends his radiance farther than his heat, and guides all that are within view, but burns only those who make too near approaches.
>
> (Johnson, 9106, *Rambler,* II, 41)

With eight passive main verbs in 16 lines (plus a passive participial adjective—"complicated"), this passage has to be some kind of record holder outside the social sciences. The passage, even for Johnson, is exceptional in its density of passives, but it points up the ironic position of those in the profession (myself included) who have, at times, preached against the passive voice out of one side of their mouths, and preached in favor of "the Great Style of Johnson" out of the other.

From Gibbon we can produce an example more typical of the writer:

> Beyond the Rhine and Danube the northern countries of Europe and Asia were *filled* with innumerable tribes of hunters and shepherds, poor, voracious, and turbulent; bold in arms, and impatient to ravish the fruits of industry. The barbarian world was *agitated* by the rapid impulse of war; and the peace of Gaul or Italy was *shaken* by the distant revolutions of China. The Huns, who fled before a victorious enemy, directed their march towards the West; and the torrent was *swelled* by the gradual accession of captives and allies. The flying tribes who yielded to the Huns assumed in their turn the spirit of conquest; the endless column of barbarians pressed on the Roman empire with accumulated weight; and, if the foremost were *destroyed,* the vacant space was instantly *replenished* by new assailants.
>
> (Gibbon, 9102, *Decline and Fall,* II, 92–93).

Notice that of eleven main verbs in the passage, six are passives. This figure from a chosen example suggests our overall figures for the Gibbon sample, wherein there are three passive verbs for every five active ones.

It occurred to me *ex hypothesi* that the habit of passive predication might be correlated with the use of passives in other areas of the verb system. Our percentages in Figure 5.11b suggest only a weak correlation at best. Gibbon, our high man in passive main verbs, is low man in passive verbals. To be sure, he is low man in verbals overall, but his passive-active ratio of 3:5 among the main verbs moves among the verbals to 1:10. Conversely, Boyle, not a notably passive predicator, becomes the most passive of our writers when he moves from the verbs to the verbal system. The reason for the density of passive verbals is that he has occasional sinking spells of postmodification, like that in the passage below:

> Whereas to the Author of the Scripture-Morals, the Frame, and Springs, and Faculties of our souls, being Intuitively and most Perfectly *known;* the most proper and Powerful ways of Working on them, cannot be unknown to him: and then certainly, one *unacquainted* with the Trade, will be much less likely to mend a Watch, that's out of order, than a Watchmaker. And indeed, ev'n in reference to that other

Figure 5.11a PASSIVE MAIN VERBS

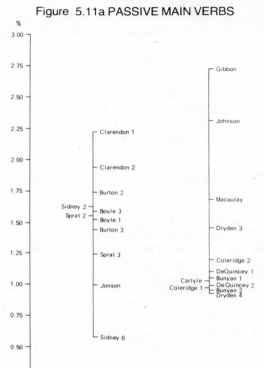

sort of Virtues which are wont in the most confin'd sense of the Word to be call'd Moral, there are I know not how many excellent Notions and Directions relating to them, *dispers'd* up and down in the Scripture, though by Reason of their not being *drawn* up by themselves, and of their being *mingl'd* with other Matters, they are not so readily taken notice of by Ordinary Readers.

(Boyle, 9075, *Holy Scriptures,* 1:2)

After the last three citations, which must have poor old Will Strunk and George Orwell wincing in their graves, it is only fair to present a style—and a noted one—that eschews the passive voice almost to the extent advocated by the schoolbooks. It is ironic and interesting: if we look not only at form[33] but at meaning, the Jonson passage below might tell us why the campaign against the passive voice was doomed to fail:

Custom is the most certain mistress of language, as the public stamp makes the current money. But we must not be too frequent with the

Figure 5.11b PASSIVE VERBALS

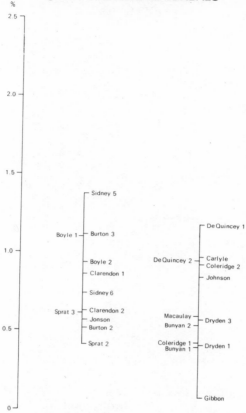

mint, every day coining; nor fetch words from the extreme and utmost ages, since the chief virtue of style is perspicuity and nothing so vicious in it as to need an interpreter. Words *borrowed* of antiquity do lend a kind of majesty to style and are not without their delight sometimes, for they have the authority of years and out of their intermission do win to themselves a kind of grace like newness; but the eldest of the present and newest of the past language is the best. For what was the ancient language, which some men so dote upon, but the ancient custom? Yet when I name custom, I understand not the vulgar custom, for that were a precept no less dangerous to language than life if we should speak or live after the manners of the vulgar; but that I call custom of speech which is the consent of the learned, as custom of life, which is the consent of the good.

(Jonson, 9024, *Timber,* 42–43)

Jonson's passage truly speaks to a pedagogic issue of our time: it is custom and not the schoolmarm that is the certain mistress of language, and to campaign against the passive voice in our time is as fu-

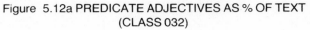

Figure 5.12a PREDICATE ADJECTIVES AS % OF TEXT
(CLASS 032)

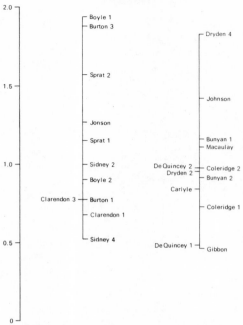

tile as it was to campaign against "inkhorn terms" in the age before Jonson's own.

Recurring again to Figures 5.11a and 5.11b (passive verbs, passive verbals), we can see how truly individual the matter is. Some are high in one, low in the other, or low in one, high in the other. Some, like Bunyan and Jonson, eschew passives wherever possible. In any case, passive verbs and passive verbals, at least in literary prose, do not seem to be positively related to each other. It is natural to ask at this point whether the use of passive main verbs correlates with the use of predicate complementation. The plausibility of such a question arises from the fact that we often encounter sentences like the following:

They were beaten 21–7 and very despondent.

He was angered and red in the face.

In both these cases, a spurious compound is made between the passive main verb and a predicate adjective. The two constructions would seem to be considered by some writers to be interchangeable. Figure 5.12a gives the percentage of predicate adjectives in each of our 33 samples. Figure 5.12b gives the total of predicate adjectives and predicate nouns.

The relationship between passives and complementation is very

Figure 5.12b COMPLEMENTS AS % OF TEXT
032+014

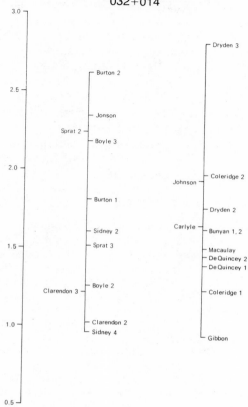

weak. Our most passive writer, Gibbon, is lowest in both adjectival (Figure 5.12a) and total (Figure 5.12b) complementation, and our third most passive writer, Clarendon, is third lowest in one, second lowest in the other. Only Johnson seems strong in both passives and predicate adjectives (his sample ranks seventh of the 33 in the latter category), although in overall complementation he is near the middle of the group. Figure 5.12 has its strongest affinities with Figure 5.7a ("be" main verbs), exactly as common sense should lead us to expect. Although by this point we might be wary of commonsense answers, we should (I hope) still be content in that rare instance when one of them proves out.

MODIFYING STYLES

Gibbon's tendency to nominalize things, Macaulay's love of proper names, Burton's irrepressible drive toward noun seriation, Johnson's habitual doubling of predicates and verbals, Dryden's peculiar density of "be" as a main verb, Clarendon's affinity for the passive voice, Boyle's for the passive verbals—all of these can be seen as manifestations of a tendency in each writer to generate sentences and to formalize meaning in certain *patterned* ways. Is it possible to see a great density of the modifying words in the same way—i.e., a density of the adjectives, adverbs, function adverbs, and intensifiers? It is possible to do so, but one must be cautious. No great change in syntax is required for a writer or an editor to slip in a *very* (class 33) before an adjective, or a *perhaps* (34) here and there, or to change *the man* to *the particular man, they came* to *they came quickly*. On the other hand, to write a Gibbonesque sentence or a sentence in Johnsonese is a mighty task that requires a sentence-generating process that starts from scratch. Let's try it.

Normal or de-styled sentence	*Johnson*
The major advantage that these fictions have over real life is that their authors can focus on objects worthy of our attention.	The chief advantage which these fictions have over real life is, that their authors are at liberty, tho' not to invent, yet to select objects, and to cull from the mass of mankind, those individuals upon which the attention ought most to be employ'd.

	Gibbon
When the prophecy came true almost at once, Philip viewed Decius with a new kind of respect . . .	The speedy completion of the prophecy inspired Philip with a just esteem for so able a counsellor . . .

Bearing in mind this fact—that of all words the modifying words can most easily be *edited* in or out—and according it due respect, we can entertain the question of "modifying" styles.

Figures 5.13a and 5.13b show intensifiers and function adverbs, respectively. We should note that in this coding system intensifiers usually do not appear as part of a normal distribution[34] and that the only samples that appear outside the narrow range of 0.5 to 1.4 are from five very distinctive writers: Sidney, Sprat, Coleridge, Macaulay, and Gibbon. The function adverbs, however, are a different matter. Each of our writers seems to stake out his own area of the scale.

Bunyan's high sample offers some extraordinary flights within this class (34), as in the passage below:

> But I thought this did not become Religion neither, yet I forced my self and would look on *still;* but quickly *after,* I began to think, How, if one of the Bells should fall? then I chose to stand under a main Beam that

lay over thwart the Steeple from side to side, thinking *there* I might stand sure: But *then* I should think *again,* Should the Bell fall with a swing, it might *first* hit the Wall, and *then* rebounding upon me, might kill me for all this Beam; this made me Stand in the Steeple door, and *now* thought I, I am safe *enough,* for if a Bell should *then* fall, I can slip out behind these thick Walls, and so be preserved notwithstanding.

(Bunyan, 9065, *Grace Abounding,* 15)

Jonson offers a marked contrast in the opposite direction:

Under this virtue may come plainness, which is not to be curious in the order, as to answer a letter as if you were to answer to interrogatories (as to the first, first; and to the second, secondly, etc.), but both in method and words to use, as ladies do in their attire, a diligent kind of negligence and their sportive freedom. Though with some men you are not to jest or practise tricks, yet the delivery of the most important things may be carried with such a grace as that it may yield a pleasure to the conceit of the reader.

(Jonson, 9024, *Timber,* 99)

Part of the difference between Jonson and Bunyan is the difference between their respective styles, but part of it is also a matter of genres: narrative after all is more likely to be concerned with questions of time and place than is a set of magisterial aphorisms or an oration. Hence narrative is likely to produce more function adverbs. This probability is supported by the relationships among the Sidney samples: the letters and the *Defence* are clearly marked off from both *Arcadias,* with no overlap, and the respective mean percentages are 2.5 and 3.1.

The possibility arises of a correlation between the function adverbs and the adjectives, such as indeed there is—to a degree. A comparison of Figure 5.13b with Figure 5.5b shows general similarities: Sprat, Carlyle, Boyle, DeQuincey, Dryden, Jonson, and Burton show almost identically in the two Figures. Other writers show less so, and two (Bunyan and Gibbon) show as total opposites in the two Figures. A look at the list of function adverbs[35] will show why they should, on their face, be coupled in train with adjectives, but once again we are up against a probability rather than an iron-bound law.

Figure 5.14a gives total percentages for descriptive adverbs (04) in each of our samples. As has been noted in previous studies,[36] this class is a volatile one and is not by itself of sufficient size to discriminate author from author.

Of all the indices of modification, the one that best separates writer from writer consistently is the "M" statistic, arrived at by addition of the four modifier types that we have had under discussion. "M" statistics for all our samples are given in Figure 5.14b.

On these samples, Carlyle looks like the most modifier-prone writer ever. Prior to 1900 he probably is. If we were to include samples

Figure 5.13a INTENSIFIERS AS % OF TEXT
(CLASS 033)

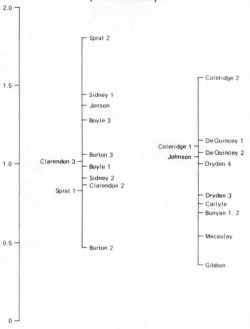

from Sprat's sermons, permitting him to rise on wings of homily, Sprat might possibly catch him in mid-hot-air.[37] In view of the prodigious frequency of rhetorical questions and exclamations in both Carlyle and Sprat's sermons,[38] one might speculate that a high "M" statistic is related to attempts to overmanage one's audience with other devices of emphasis, but, on the evidence we have, speculation is all that we can muster. In any case, we do have a writer clearly demarked from all the others, and we should stand back and watch him perform:

> That in the environment, *here mysteriously enough* shadowed forth Teufelsdrockh must have felt *ill* at ease, cannot be *doubtful.* 'The *hungry* young,' he says, 'looked up to their *spiritual* Nurses; and, for food, were bidden eat the *east*-wind. What *vain* jargon of *controversial* Metaphysics, Etymology, and *mechanical* Manipulation *falsely* named Science, was *current there,* I *indeed* learned, *better perhaps* than the most.'

> (Carlyle, 9110, *Sartor,* 91)

This may look like a tendentious selection, with roughly one word in five a modifier. The "M" statistic in *Sartor* (611) represents over

Figure 5.13b FUNCTION ADVERBS AS % OF TEXT

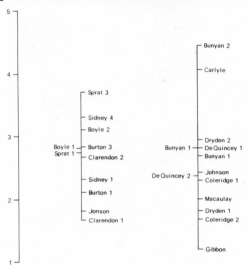

17% of the words, however; the selection above is not such a self-caricature as it might at first seem.

A further interesting note on Figure 5.14b is that Bunyan, with a mean "M" of 348, is the most "chaste" and "biblical" writer of our group.[39] But before we go on and conclude that a low "M" makes for chastity and a high one for floridity, we should pause a moment. Sprat, of course, has been again and again identified with the reform of prose style in the seventeenth century, and with "simplification," "chastity," "manliness," and other things hard to pin down but clear in direction (away from ornateness, whatever ornateness is). And yet, Sprat is one of our leaders in total modifiers. Perhaps, as Carlyle was the Casanova of modification, Sprat was the Elmer Gantry. But it would be simple-minded to make a direct connection between "M" and floridity or simplicity. Even though it might hold up in cases like Jonson, Bunyan, Carlyle, and the King James Bible, it would—like the other tentative typological connections that we have tried in this chapter—collapse sooner or later. Whatever the biographical facts surrounding it, nobody—even on the basis of a sub-400 "M" statistic—is going to call Gibbon's style "chaste."

A final point is that of all the "M" statistics given, Sidney's is the richest in the three kinds of adverbs. This fact is related to the strong verb component in his style, a matter to which we shall return in Chapter 6.

Figure 5.14a ADVERBS

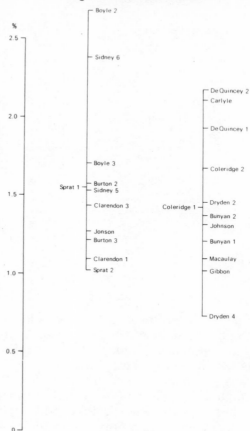

CONCLUSIONS

Even though we have eschewed stylistic types that are either imagi-
nary ("rough," "sprightly," "jejune") or paradigmatic (Senecan,
Ciceronian, Tacitean), and even though we have stayed with types
that at least have some element of linguistic referent, we have found
stylistic typology to be of limited use in this chapter. As soon as a
type can be named, it breaks down in confrontation with the textual
facts. To return to where we began this chapter, the so-called nominal style quickly breaks down into the nominalizing nominal (Gibbon), the seriating nominal (Burton), and the anaphoric nominal
(Macaulay). Move forward a few years and take in another nominal-
izer—say, Lytton Strachey[40]—and we shall need yet a fourth (ironic

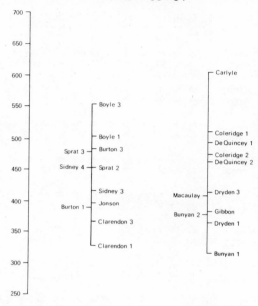

Figure 5.14b "M" STATISTIC
03+04+33+34

nominal?). Soon we shall run out of typological categories. But why make categories or types at all? Is it not enough to describe the constant forms that operate within the style in such a way that other readers might recognize them?

Table 5.2 STATISTICS FOR CHAPTER 5

CATEGORY	Sidney 9004	Sidney 9005	Sidney 9006	Sidney 9007	Sidney 9008	Sidney 9009	Burton 9028	Burton 9029	Burton 9030	Jonson 9024	Clarendon 9031	Clarendon 9032	Clarendon 9033	Boyle 9075	Boyle 9076	Boyle 9077
01	19.4	18.4	18.1	17.8	17.6	16.4	23.3	22.2	22.2	20.8	21.9	20.6	20.2	17.6	18.6	17.4
02	8.2	8.1	8.9	8.6	8.8	8.1	7.7	9.2	8.5	8.3	7.0	7.7	8.4	6.5	7.1	7.3
03	7.3	6.8	6.4	6.0	7.0	6.4	7.0	7.7	9.1	6.8	5.7	5.4	5.3	8.9	8.3	9.4
04	1.8	1.6	1.7	2.2	1.5	2.4	1.5	1.6	1.2	1.3	1.1	1.2	1.4	2.3	2.6	1.7
05	1.8	2.4	2.5	2.5	2.6	2.6	3.5	1.7	1.4	1.9	2.3	1.7	2.0	2.0	1.5	1.3
06	1.4	2.2	1.8	2.3	2.5	.9	1.0	.5	1.5	.7	1.2	.6	1.0	.9	1.3	1.8
07	.8	.7	.9	.6	.8	.9	.1	.1	.4	1.2	.7	.4	.6	1.1	.6	.5
11	7.3	10.3	9.2	10.3	10.5	11.5	7.0	8.0	7.0	7.5	6.0	7.7	7.3	6.7	7.8	7.0
21	8.3	5.9	7.4	6.3	6.1	7.3	5.5	7.3	5.3	6.8	7.0	7.4	8.2	7.6	6.9	8.0
31	11.0	13.0	12.0	11.7	11.1	11.1	10.0	10.9	10.7	12.2	14.2	14.0	13.9	11.6	11.7	11.5
33	1.4	.9	1.1	.9	.9	.9	.7	.5	1.1	1.4	1.0	.9	1.1	1.0	1.2	1.2
34	2.4	3.1	2.8	3.4	2.9	2.7	2.2	2.3	2.8	1.8	1.7	2.7	2.6	2.8	3.1	2.8
35	1.0	.8	.8	.7	.7	1.0	.7	.8	.6	1.2	.8	.6	.9	1.4	.7	1.1
41	4.0	3.2	3.4	4.1	4.0	3.8	5.8	5.5	5.5	5.0	6.1	5.4	5.0	4.5	5.2	5.2
42	3.6	3.0	3.0	3.7	3.7	2.8	2.1	2.5	2.6	2.2	2.2	2.9	2.4	2.8	1.1	2.9
43	2.4	1.8	2.0	1.6	1.4	2.3	1.5	1.8	1.1	2.0	2.4	2.3	3.2	3.2	2.2	2.3
44	.1	.1	.3	.1	.1	.0	.2	.3	.1	.1	.1	.0	.0	.0	.0	.0

45	1.2	.6	1.2	1.2	1.5	1.6	.2	.5	.3	.7	.5	.6	.3	1.4	1.2	1.4
51	11.1	11.6	11.2	11.9	10.6	11.8	9.6	10.2	11.4	11.4	14.0	13.5	12.5	12.9	12.8	12.2
61	.8	.5	.4	.5	.5	.7	.3	.5	.3	.5	.6	.8	.5	1.0	.3	.4
62	1.8	2.2	2.3	2.4	2.3	2.3	1.9	1.6	1.1	1.7	2.4	2.1	2.1	2.0	1.6	1.6
91	1.5	.9	.9	.5	1.2	1.0	.4	.6	.5	.9	.5	.4	.4	1.0	.6	1.4
51-31-01	97	119	123	112	108	116	9	105	100	119	224	188	166	141	120	97
Strings	58	79	58	84	61	91	44	52	71	63	144	104	90	60	105	67
Strings w/out determiner	17	33	27	31	27	42	20	24	42	33	154	29	33	40	39	15
51-03-01	23	22	17	19	26	13	15	6	21	15	24	15	17	26	23	27
213 as%	3.0	1.9	1.5	1.2	1.7	2.4	1.8	2.5	2.0	3.2	1.6	2.0	1.9	2.4	1.2	1.8
022	36	54	40	33	28	22	50	60	50	35	79	69	71	54	55	56
062 & 052 & 072	39	33	31	42	48	26	30	20	38	20	27	23	24	37	34	19
Total passives	75	87	71	75	76	48	80	80	88	55	106	92	95	91	89	75
032	32	35	20	18	29	30	27	53	64	44	24	25	27	67	32	55
032 & 014	47	54	37	33	40	44	62	92	81	82	39	35	44	71	45	72

Table 5.2 (continued)

CATEGORY	Macaulay 9111	Coleridge 9206	Coleridge 9205	DeQuincey 9203	DeQuincey 9201	Carlyle 9110	Gibbon 9102	Johnson 9106	Dryden 9099	Dryden 9098	Dryden 9097	Dryden 9096	Sprat 9069	Sprat 9068	Sprat 9067	Bunyan 9065	Bunyan 9064
01	24.4	22.8	21.9	22.1	21.4	22.1	27.4	20.3	20.3	20.8	19.7	18.9	19.1	18.3	19.7	15.4	15.9
02	8.7	6.0	6.1	5.9	6.5	7.6	7.5	8.9	8.4	6.5	7.6	7.8	6.6	6.8	7.2	9.6	11.4
03	7.0	8.9	10.1	8.1	8.4	10.7	8.4	6.4	6.7	7.5	6.0	6.7	8.7	8.3	8.0	4.5	4.6
04	1.1	1.7	1.5	2.2	1.9	2.1	1.1	1.4	.8	1.4	1.5	1.4	1.4	1.1	1.6	1.4	1.2
05	1.3	1.1	1.1	1.4	1.3	.6	1.0	2.3	1.5	1.3	1.4	2.0	2.3	2.5	1.6	1.9	2.0
06	.7	1.3	.7	1.7	1.7	1.6	.1	.8	.5	.8	1.0	.5	.8	.3	.6	.9	.7
07	.9	.4	.2	.8	.6	.5	.4	.8	.6	.6	.5	.6	1.1	.9	.6	.4	.6
11	5.2	4.4	5.4	6.2	5.9	5.4	1.9	6.5	9.3	7.8	9.8	9.3	7.2	7.9	8.6	12.4	13.0
21	6.5	6.9	5.6	6.7	6.5	6.2	5.4	7.6	7.7	8.3	6.7	8.2	7.3	8.9	6.7	8.0	7.4
31	13.4	14.2	13.8	13.3	13.2	11.6	18.0	12.4	13.1	13.5	12.8	12.9	12.8	13.2	14.2	10.5	11.4
33	.6	1.5	1.2	1.1	1.2	.8	.1	1.1	1.0	.8	.8	.9	1.1	.9	.9	.7	.7
34	2.0	1.7	2.4	2.3	2.9	4.1	1.2	2.5	2.6	2.5	3.0	1.8	3.7	2.9	2.8	4.4	2.7
35	.7	.9	.5	.8	.4	.6	.2	.7	.9	1.0	.8	.9	.5	1.2	.4	1.0	.9
41	4.2	5.3	5.3	3.5	4.3	5.1	6.5	5.0	4.9	4.9	4.4	5.6	5.3	4.6	4.2	5.0	5.6
42	2.1	1.9	1.9	2.0	2.2	1.6	1.2	2.6	2.7	2.7	2.3	2.5	2.3	2.4	1.9	3.4	3.6
43	1.6	1.8	1.7	1.1	1.2	1.6	1.6	2.4	2.0	1.9	2.7	2.3	1.7	2.1	2.1	1.1	1.5
44	.0	.2	.1	.2	.0	1.3	.0	.0	.1	.1	.1	.1	.2	.3	.0	.0	.4

45	.3	1.5	.8	.5	.5	.6	.6	.5	.4	.8	.2	.5	.6	.6	.8	.8	.7	.2
51	9.9	10.9	13.6	12.5	12.1	11.6	13.2	12.9	12.5	12.9	15.3	12.1	14.2	14.0	14.8	14.8	14.3	14.6
61	.4	.4	.8	1.1	1.0	.8	.5	.8	.7	.8	.2	1.0	.7	.4	.5	.9	.6	.4
62	1.6	1.6	1.9	2.4	2.2	2.3	1.5	1.5	1.4	2.6	.9	.6	1.5	1.6	.9	.9	1.4	1.6
91	2.0	1.8	.8	.8	.8	1.1	.5	.4	.7	.3	0	.3	.4	.9	.3	.3	.4	.3
51-31-01	145	141	169	128	125	122	134	148	129	148	215	90	141	137	135	135	147	156
Strings	60	79	136	98	101	76	89	106	95	110	133	88	109	100	138	138	132	140
Strings w/out determiner	24	30	47	27	34	33	37	42	42	50	30	41	45	36	54	54	57	69
51-03-01	17	16	23	18	27	16	20	10	14	42	23	35	38	29	39	39	34	30
213 as %	2.4	2.3	2.0	2.5	2.0	3.0	2.5	3.6	2.5	2.1	.6	2.1	1.7	2.1	1.3	1.3	2.0	1.6
022	35	32	53	54	43	31	31	50	31	84	93	37	38	33	31	31	40	57
062 & 052 & 072	14	19	16	15	22	16	16	19	15	30	3	34	39	33	15	15	32	21
Total passives	49	41	69	69	65	47	47	69	46	114	96	71	77	66	46	46	72	78
032	39	31	40	54	43	41	46	63	31	50	16	29	26	16	26	26	34	37
032 & 014	56	56	66	72	56	84	72	99	60	66	29	57	49	47	46	46	66	53

*Where, what befell unto them, what valyant actes they did . . . how
many Ladyes they defended from wronges, and disinherited persons
restored to theyre Right, yt ys a worke for a higher style than myne:
This onely shall suffice, that, theyre fame returned . . .*

Sir Philip Sidney, Old Arcadia

Chapter 6

SIDNEY AND THE ELIZABETHAN NOVELISTS

IN THIS volume, we have already encountered the style of Sir Philip Sidney several times in examining how the materials of the York Inventory can be used. It has been easy to demonstrate that Sidney is more syndetic than Macaulay, more suspensive then Clarendon, more various than Gibbon, and richer in verbals than Burton; these distinctions can almost be made without the aid of extensive analysis, since they involve historical differences as well as individual ones. It is less easy to discriminate Sidney from other writers of prose fiction contemporary to him, although it undeniably can be done, and the doing of it is an appropriate test of the materials of the York Inventory.

Literary historians often lump together as a classifiable group the "Elizabethan Novelists"—that group of writers loosely connected by the fact that they wrote prose fiction or romance between 1570 and 1605—of whom the most notable practitioners were Lyly, Sidney, Greene, and Nashe. Sometimes their being grouped together goes beyond generic considerations; in Croll, for example, these novelists are manifestations of the Zeitgeist[1] and in the anthologists White, Wallerstein, and Quintana[2] they seem to form a major target for "anti-Ciceronianism." In any case, time and genre alone would be sufficient to warrant our considering these men together. Listed in Table 6.1 are the samples on which this chapter is based.

We can make some observations on what generic resemblances to one another these various works tend to show, in addition to the elements of travel, exoticism, didacticism, and such that have been noted in previous commentary.[3] Among our samples from the seven

Table 6.1 SAMPLES FOR CHAPTER 6[a]

9001	Lodge	Rosalind
9002	Lyly	Euphues, Anatomy of Wit
9003	Lyly	Euphues and His England
9005	Sidney	Old Arcadia
9006	Sidney	Old Arcadia
9007	Sidney	New Arcadia
9008	Sidney	New Arcadia
9010	Nashe	Peirce Penniless
9011	Nashe	Unfortunate Traveler

[a]All references to primary text are by author, sample number, work, and page. A full catalog of the samples is given in Appendix B.

works listed in Table 6.1, there is common distortion of the language frame away from certain word classes and toward others. The word classes in which these novels are abnormally plentiful are the verbs (both 01 and 21) and pronouns (11). This is a fact easily anticipated. After all, these works deal with actions, and the actions are performed by people. The word classes in which these novels are unusually sparse are the adjective, the descriptive adverb, and the preposition. These are surprising facts in some ways. The lushness that tends to be associated with Elizabethan fiction would lead us to expect a fecundity of modifiers; perhaps this is a mystery that can be solved before the end of the chapter. Using the non-Sidneyan samples of Chapter 5 as a norm, Figure 6.1 shows where our five control samples stand in each of these three classes.

In addition to these contrasts with the norms generated by other users of the language as they developed in the 250 years after Nashe died, there are contrasts with language of other genres written in the period 1595 to 1620. The period length of the novels other than Sidney's can be said to be generally shorter than that of expository prose and sermons written about the same time, and there seems to be less initial connection than in the genres that are didactic or expository. Figure 6.2 shows the contrast between the three "control" novelists on the one hand and Bacon, Donne, Jonson, Ascham, and Burton on the other. These differences, like those of verb and pronoun density, could have been anticipated. Philosophical matters will generally call forth a more elaborate and extended sentence than will narrative, whereas argument, carried by cognitive signals, will probably introduce more of its sentences with explicit signals of connection

Figure 6.1 ADJECTIVES, ADVERBS, PREPOSITIONS, NOVELS VS.
OTHER WRITINGS

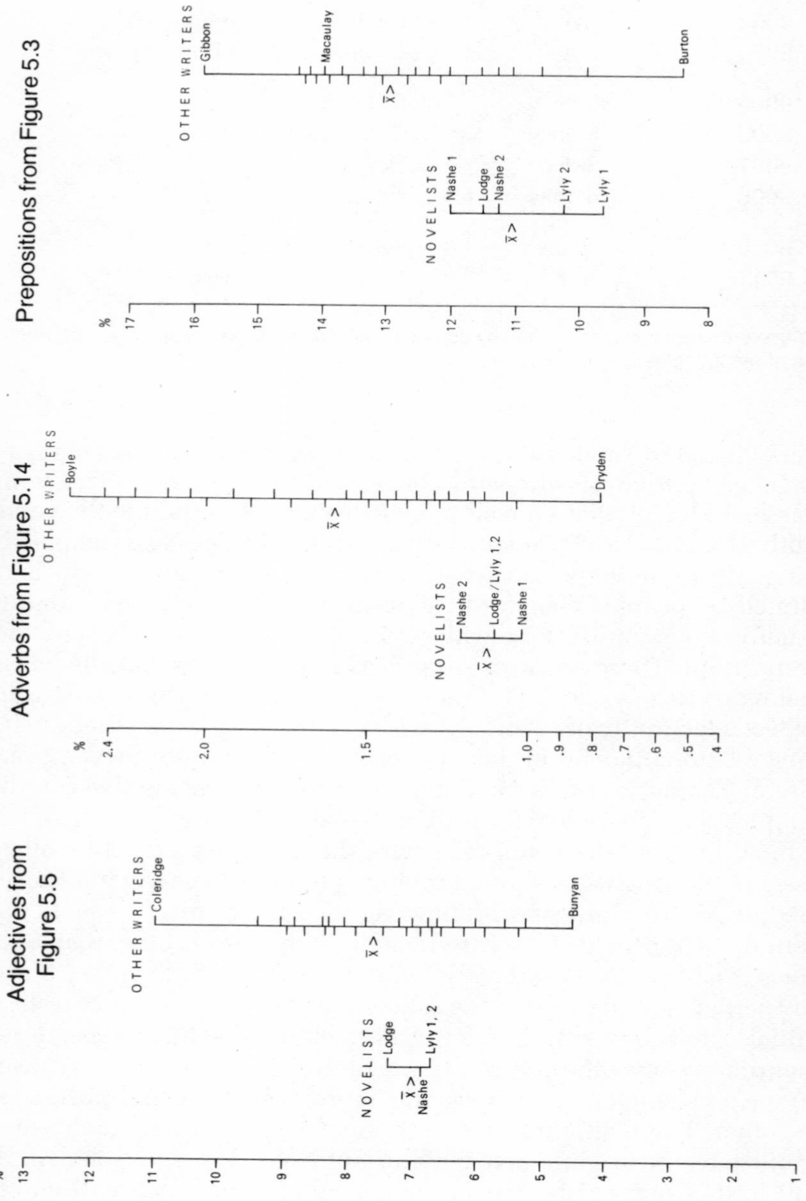

Adjectives from
Figure 5.5

Adverbs from Figure 5.14

Prepositions from Figure 5.3

Figure 6.2 PERIOD LENGTH, INITIAL CONNECTION, NOVEL VS.
OTHER WRITINGS TO 1625

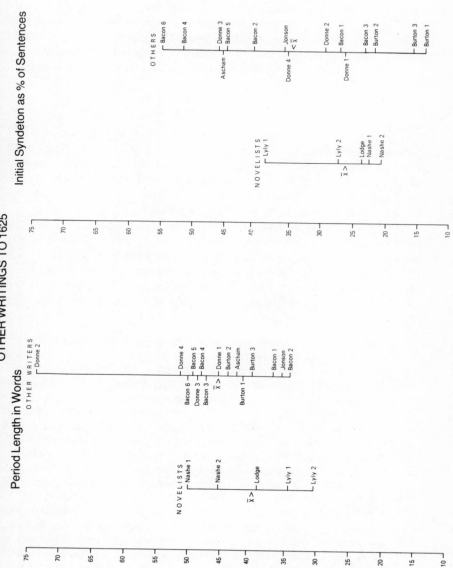

than will narrative, which tends to be carried along by objects, places, and actions.

Finally, there are some obvious differences in some of the other more obvious categories. In comparison to the other literature, the novels abound in exclamations and nominatives of address, and they also tend to contain more exclamation points and question marks. Within these constraints of genre that our taxonomy has been able to discern, we will find that each of our novelists has great distinctiveness, particularly Sidney, with whom this chapter is principally concerned.

SYNTAX

Sidney's period is generally longer than those of his contemporaries; even the shortened periods of the "New" *Arcadia* are at the long end of the range established by our five control samples. The mean length for our four Sidney samples is 56.6 words; the mean for the control samples is 38.7, as shown in Figure 6.3a.

More than half the time in our samples (55.4% vs. 24.1% for the controls), Sidney's sentence is introduced by one of the syndetic words (classes 41, 42, 91), usually a coordinator. In this respect, Sidney deviates markedly from other practitioners of the genre; he is clearly marked off from Lyly, the writer closest to him, and even two brief passages will illustrate their differences, which are shown in Figure 6.3b.

> Much talk there was in the way, which much shortened their way. And at the last they came to London, where they met divers strangers of their friends, who in small space brought them familiarly acquainted with certain English gentlemen; who much delighted in the company of Euphues, whom they found both sober and wise, yet sometimes merry and pleasant. They were brought into all places of the city and lodged at the last in a merchant's house, where they continued till a certain breach. They used continually the Court: in the which Euphues took such delight that he accounted all the praises he heard of it before rather to be envious than otherwise, and to be partial in not giving so much as it deserved, and yet to be pardoned because they could not.
>
> It happened that these English gentlemen conducted these two strangers to a place where divers gentlewomen were, some courtiers, others of the country. Where being welcome they frequented almost every day for the space of one month, entertaining of time in courtly pastimes, though not in the Court: insomuch that if they came not they were sent for, and so used as they had been countrymen not strangers.
>
> (Lyly, 9002, *Euphues, Anatomy of Wit*, 290)

> Now we being brought known unto her . . . For, with equal ardor she affected us both: and so did her greatness disdain shamefastness,

that she was content to acknowledge it to both. For, (having many times torn the veil of modesty) it seemed, for a last delight, that she delighted in infamy: which often she had used to her husband's shame, filling all men's cares (but his) with reproach; while he (hoodwinked with kindness) least of all me knew who strake him. But her first degree was, by setting forth her beauties, (truly in nature by art) thereby to bring us (as willingly-caught fishes) to bite at her bait. And thereto had she that scutcheon of her desires supported by certain badly-diligent ministers, who often cloyed our ears with her praises, & would needs teach us a way of felicity by seeking her favor. But when she found, that we were as deaf to them, as dumb to her . . .

(Sidney, 9007, New *Arcadia*, 298–299)

We should notice again, as we noticed in Chapter 4, the variety in the Sidney openings as well as the strong tendency toward syndetic beginnings.

Within this long, initially-syndetic period, Sidney exploits a syntax that is varied, asymmetrical, and extremely hypotactic; despite the greater length of his period, it has not many more *internal* full stops[4] than do those of the controls (34.0 per sample vs. 30.2, an inconsequential difference). Hence, we can assume that, in addition to hypotaxis, greater length of member and of syntactic interruption is a general characteristic of the Sidney samples. The two citations just used give an excellent glimpse of the degree to which Sidney tended to suspend and interrupt his sentences in comparison with Lyly. Consider some of Sidney's interruptions:

Line number	Text	Point of interruption or suspension
3–4	*For,* (having many times torne the veil of modesty), *it*	Frontal suspension
4	*seemed,* for a last delight, *that*	Verb/Complement interruption
6–7	*he* (hoodwinked with kindness) least of all me *knew*	Subject/Verb interruption
8	*was,* by setting forth her beauties, (truly in nature by art) *thereby*	Verb/Complement interruption

There is nothing comparable to these four examples in the Lyly passage, which contains one modest (three-word) frontal suspension in its last sentence. And the list above does not even include the long frontal suspensions of the first and last sentences of the Sidney paragraph. The contrast between Sidney and Nashe is similar, as we can see from the following Nashe passage:

But this strife must be so tempered that we fall not from the eagerness of praise to the envying of their persons; for then we leave running to the goal of glory to spurn at a stone that lies in our way—and

Figure 6.3a PERIOD LENGTH IN WORDS

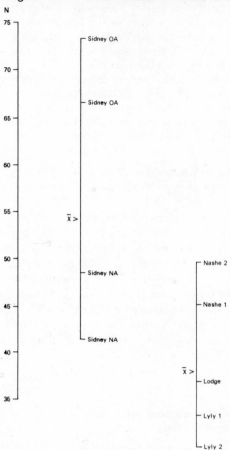

so did Atalanta in the midst of her course stoop to take up the golden apple that her enemy scattered in her way, and was outrun by Hippomenes. The contrary to this contention and emulation is security, peace, quiet, tranquility; when we have no adversary to pry into our actions, no malicious eye whose pursuing our private behaviour might make us more vigilant over our imperfections than otherwise we would be.

That state or kingdom that is in league with all the world and hath no foreign sword to vex it is not half so strong or confirmed to endure as that which lives every hour in fear of invasion. There is a certain waste of the people for whom there is no use but war, and these men must have some employment still to cut them off. *Nam si foras hostem*

Figure 6.3b INITIAL SYNDETON AS % OF SENTENCES

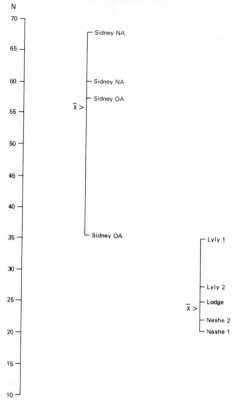

non habent, domi invenient—"if they have no service abroad, they
will make mutinies at home." Or if the affairs of the state be such as
cannot exhale all these corrupt excrements, it is very expedient they
have some light toys to busy their heads withal, cast before them as
bones to gnaw upon which may keep them from having leisure to in-
termeddle with higher matters.

(Nashe, 9010, *Peirce Penniless,* 56)

As in the case of Lyly, we have one frontal suspension (last sentence)
in two paragraphs of Nashe.

In quantitative terms, the variety of Sidney's syntax can be inferred from several corroborative sources. First of these is the Milic
"D" statistic. Generally, "D" statistics tend to be higher as one
moves back in time, and the "D" statistics for 20 of our 97 samples

prior to 1700 exceed 1,000: Sidney's six are among these 20. More-over, he is the only writer for whom four or more samples were tak-en, all of whose samples exceeded 1,000 on the "D" scale; he is the only writer in the Inventory except Ascham whose "D" ever exceed-ed 1,000 in under 3,000 words, as it did in four of his six samples, and finally he is the only novelist whose "D" exceeded 1,000 at all. All these facts clearly establish his pre-eminence in this respect. Fig-ure 6.4 shows Sidney in comparison with the controls.

Once again, Lyly offers a demonstrable contrast with Sidney; translations into two-digit code to the 95th word are given below in the passages:

> But certainly, so did the boldness of their affirmation accompany the greatness of what they did affirm (even descending to particularities, what kingdoms he should overcome) that the King of Phrygia (who over-superstitiously thought him self touched in the matter) sought by force to destroy the infant, to prevent his after-expectations: because a skillful man (having compared his nativity with the child) so told him. Foolish man, either vainly fearing what was not to be feared, or not considering, that if it were a work of the superior powers, the heavens at length are never children. But so he did, & by the aid of the Kings of Lydia and Crete (joining together their armies) invaded Thessalia, and brought Dorilaus to some behind-hand of fortune, when his faithful friend & brother Euarchus came so mightily to his succor, that with some interchanging changes of fortune, they begat of a just war, the best child, peace.
>
> (Sidney, 9008, New *Arcadia*, 188)

Sidney:

```
41 04 34 21 31 01 51 31 01 02 31 01 51 43 11 21 02 34 06 51 01 43 01
11 21 02 42 31 01 51 01 43 33 04 02 11 06 51 31 01 02 51 01 62 05 31
01 62 05 31 03 01 42 31 03 01 21 06 31 01 51 31 01 04 02 11 99 03 01
45 04 06 43 21 35 62 21 05 45 35 06 42 42 11 21 31 01 51 31 01 01 31
01 34 21 34 01 99
```

> Be not curious to curl thy hair, nor careful to be neat in thine appar-el; be not prodigal of thy gold, nor precise in thy going; be not like the Englishman, which preferreth every strange fashion before the use of his country; be thou dissolute, lest thy lady think thee foolish in fram-ing thyself to every fashion for her sake. Believe not their oaths and solemn protestations, their exorcisms and conjurations, their tears which they have at commandment, their alluring looks, their treading on the toe, their unsavory toys. Let every one loathe his lady, and be ashamed to be her servant. It is riches and ease that nourisheth affec-tion, it is play, wine, and wantoness that feedeth a lover as fat as a fool; refrain from all such meats as shall provoke thine appetite to lust, and all such means as may allure thy mind to folly.
>
> (Lyly, 9002, *Euphues, Anatomy of Wit*, 106)

Figure 6.4 "D" STATISTIC PER SAMPLE

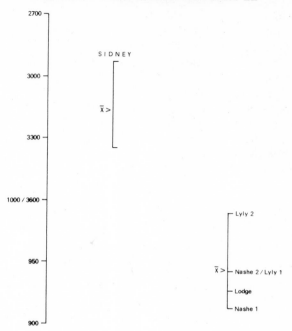

21 35 03 62 05 31 01 41 03 62 21 03 51 31 01 <u>98</u> 21 35 03 51 31 01 41
03 41 31 07 <u>98</u> 21 35 51 31 01 43 02 31 03 01 51 31 01 51 31 01 <u>98</u> 21
11 03 42 31 01 02 11 03 51 07 11 51 31 01 51 31 01 <u>99</u> 02 35 31 01 41
03 01 31 01 41 01 31 01 43 11 02 51 01 31 03 01 31 07 51 31 01 31 03
01 <u>99</u> 21 11 02 31 01 41 21 02

There is much to be said about the two passages. Lyly's parallelism
(in anaphoric form) is immediately visible even to the untrained eye:
"Be not," "be not," "be not," "be thou," "believe not"; "it is
riches . . . it is play . . . ." Also, in the Lyly passage, despite the
punching-bag effect of the repeated openings, there is a certain variety in many of the parallelisms in that many elements parallel to
each other are not precisely symmetrical. For example, "to curl thy
hair," an infinitive phrase, is an element parallel to "to be neat in
thine apparel," but there is a slightly skewed symmetry between the
first element (62-05-31-01) and the second (62-21-03-51-31-01). Despite syllabic parity (isocolon), there is a similar syntactic skewing
between "their oaths and solemn protestations" (31-01-41-03-01)
and "their exorcisms and conjurations" (31-01-41-01). Even though

instances of such asymmetry are common in his prose, Lyly writes a relatively unvaried style in comparison to Sidney. Counting to the 95th word in each, the respective "D" statistics for the passages above are 77 (Sidney) and 49 (Lyly). Some of this difference is due to differences in the use of terminal punctuation: in the first 95 words of Lyly there are five stops, and over the same space in Sidney there are only two, with the result that there are 83 *total* three-class patterns in Lyly and 91 in Sidney. Most of the difference, however, derives from the fact that whereas Lyly is much more varied than, say, the King James Bible or Gibbon, he is much more repetitive than Sidney. Listed below are the repeated patterns (and their incidence) up to the 95th word in each passage:

Sidney		*Lyly*	
31-01-51	(5)	51-31-01	(8)
51-31-01	(3)	31-01-41	(5)
31-03-01	(3)	01-41-03	(3)
01-51-31	(3)	03-01-31	(3)
51-01-43	(2)	01-51-31	(3)
01-62-05	(2)	31-03-01	(3)
62-05-31	(2)	01-31-01	(2)
11-21-02	(2)	31-01-43	(2)
		03-51-31	(2)
		01-31-03	(2)
		31-01-51	(2)

Tested against the other novelists, Sidney's distinctiveness will appear to be only sightly less magnified. Figure 6.4 suggests that our three control writers are very similar to one another in syntactic variety as measured by the "D" statistic. Together with this kind of syntactic richness there worked in Sidney's style a conscious avoidance of exactly parallel forms. Unlike Lyly's, his samples offer no suggestion of extensive initial anaphora; they yield very few parallel prepositional phrases (a mean of 5.5 per sample, vs. 9.0 for Lodge, 20.5 for Lyly, 4.5 for Nashe), and they are very sparse in our 44 configuations of word parallelism.[5] Figure 6.5 suggests how strong this avoidance was.

In the treatment of the "D" statistic both in Chapter 4 and in the present chapter, we have observed the subtly skewed asymmetries of Sidney's style. It is important to note that he presses this asymmetry even in writing passages that seem deliberately parallelistic, such as the one below:

> Those two Princes, as well to help the weaker, as for the natural hate the Grecians bare Persians, did so much with their incomparable valor, as that they got into the City, and by their presence much repelled Otanes' assaults: which he understanding to be occasioned by them, made a Challenge of three Princes in his Retinue, against those two

Princes & Antiphilus. And that, thereupon, the matter should be decided, with Compact, that neither should help his fellows, but of whose side the more overcame, with him the victory should remain. . . .

(Sidney, 9005, Old *Arcadia*, 68)

Notice that there are two clearly (contrivedly?) parallel sets, each of which could have had its members identically sequenced:

as well to help the weaker	45-62-05-31-03
as for the natural hate the	45-51-31-03-01-00-31
Grecians bare Persians	-01-02-01

and

of whose side the more overcame,	51-43-01-31-33-02
with him the victory should	51-11-31-01-21
remain	-02

The asymmetry of the first example needs no comment. Of the second we can note that the lines are parallel not only syntactically (beginning and ending in parallelism) but also in syllabic quantity (eight per member in the first, nine in the second), and in the near-rhyme of their last syllables. Nevertheless, between the beginning preposition and the terminating verb there is a considerable syntactic difference.

Figure 6.5a clearly shows Sidney's avoidance of single-word parallelism in serial form. Partly because of this avoidance and partly because of his elaborate techniques of embedding, interrupting, and suspending sentences, Sidney—within a sentence that we should remember is relatively long—used far less internal coordination than his contemporaries. This is a major and noteworthy point of distinction; the historical tendency in English is toward a strong correlation between long sentences and compounding with coordinated elements.[6] Sidney is the first case that I have known who is distinctively high in sentence length and uniquely low in internal coordination.[7] If we take the total number of coordinators per sample and subtract from that the number of initial coordinators (Table 6.2), we can derive a figure for non-frontal or internal coordinators, as is done in Figure 6.6. The mean for the Sidney samples is 100.5; the mean for the controls is 134.2. In samples of roughly 3,500 words, this is a large difference. To observe what it means in terms of internal connection, we can examine two passages, one from Sidney and one from Nashe, each of which is this dimension is almost exactly representative of the sample from which it is taken:

And as for Dametas, taking from him the keys of both the Lodges calling him the Moth of the Princes' estate, and only spot of his wife

Figure 6.5a WORD PARALLELISMS

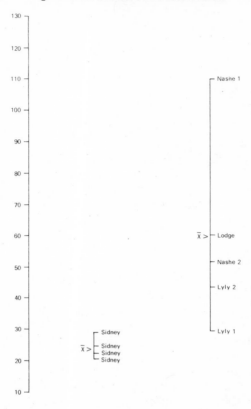

and Daughter to be fettered up in as many Chains and Clogs as they could bear; And every third hour to be cruelly whipped, till the determined Judgment should be given of all those matters, that done, having sent already at his first coming to all the quarters of the Country to seek Pamela, although with small hope of overtaking them, he himself went, well accompanied to the Lodge, where the two unfortunate Lovers were attending a cruel Conclusion of their long painfull late pleasant affection. Dametas' Clownish eyes having been only the Discoverers of Pyrocles' Strategem, he had no sooner taken a full view of them (which in some sights would rather have anything than an accusing mind), and locked the Door upon those two young folks, now made Prisoners for Love, as before they had been Prisoners to Love: But that, immediately upon his going down whither with noise that Dametas made, or with the Creeping in of the Light, or rather as I think that he had but little slept that Night, so, the sweet embracement he enjoyed gave his senses a very easy salve to come to themselves. But, so it was that Pyrocles awaked, grudging in himself, that sleep (though very

Figure 6.5b TOTAL INDICES OF SYMMETRICAL PARALLELISM

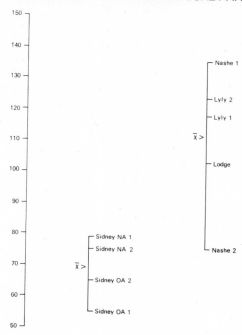

short) had robbed him, of any part of those his highest Contentments, especially Considering that he was then to prepare himself to return to the Duke's bed, and at his Coming, to set such a Comical face of the Matter, as he should find by the speeches of Basilius and Gynecia should be most Convenient: By being now fully awaked, he might hear a great noise under the Lodge, which (as affection is full of Doubts) made him leap out of his Bed.

(Sidney, 9006, Old *Arcadia*, 269)

Bona fide, it is a great mixture that we have not men swine as well as beasts; for then we should have pork that hath no more bones than a pudding, and a side of bacon that you might lay under your head instead of a bolster.

It is not for nothing that other countries whom we upbraid with drunkenness call us bursten-bellied gluttons; for we make our greedy paunches powdering-tube of beef, and eat more meat at one meal than the Spaniard or Italian in a month. Good thrifty men, they draw out a dinner with sallets like a swart-rutter's suit, and make Madonna Nature their best caterer. We must have our tables furnished like poulter's stalls, or as though we were to victual Noah's Ark again, wherein there was all sorts of living creatures.

(Nashe, 9010, *Peirce Penniless*, 56)

Figure 6.6 NON-FRONTAL COORDINATORS PER SAMPLE
(CLASS 41)

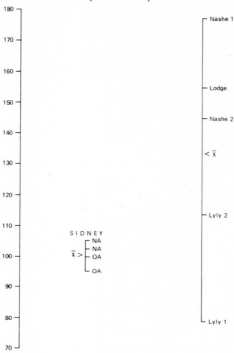

In the Sidney passage, there are two initial and nine internal coordinators over a space of 320 words; in the Nashe passage, there are no initial and eight internal coordinators in 145 words of text. Normalized to 3,500 words, the passages have densities of roughly 100 and 190 internal coordinators, very close to the samples from which they are taken (Figure 6.6.). A second look at the first sentences of the preceding passages is perhaps in order. Internal coordinators are italicized; verbals and subordinations are noted in the margin.

06	And as for Dametas, taking from him the keys of both the
06	Lodges calling him the Moth of the Princes' estate, *and* on-
05	ly spot of his wife *and* Daughter to be fettered up in as
42	many Chains and Clogs as they could bear; And every
05	third hour to be cruelly whipped, till the determined
45	Judgement should be given of all those matters, that done,
06 06	having sent already at his first coming to all the quarters of
07	the Country to seek Pamela, although with small hope of
05 07	overtaking them, he himself went, well accompanied to
06	the Lodge, where the two unfortunate Lovers were attend-
	ing a cruel Conclusion of their long painful late pleasant
43	affection.

42   Bona fide, it is a great mixture that we have not men
43   swine *as well as* beasts; *for* then we should have pork that

43   hath no more bones than a pudding, *and* a side of bacon
that you might lay under your head instead of a bolster.

The Nashe sentence has three internal coordinators, the Sidney four. The Sidney passage, however, is over two and a half times as long.

A further representative feature both of this sentence and of the Sidney passage in general is the extent to which it is embedded, suspended, and interrupted—not only by conventional hypotaxis (subordinate clauses) but by the extensive use of verbal phrases. In the first sentence of the Sidney passage, just quoted, there are ten verbals and two subordinate clauses *before we get to the main clause.* Similarly, the second sentence is suspended by an absolute participial phrase; the third sentence, although not initially suspended, does not proceed for more than a line before we have an interrupting included element. Suspension, interruption, and inclusion are the rule in Sidney's style; in conjunction with the avoidance of coordinators, they may account for the frequent complaint that I hear from third-year undergraduates—that interesting as Sidney is, he is the most dense and difficult reading they have ever encountered.

Although the York Inventory program cannot get directly at a full description of the embedding, interruption, and suspension in each sentence of our samples, it can make an assessment of two things: (1) the placement of initial subordinate clause suspensions, together with the number of unsubordinated sentences; and (2) the density of indices of complexity (rank shifting)—subordinators, unsignaled subordinations, and verbals. Figure 6.7 gives, in biaxial form, the mean point of first subordination in each of our nine samples. As in Figure 4.9, the points tend to fall along a line. The point of first subordination and the sentence length are positively related. Unlike the samples in Figure 4.9, these samples tend to be more homogeneous—as they should, being samples from the same genre during the same era. Despite this unifying influence of genre, Sidney is distinguished from these controls in the same way as he is from the controls in Chapter 4: for the same point of first subordination he writes a longer sentence, and for the same length of sentence he has an earlier point of first subordination. Of the three control writers, the only one who subordinates earlier than Sidney is Lyly (roughly the fourteenth word in Lyly, vs. the sixteenth in our New *Arcadia* samples, vs. the twentieth in our Old *Arcadia* samples), and Lyly's sentences are considerably shorter (31.9 words vs. 44.7 in the New *Arcadia).*

The pair of lines drawn in Figure 6.7 at an angle of approximately 50 degrees indicates the area within which fell 18 of the Inventory's first 24 samples; the six exceptions were the five samples from Sid-

Figure 6.7 INITIAL SUBORDINATION

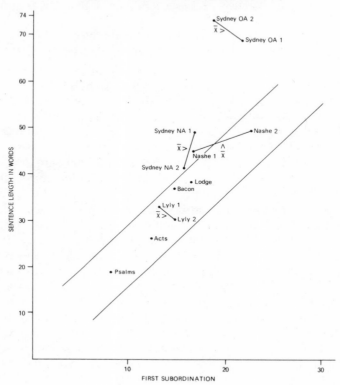

ney, the *Defence* and four *Arcadias,* and the first sample of Nashe. The area within the 50-degree lines offers merely one more indication that at any given sentence length Sidney was likely to subordinate perceptibly earlier than the norm. Figure 6.8a depicts the total number of unsubordinated sentences in our nine samples. Just as we should expect, Sidney is again clearly distinguished from the others in the direction of complexity. To some extent this distinctiveness is a function of his sentence length: after all, how many unsubordinated sentences do we see with 60 or more words in them? But it is possible that the reverse is also true, that Sidney's sentence length is a product not only of his strong tendency toward *copia* but of his unremitting impulse to avoid symmetry and coordination in favor of asymmetry, hierarchy, and complexity: in a subtle mind, if everything is to have its place, then there must be many *things,* to show the nicety of the gradations.

We can obtain some idea of the degree of Sidney's complexity by adding together a number of indices of rank shifting: verbals, subordinators, and unsignalled subordinations (Figure 6.8b). Nearly any passage in Sidney will illustrate the tendencies that Figure 6.8b shows. He will even stand out against a passage from Lyly that is, for Lyly, relatively complex:

> Philoclea fearing lest refusal would turn him back again to his violent refuge gave him a certain Countenance, that might show she did yield to his request: The later part whereof indeed she meant for his sake to perform neither could they spend more words together. For Philanax with Twenty of the Noblest personages of Arcadia after him, were come into the Lodge, Philanax making the rest stay below: For the Reverence he bore to womanhood, as stilly as he could came to the door and opening it, drew the eyes of those two Doleful Lovers upon him, Philoclea closing again for modesty's sake the Riches of her beauties, but Pyrocles took hold of his Bar minding at least to die before the excellent Philoclea should receive any outrage.
>
> (Sidney, 9006, Old *Arcadia,* 280)

> It is wit that flourisheth when beauty fadeth, that waxeth young when age approacheth, and resembleth the ivy leaf, who although it be dead continueth green. And because of all creatures the woman's wit is most excellent, therefore have the poets feigned the muses to be women, the nymphs, the goddesses; ensamples of whose rare wisdoms and sharp capacities would nothing but make me commit idolatry with my daughter. I never heard but of three things which argued a fine wit: invention, conceiving, answering. Which have all been found so common in women that, were it not I should flatter them, I should think them singular.
>
> Then this sufficeth me that my second daughter shall not lead apes in hell, though she have not a penny for the priest, because she is witty; which bindeth weak things, and looseth strong things, and worketh all things in those that have either wit themselves or love wit in others.
>
> (Lyly, 9002, *Euphues, Anatomy of Wit,* 45)

We should note that the Lyly passage, although shorter, has more clausal subordination (classes 42 and 43) than the Sidney, and *that this is typical of the contrast between the two writers.* The Sidney passage, however, with its longer periods, longer interruptions, more frequent suspensions, more numerous unsignalled subordinations, and heavier use of verbals, is much the more complicated in its architecture.

In the light of Figure 6.8, and in the light of the illustrative passages, it is irresistible to recall how often one hears Sidney's style contrasted as "hypotactic" to the allegedly "paratactic" style of Lyly. Not only in our illustrations but in our entire six Lyly-Sidney samples, there is very little difference between these two men in the mere number of subordinate clauses (Sidney's four samples yield a mean of 116.7 clausal subordinators, Lyly's two samples a mean of 109.5). This difference is more than compensated by the difference

Figure 6.8a UNSUBORDINATED SENTENCES PER 3,500 WORDS

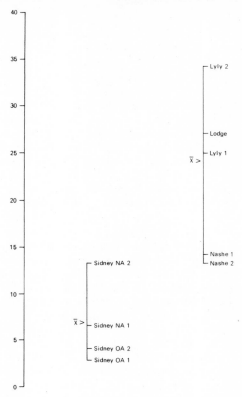

between them in relative clauses: Lyly's two samples yield a mean of 85, Sidney's four a mean of 60 per sample. There is a measure of truth (although imprecise truth) in the conventional hypotactic-paratactic antithesis: it lies in Sidney's extensive use of verbals, especially for interruption, and in Lyly's extensive use of anaphora. We would be more accurate if we dispensed with the old antithesis and acknowledged that both men wrote very hypotactic styles but that Sidney's was hypotactic in a way that is irregular, interrupted, and without internal connection and that Lyly's was hypotactic in a way that is symmetrical, anaphoric, and seriated.

We can now direct our attention to Sidney's extremely distinctive use of the verb system as a whole. The Elizabethan novel itself is in its time an unusually verb-rich genre. Sidney did not overgo his peers in this respect, although he had an enormous pre-eminence in the use of the verbals (Figure 6.9b). One kind of verbal of which he is a particularly heavy user is the passive participle (Figure 6.9a).

Other areas where Sidney's use of the verb system is distinctive

Figure 6.8b INDICES OF COMPLEXITY TOTAL PER SAMPLE
42+43+05+06+07

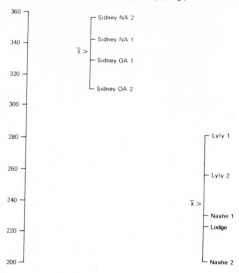

are use of the passive voice and complementation (nouns and adjectives in complement position). The "energetick prose" of Sidney's fiction is one of those rare felicitous cases of a renowned prose style that conforms to commonplace prejudices about neutral and passive verbs: in comparison with the controls, Sidney used very few "be" main verbs, little complementation, and few passive main verbs. Figure 6.10 compares him with the controls in these respects. Notice that the mean for the Sidney samples is in each category some 20% to 40% below the mean for the controls. Although not all the Sidney samples stand fully clear of all the control samples in each category, the Sidney syndrome is clearly depicted—at least a large part of it is. That depiction gains further clarity when we remind ourselves of Sidney's anomalously heavy use of passive participles.

Apart from demonstrating anew that there is no positive correlation between a writer's use of the passive voice and his use of passive participles, Figure 6.9a points to an important feature of Sidney's use of interruptive participial elements. We should not need to be reminded of how often the reader of Sidney encounters interrupting (passive) elements like the following:

> Then forthwith Erona (being seized of the Crown). . . .

> . . . there had landed in Lydia (driven thither by tempest) two excellent young Princes. . . .

> For the People (tired already with their Divisions, of which his Complaining had been principal Nurse). . . .

Figure 6.9a PASSIVE PARTICIPLES
(CLASS 062)

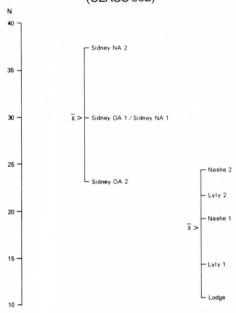

Reassembling the concrete features of Sidney's style that have been thus far discussed, we can classify nearly all of them under three overlapping general heads: (1) complexity, (2) asymmetry, and (3) energy (in the sense of extensive and *active* exploitation of the verb system). To the first two we have already ascribed some of the difficulty that students have when they try to read Sidney for the first time; perhaps we could make a similar ascription to the third . After all, in a Sidney narrative, more is *happening,* people are *doing* more, and there is significantly more activity for us readers to keep in our heads.

SIDNEY'S WORD CLASSES

It has been said by more than one commentator that Sidney writes in a "rich, adjectival style." This may well be true of Sidney, but if so it is true also of Lodge, Lyly, and Nashe. Each of our nine samples produced between 209 and 252 adjectives, or between 6.0% and 7.2% of the total text. This percentage is quite average for the period 1570 to 1700: well above "heavy" styles like those of Lord Clarendon and John Donne, well below the extreme-unctuous styles of Sprat and other Restoration figures.[8] But there are very distinctive elements in Sidney's use of modifiers.

Figure 6.9b VERBALS PER 3500 WORDS
05+06+07

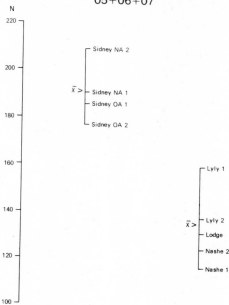

We cannot properly consider Sidney's habits of modification without first observing that he is the least nominal writer of our four. Figure 6.11 compares Sidney, with a mean total of 629 nouns per sample, with the control writers, who average a total of 711 nouns per sample. We can note that both Sidney's and Lyly's are among those very unusual English styles in which the percentage of nouns consistently runs less than 20%.[9]

This anti-nominal tendency in Sidney's style is the other side of a coin that we looked at earlier: his avoidance of word parallelism (Figures 6.5a and 6.5b), for it is nouns that are the items most frequently doubled and trebled in series. Nashe gets much of his high figure for nouns from multiplication in series (a mean of 80.5); Sidney's low figure partly derives from his studious avoidance of parallelism in its shorter forms (23, 22, 29, and 21 series in his four samples). Once again, a look at a piece of text can be illuminating:

> For now indeed, Love paid off his mask, and showed his face unto her, and told her plainly, that she was his prisoner. Then needed she no more paint her face with passions; for passions shone through her face; Then her rosey color was often increased with extraordinary blushing; and so another time, perfect whiteness ascended to a degree of paleness; now hot, then cold, desiring she knew not what, nor how, if she knew what.

> (Sidney, 9008, New *Arcadia*, 171)

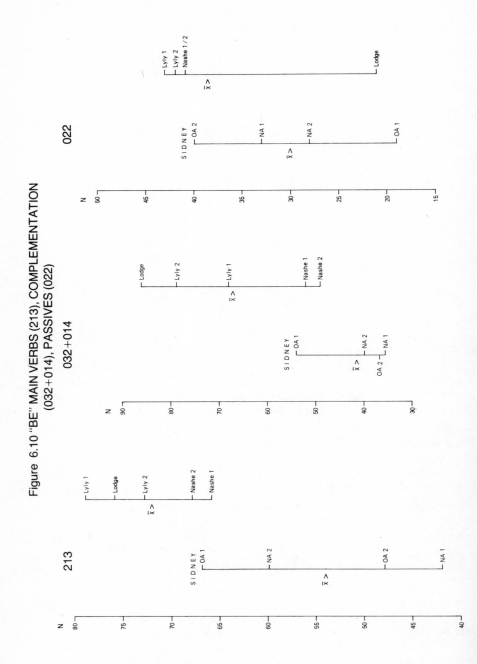

Figure 6.10 "BE" MAIN VERBS (213), COMPLEMENTATION (032+014), PASSIVES (022)

They wander through lakes, fish ponds, and fens, and overwhelm ships, cast boats upon anchors, and drown men that are swimming; therefore are they counted the most pestilent, troublesome, and guileful spirits that are; for by the help of Alrynach (a spirit of the west) they will raise storms, cause earthquakes, whirlwinds, rain, hail, or snow in the clearest day that is; and if ever they appear to any man, they come in women's apparel.

(Nashe, 9010, *Peirce Penniless,* 78)

There is, to be sure, parallelism in the Sidney passage, but at the level of the full predicate; there are no word seriations. By contrast, the Nashe passage has three such seriations, of which two are of nouns: "lakes, fishponds, and fens," "pestilent, troublesome, and guileful," and "earthquakes, whirlwinds, rain, hail, or snow."

Lyly's samples have slightly more nouns than Sidney's (a mean of 639.5 to Sidney's 628.7) and slightly more adjectives (233.5 to 228.2). But there is a very large difference in the number of adjectives used as verb complements (classes 032 and 034): Lyly's samples produced means of 57.5 for class 032 (predicate adjective) and 19.0 for class 034 (subjective or objective complement); Sidney's produced means of 25.5 and 11.0. Totalled, the two means are 76.5 for Lyly, 36.5 for Sidney. The mean *net* total of non-complement adjectives per sample is in Lyly's case 157, in Sidney's case 192; stated as percentages of all nouns, these are 24.6% for the Lyly samples and 30.5% for the Sidney samples. These figures, plus others below, suggest that, certainly of our four novelists and probably of all prose writers from 1580 to 1640, Sidney had the highest density of attributive adjectives per noun. Notice in the second half of the Sidney passage just cited, it is not enough that her color was "often increased with blushing" or that her whiteness "ascended to a degree of paleness"; instead, we have "rosey colour," "extraordinary blushing," and "perfect whiteness."

In this, we are sure, Sidney was distinctively copious. Corroborating evidence comes from the frequency-ordered listing of three-class patterns that follows in our output the computation of the "D" statistic. The three-class pattern 31-03-01 (determiner-adjective-noun: "the splendid castle," "the noble warrior," "the sullen shepherd," etc.) is frequent among the novelists: in Lodge's sample it occurs 71 times; in Lyly's, a mean of 67; in Nashe's, a mean of 87; in Sidney it occurs a mean of 75 times in samples that were less than 85% counted because of the 1,000 limit on the computer's counting of the "D" statistic. By extrapolating, we can see that the 31-03-01 pattern would occur 88 times in 3,500 words for Sidney. This is not a consequential difference with Nashe for this pattern considered alone, but if we recall that Nashe's prose has over 120 more nouns per sample,

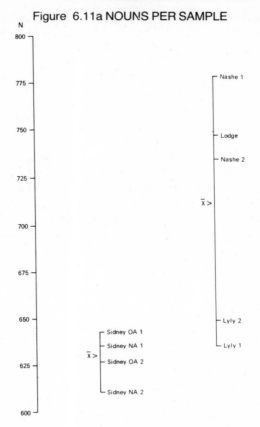

Figure 6.11a NOUNS PER SAMPLE

we can see that these figures are concurring evidence with the percentages above.

Further corroboration comes from the count of strung prepositional phrases. From the *total* count of these strings, nothing distinctive emerges for any of our novelists. For the three strings that included attributive adjectives, however, Sidney was high man. The three strings were:

51	03	01	51				in heavy armor at
51	31	03	01	51			at the large house of
51	31	03	41	03	01	51	in the large and verdant meadow in

Sidney's mean for these three groups was 15.5 per sample, compared to a mean of 13.5 for Nashe, 9.5 for Lyly, and 8 for Lodge. These are given in graph form in Figure 6.11b.

Below, we can see (at full throttle) Sidney's tendency to attach modifiers to nouns contrasted with those of Lodge and Lyly, in passages of rather similar length.

Figure 6.11b "ADJECTIVAL" STRINGS PER SAMPLE

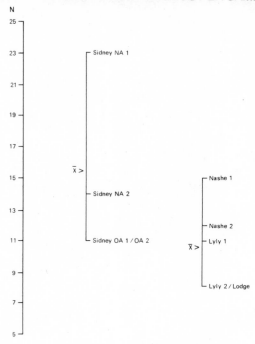

Where again leaving them all to lament his departure, he by enquiry got to the *wel-known* house of Kalander: There was he received with *loving* joys of Kalander, with *joyful* love of Palladius, with *humble* (though *doulful*) demeanor of Argalus (him specially both he and Palladius regarded) with *grateful* servisableness of Clitophon, and *honorable* admiration of all.

(Sidney, 9008, New *Arcadia,* 48)

Sir JOHN (that with the Phoenix knew the term of his life was now expired, and could with the Swan discover his end by her songs) having three sons by his wife LYNIDA, the *very* pride of all his *forepassed* years, thought now (seeing death by constraint would compel him to leave them) to bestow upon them such a legacy as might betray his love, and increase the *ensuing* amity.

(Lodge, 9001, *Rosalind,* 10)

But things past are past calling again, it is too late to shut the stable door when the steed is stolen. The Trojans repented too late when their town was spoiled. Yet the remembrance of thy *former* follies might breed in thee a remorse of conscience and be a remedy against *further* concupiscence.

(Lyly, 9002, *Euphues, Anatomy of Wit,* 15)

Figure 6.12a DETERMINERS PER SAMPLE
(CLASS 31)

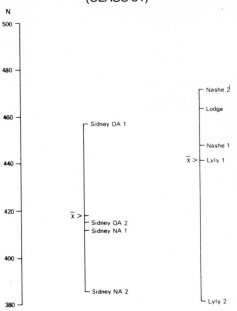

Notice that the proportion of nouns with attributive modifiers to those without is, respectively, 6:6 in Sidney, 3:13 in Lodge, and 2:11 in Lyly.

While speaking of Sidney's use of the modifier system within noun clusters, we should turn our attention briefly to his use of the determiners. Although Sidney had fewer determiners per sample than any other novelist except Lyly (Figure 6.12a), he had more determiners per noun than did any of the controls. Sidney averaged 66.5 determiners per 100 nouns, vs. 64.3 for Lyly, 61.9 for Lodge, and 60.6 for Nashe. These figures *per se* are not earth shaking, but they develop considerable interest when we consider the sparseness with which he used the indefinite determiners, *a, an, any* (Figure 6.12b). Figure 6.12 suggests Sidney's heavy reliance on the definite and demonstrative articles (the, this, that, these, those) and on the possessive pronouns. In fact, the ratio between the other determiners and the indefinite ones in Sidney is roughly 7:1 vs. a ratio of 4:1 in the controls. This is a startling difference of proportion in a word class that should be, *ex hypothesi,* rather genre-sensitive. What it suggests is that Sidney probably wrote at a more specific and personal level than did the controls and that when he did rise in the pulpit to puff off a few moralizations he did it with a technique different at least from Lyly's, as we can see below.

Figure 6.12b INDEFINITE DETERMINERS PER SAMPLE
(CLASS 313)

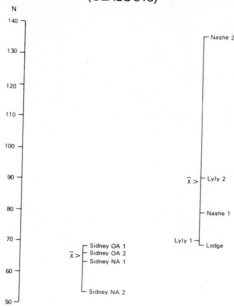

Insomuch that those things which often times the best sort think re-
wards of Virtue, he held them not at so a high a price, but esteemed
them Servants to well doing: The Reward of virtue being in itself, on
which his Inward love was so fixed, that never was it dissolved into
other desires, but keeping his thoughts true to themselves, was neither
beguiled with painted glass of pleasure, nor dazzled with the false
light of Ambition.

(Sidney, 9005, Old Arcadia, 331)

Not for Sidney lines like "A Lover is like the herb Helio-
tropium. . . ."[10] Not for Sidney either the indefiniteness of Nashe's
unfortunate traveler:

A company of cloystrell Clearkes (who were in band with Sathan, and
not of any Soldiers collar nor hat-band) pincht a number of good
minds to God-ward of their provant.

(Nashe, 9011, Unfortunate Traveler, 279)

Moving from noun clusters to verb clusters, we can see that here,
too, Sidney is unique. Figure 6.13a, which takes main verbs (other
than "be" main verbs) and verbals (other than "be" verbals) together,
shows the extent of Sidney's use of the verb system. Combined with
the verbal richness is, as we might expect, a considerable adverbial
richness, which is shown in Figure 6.13b. It is this adverbial richness, plus Sidney's reliance on intensifiers (33.5 per sample, vs. 23

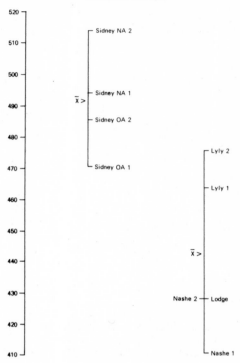

Figure 6.13a VERBS AND VERBALS PER SAMPLE
02+05+06+07

for Lyly, 16 for Lodge, and 9 for Nashe) that gives Sidney his abnormally high "M" statistic—the total of all adjectives, adverbs, intensifiers, and function adverbs. He is the only prose writer from 1575 to 1640 whose "M" for every sample exceeds 400, and he is the only writer in that era other than Burton whose mean "M" is over 400. Figure 6.14 illustrates his relationship with the other novelists.

A passage from Sidney will illustrate his adverbial density:

> Although his fair sister Artaxia (who accompanied him in the Army) sought all means to mollify his Rage: Till *lastly* he besieged Erona in her best City, vowing he would have her, either for force or *otherwise*. And to the extremity he had brought her, when there had landed in Lidia (driven *thither* by tempest) two excellent young Princes, as Plangus named them, Pyrocles, Prince of Macedon, and Musidorus, Duke of Thessalia; At these words a man might *easily* have perceived a starting and blushing both in Cleophila, and Dorus, but being *utterly* unsuspected to be such they were unmarked.
>
> (Sidney, 9006, Old *Arcadia,* 64)

Figure 6.13b ADVERBS PER SAMPLE
(CLASS 04)

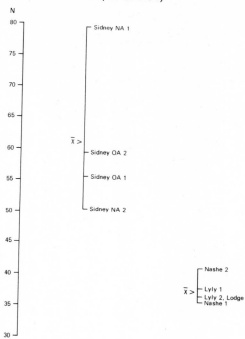

What intrigues me about this passage is that it contains five adverbial modifiers (italicized)—above normal for the time and genre; yet
their presence escaped my notice on the first half dozen or so read-
ings. The reason for this fact is not hard to find: there is so much activity in Sidney's style—the exquisite sentence architecture, the subtle asymmetries, the richness of metaphor—that above-normal occurrences of certain word classes do not strike one as forcibly as they
would in other writers, that is to say in *any* other writers, for when it
comes to complexity, Sidney is in a class by himself.

CONCLUSIONS

A certain fuss is made from time to time over Sidney's alleged
change of style between the Old and the New *Arcadia*. There is no
doubt that he or his printer dramatically shortened his periods, that
his already heavily syndetic sentence openings became more so, that
his reliance on verbals became more pronounced, and that he reduced the already low number of indefinite determiners.[11] Neverthe-

Figure 6.14 "M" STATISTIC
03+04+33+34

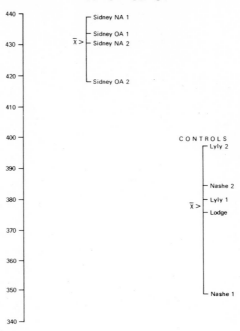

less, excepting only the category of period length, the New *Ar-cadia's* closest relative in all the categories that we have here discussed—and do not forget that these are Sidney-defining categories—is the Old *Arcadia.* In most of the parameters that we have examined, the two works are virtually indistinguishable. Both are marked by the clear manifestations of the unique complexity, asymmetry, and energy that characterize Sidney's style.

I find it hard to believe that any stylistician could read Sidney's prose without feeling enriched if not surfeited by the experience. The voice is as unique, as idiosyncratic, and as self-conscious as Gibbon's; at the same time it seems to me to lack the singular drawback of Gibbon's—the monotony that, for me, arises from the historian's ample use of certain Francophone mannerisms. Sidney was an heir to a self-conscious movement to bring English up to the level of the world's great rhetorical languages, especially in its sentence architecture. The unique richness and complexity he brought to his task might evoke from the modern reader nothing but wonder and admiration were it not for the brevity of the average attention span in our time. Surely styles—especially a style as good as this one—are to be admired as well as counted.

At the same time, it does our admiration no harm if it is chastened occasionally with a few hard facts about what exactly is in the text. And what we can enumerate in careful analysis of the syntax is as rich and distinctive as our intuition tells us it is when we simply let Sidney's language—at all its levels—take us by force.

Table 6.2 STATISTICS FOR CHAPTER 6

	00	01	02	03	04	05	06	07	11	21	31	32
Lodge	15	749	300	252	37	63	51	14	277	198	464	22
ROS	.4	22.0	8.8	7.4	1.1	1.9	1.5	.4	8.1	5.8	13.6	.6
Lyly	12	634	305	236	38	98	34	27	334	285	441	15
EAW	.4	18.3	8.8	6.8	1.1	2.8	1.0	.8	9.7	8.2	12.7	.4
Lyly	19	645	342	231	37	74	48	12	315	230	381	12
E&E	.6	18.9	10.0	6.8	1.1	2.2	1.4	.4	9.2	6.7	11.1	.4
Sidney	39	645	206	237	56	85	78	23	359	208	456	29
OAI	1.1	18.4	8.1	6.8	1.6	2.4	2.2	.7	10.3	5.9	13.0	.8
Sidney	30	628	309	223	58	85	62	31	319	255	415	27
OA2	.9	18.1	8.9	6.4	1.7	2.5	1.8	.9	9.2	7.4	12.0	.8
Sidney	26	629	305	209	79	88	81	20	363	224	413	20
NA1	.7	17.8	8.6	6.0	2.2	2.5	2.3	.6	10.3	6.3	11.7	.6
Sidney	23	613	308	244	53	90	86	29	365	214	387	26
NA2	.7	17.1	8.8	7.0	1.5	2.6	2.5	.8	10.5	6.1	11.1	.8
Nashe	13	782	293	241	36	58	42	15	253	213	448	24
PP	.4	22.4	8.4	6.9	1.0	1.7	1.2	.4	7.3	6.1	12.9	.7
Nashe	27	735	305	239	41	85	32	6	321	223	471	34
UT	.3	21.2	8.8	6.9	1.2	2.5	.9	.2	9.3	6.4	13.6	1.0

Note: For each sample, the first figure is the *number* of words of a class; that class as a *percentage* of the total words in the sample is given next.

Table 6.2 (continued)

33	34	35	41	42	43	45	51	61	62	71	91	
16	72	19	161	82	42	33	392	10	67	41	30	Lodge
.5	2.1	.6	4.7	2.4	1.2	1.0	11.5	.5	2.0	1.2	.9	ROS
21	85	30	105	115	63	76	333	13	102	34	28	Lyly
.6	2.5	.9	3.0	3.3	1.8	2.2	9.6	.4	3.0	1.0	.8	EAW
25	106	53	137	104	107	48	347	26	73	35	16	Lyly
.7	3.1	1.6	4.0	3.0	3.1	1.4	10.2	.8	2.1	1.0	.5	E&E
32	108	29	111	105	64	22	407	17	78	21	33	Sidney
.9	3.1	.8	3.2	3.0	1.8	.6	11.6	.5	2.2	.6	.9	OA1
38	99	26	119	105	68	42	389	13	79	21	31	Sidney
1.1	2.9	.8	3.4	3.0	2.0	1.2	11.2	.4	2.3	.6	.9	OA2
32	118	23	144	130	58	44	419	18	85	11	17	Sidney
.9	3.4	.7	4.1	3.7	1.6	1.2	11.9	.5	2.4	.3	.5	NA1
32	102	25	138	127	49	51	369	18	79	17	41	Sidney
.9	2.9	.7	4.0	3.7	1.4	1.5	10.6	.5	2.3	.5	1.2	NA2
10	71	30	188	77	94	20	417	23	58	7	13	Nashe
.3	2.0	.9	5.4	2.2	2.7	.6	12.0	.7	1.7	.2	.4	PP
8	94	35	151	78	49	22	386	18	65	13	20	Nashe
.2	2.7	1.0	4.4	2.3	1.4	.6	11.1	.5	1.9	.4	.6	UT

Table 6.2 (continued)

	Period Length	First Subordinator ($\bar{X}$)	Unsubordinated Sent	N Sent	Initial Syndeton %	"D" Statistic	Word Parallelisms	Nonfrontal Coordinators	Total indices of symmetric parallelism	Adjectival Strings
Lodge ROS	38.1	16.1	27	91	22.0	932	60	155	102	8
Lyly EAW	33.6	13.2	25	104	34.4	946	28	79	119	11
Lyly E&E	30.3	14.9	34	114	25.4	989	47	113	121	8
Sidney OA1	68.9	21.8	3	52	58.4	$\frac{1000}{3323}$	22	100	55	11
Sidney OA2	73.8	18.8	4	48	38.4	$\frac{1000}{2977}$	23	96	65	11
Sidney NA1	49.1	16.9	7	73	68.5	$\frac{1000}{3214}$	29	104	79	23
Sidney NA2	41.6	15.8	13	85	60.0	$\frac{1000}{2987}$	21	102	76	14
Nashe PP	45.2	16.8	14	78	20.5	916	110	178	134	15
Nashe UT	49.7	22.7	13	71	22.0	946	51	146	78	12

Table 6.2 (continued)

Class 062	Class 213	032 +014 Complements	Passive Verbs class 022	Indefinite Determiners (313)	
11	76	86	21	70	Lodge ROS
14	79	68	43	72	Lyly EAW
22	73	79	42	91	Lyly E&E
30	67	54	19	68	Sidney OA1
23	48	37	40	67	Sidney OA2
30	42	33	33	64	Sidney NA1
37	60	40	28	53	Sidney NA2
19	66	52	41	80	Nashe PP
24	68	49	41	136	Nashe UT

The great thing is to last and get your work done and see and hear and learn and understand: and write when there is something that you know; and not before; and not too damned much after . . . No. It is not enough . . . but still there were a few things to be said. There were a few practical things to be said.

Ernest Hemingway, Death in the Afternoon

Chapter 7
STYLE IN THE AFTERNOON: Hemingway at Mid-Career

T HE violin playing of Paganini contained elements of technical virtuosity so fast and so subtle as to elude the eyes of even the most astute observers among his audience. The story arose—to be instantly and universally believed—that the devil had been seen guiding his bow. The violinist himself, a man with a shrewd sense of what makes art marketable, did all he could to encourage his public in the belief. The case has been similar with Hemingway's style, which has attracted stylisticians, both pros and hodads, Villaltas and Caganchos, much as Paganini's playing attracted music lovers and admirers of musicianship. These, too, have seen a supernatural something guiding the hand of the artist: in Hemingway's case, the goddess Simplicity. And the author himself, by suggesting that everything he did was simple and unforced and unselfconscious, sustained the commentators in their most cherished beliefs about how he wrote.

The consensus clearly says he wrote in some variety of plain: terse, staccato, concrete, understated, masculine, indirect, and clipped are possibly the adjectives one has heard most frequently over the years, although "hard-boiled" had a vogue in England in the 1930's.[1] "Biblical" had a great vogue among American teachers during the 1950's, after *The Old Man and the Sea,* and Richard Bridgman has managed to fasten "colloquial" on him.[2] Acting in concert with typological adjectives associated with the plainness syndrome have been some highly perceptive statements about individual works—George Steiner's remark, for example, that in *The*

Killers Hemingway retrenched "language to a kind of powerful, lyric shorthand."[3] To this point, except to the extent that stylistic typology is insidious,[4] nothing that we have noted is disturbingly amiss. Alas, however, Hemingway's commentators have often been tempted into the rediscovery of what is widely believed on faith and by doing so have reinforced the faith. The technique is as follows. The commentator finds a passage in Hemingway's fiction (usually an initial, a terminal, or a climactic passage, since it is in these places that Hemingway tends to get most terse), displays it, and describes it in some variation of the received criticism. For example, Earl Rovit, in a generally sound survey of Hemingway's life and work, brings out a passage from *In Our Time* as a typical example of the man's fully developed art and style. Of it he notes:

> The simplicity of the sentence structure and of the diction is reinforced by the minimal use of adjectives and adverbs. There are no metaphors, similes or descriptive relative clauses. In other words the traditional techniques of pictorial description have been sedulously avoided.[5]

Similarly, William Barrett brings out the opening passages of *A Farewell to Arms,* of which he remarks:

> . . . The abstraction, the universal under which the sensory particulars are to be subsumed, has become meaningless. The honest observer is left only with those sensory fragments.
>   Accordingly, the syntax itself has a minimum of grammatical subordinating structures (paratactic rather than hypotactic, as the grammarians would put it). Everything in this world must be put on the same level, and any trace of hierarchial order, even in language, must be abolished.[6]

These are merely two examples among many available. The cumulative effect of all these assessments is preserved for humanity and indelibly stamped in the minds of our undergraduates by our anthologists, who sedulously perform their task of perpetuating current critical orthodoxy. One example will suffice:

> . . . his most admired fiction is stripped clean, with no commentary by the author and no self-analysis by the characters. He simply tells us what was said and done, leaving the rest to implication.
>   Hence, too, his famous style. He wanted the clearness, the cleanness, of a style unmuddied by vague abstractions and pompous complexity. The syntax of his sentences must be elementally plain, a procession of simple and compound sentences, stringing *and* clauses one after another as a child does (but a very artful child). When he did use complex sentences he commonly placed the subordinate clause after the main clause. He defied the rhetoric books and the tradition on which they are based; in style, as in many other things, we should go back to the primitively natural and build on that. . . .[7]

In addition to being an immoral thing to teach to literature students, it is fatuous, of course, that a writer could ever become as rich as Hemingway[8] by defying rhetoric books and the tradition on which they are based: that tradition, after all, begins with knowing one's audience. Not merely fatuous but false, however, is this representation of his style when applied to the first paragraph of the story that immediately follows it. The first paragraph of "A Clean, Well-Lighted Place" covers eleven lines and 110 words in three sentences. Not one of the sentences is either simple or compound; there are seven subordinate clauses: two relative clauses, two noun clauses, and three adverbial clauses (of which two are frontal, i.e., *preceding* the main clause to which they are attached). There is a similar, although much less grotesque, kind of contradiction in the work of Rovit.[9] Prior to his citation of the *In Our Time* passage and his description of it, Rovit rightly notes that *Death in the Afternoon* "serves in so many ways as Hemingway's *Principles of Poetic Composition*,"[10] and he quotes two passages of it as follows:

> It is impossible to believe the emotional and spiritual intensity and pure, classic beauty that can be produced by a man, an animal and a piece of scarlet serge draped over a stick. If you do not choose to believe it possible and want to regard it all as nonsense you may be able to prove you are right by going to a bullfight in which nothing magical occurs . . . But if you should ever see the real thing you would know it. It is an experience that either you will have in your life or you will never have . . . But if you ever do see one, finished by a great estocada, you will know it and there will be many things you will forget before it will be gone.
>
> (Hemingway, *Death in the Afternoon*, 207)[11]

> Now the essence of the greatest emotional appeal of bullfighting is the feeling of immortality that the bullfighter feels in the middle of a great faena and that he gives to the spectators. He is performing a work of art and he is playing with death, bringing it closer, closer, closer, to himself, a death that you know is in the horns because you have the canvas-covered bodies of the horses on the sand to prove it. He gives the feeling of his immortality, and, as you watch it, it becomes yours. Then when it belongs to both of you, he proves it with the sword.
>
> (Hemingway, 9301, *Death in the Afternoon*, 213)

Once again there is a rash of complex sentences, many of them frontally subordinated. One can only begin to suspect that Hemingway did not write up (or down) to his stylistic reputation all the time.

The question is undeniably worthy of investigation. But where to begin? A beginning, after all, is all that a single critic can make in a single chapter of a survey. For a variety of reasons, *Death in the Afternoon* commends itself. First of all, it is virgin territory, unharrowed by legions of previous stylistic archaeologists looking for primitive artifacts. References to its style are either evasive or teasingly ambiguous (e.g., Waldhorn: "Both its diction and syntax are unexpectedly cavalier, more erratic than one might have expected . . .").[12] Second, it comes at a turning point in Hemingway's career, the point where he moved away from fiction for a while to go back to a variety of kinds of journalism. Richard Peterson, author of far and away the most sensitive treatment of Hemingway's style, suggests that the book marks the watershed of Hemingway's career—the dividing line between his early and his later style.[13] If so, the book has an enhanced interest. Third, it is the most style-conscious of Hemingway's books, with its unremitting emphasis on *how* things should be done (if they are to be done well and truly, etc., etc.). For the stylistic historian, such, of all an author's utterances, are the most interesting. Let the banderilleros begin.

THOSE STACCATO SENTENCES

The vaunted simplicity of Hemingway's staccato sentences is the central topos in the received opinion about his style. It is therefore in this place that we shall start. The method, as in the last chapter, will be to compare random samples of Hemingway in a number of aspects of his style with people more or less contemporary with him, including in this case three writers specifically identified as his preeminent models: Twain, James, and Gertrude Stein. The samples from which this chapter is developed are listed in Table 7.1. Ideally, one would prefer to have non-fiction samples from Twain, Callaghan, and Nabokov, especially from Callaghan. No such samples, however, will be incorporated into the Inventory until after this book has been published. Hemingway's syndrome of normal and idiosyncratic traits would be identified in any case by the remaining 14 control samples; no harm is done by including these three fiction samples, if only for their own intrinsic interest.

We shall start by the construction of an hypothesis. Existing folklore would lead us to expect several things from our man's staccato sentences: shortness, lack of variety, a minimum of initial connection, and a high density of sentences containing no subordination. Moreover, in accordance with the *dicta* of Forster and Falk, we should expect him to eschew frontal subordination and to be revealed in that part of our computer program that measures the first point of subordination as a late subordinator. We should expect him to have a minimum not only of subordinate and relative clauses but of other kinds of rank shifting, such as with verbals. Finally, we might also expect him (in accordance with his self-proclaimed dis-

Table 7.1 SAMPLES FOR CHAPTER 7[a]

9301	Hemingway	Death in the Afternoon
9319	Hemingway	Death in the Afternoon
9401	Orwell	four essays
9196	Orwell	A Collection of Essays
9313	Twain	Huckleberry Finn (f)
9318	Stein	Paris France
9611	Callaghan	Short Stories (f)
9323	Fitzgerald	The Crack-up
9327	Wilson	Axel's Castle
9402	Reich	The Greening of America
9336	Nabokov	Lolita (f)
9192	Strachey	Eminent Victorians
9179	James	Notes on Novelists
9614	Davies	A Voice from the Attic
9187	Woolf	The Common Reader
9166	Chesterton	Essays
9194	Burgess	The Novel Now
9617	Richler	Hunting Tigers under Glass
9329	Mumford	Technics & Civilization

[a]All references to primary text are by author, sample number, work, and page. A full catalog of the samples is given in Appendix B.

trust of both "flowery" and other language) to avoid the more complicated kinds of adverbial subordination, the kinds involving concession, condition, cause, and result.

The hypothesis is thoroughly plausible in the light of received opinion. In confrontation with our 19 samples, however, it gets some rude surprises. First of these is with regard to sentence length, as given in Figure 7.1. Notice that Hemingway sits dead in the middle of our samples, with a mean sentence length of 27.2 words, almost exactly halfway between Callaghan (at 17.2 words) and James (at 37.9). Nine of the control samples showed shorter sentences; seven showed longer. The case was similar with initial connection (41, 42, 91);[14] the mean for all samples was 14.4%, which was exactly the mean for the two Hemingway samples. Nine control samples (topped by Stein and Woolf at 23% +) exceeded Hemingway in this measure; seven (with Callaghan low man at 2.5%) were exceeded by him.

The "D" statistic seemed more promising. Hemingway's penchant

Figure 7.1 PERIOD LENGTH IN WORDS

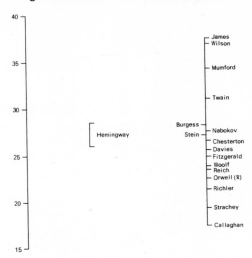

for repetitiveness not only has been much talked of but has been studied with considerable rigor by both Peterson and Gutwinski.[15] The enormous amount of lexical repetition in his prose is likely to give the reader (at least *this* reader) an insistent impression of repeated pattern, much as Gibbon in his very different way gives a similarly insistent impression. The lexical repetition *seems* to be reinforced by repetition of syntactic arrangement, which in its turn should produce in Hemingway's prose, as in Gibbon's, a low "D" statistic. The facts adduced by the samples refute the hypothesis (Figure 7.2). Once again, Hemingway comes out in the exact center of the range: he is, for the third time, the All-American (or all-twentieth-century) sentence writer.

A further feature of the simplicity hypothesis—that he probably wrote a greater number of unsubordinated sentences than did the controls—fares even worse. Figure 7.3 shows the two *Death in the Afternoon* samples to rank very low on this measure of simplicity; indeed, only three other writers, all of whom could be considered very old-fashioned,[16] rank lower. In the converse of this measure, density of subordinate clauses, the mean for the two Hemingway samples ranks him fifth among our 17 writers. In total complexity[17] (i.e., density of rank shifting: subordinators plus relatives plus all the verbals) Hemingway ranks first. These surprising—yea, stunning—data are given in Figures 7.4a and 7.4b. Surely the figures lie? Before entertaining such an hypothesis, we might do well to recur to the two *Death in the Afternoon* passages quoted by Rovit above. I would concede that Rovit's passages might not be so "typical" of the

Figure 7.2 "D" STATISTICS

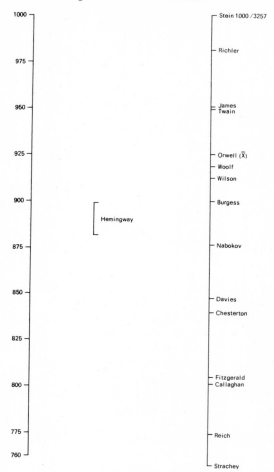

Note: Mumford, at 659, is beneath the scale.

work as a whole sequence of passages selected by random number table; they are nevertheless indicative. A re-reading of them will show nine sentences, all hypotactic, four suspended with frontal subordination.

Here again, we touch an area where Hemingway seems to excel the controls: early subordination. Figure 7.5 shows that of our controls only Orwell, who wrote a sentence 25% shorter, placed his first subordination earlier; only James joins Hemingway on the left-hand side of the 50-degree line.

Of all the statistics that we have so far unearthed, perhaps the most

Figure 7.3 UNSUBORDINATED SENTENCES AS % OF ALL
SENTENCES

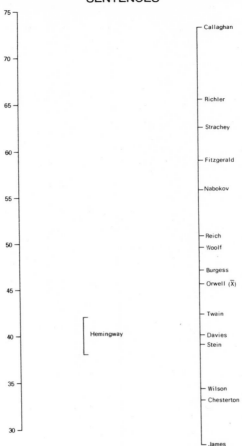

devastating to the critical stereotype of Hemingway's style is the one
related to adverbial subordination. Since my boyhood I have been
told of Hemingway's disdain for language, of his belief that three
grunts and a wineskin full of chest hair were worth a million words.
We have noted in our hypothesis that he should therefore eschew
the most complex and cognitive (rational rather than descriptive) adverbial forms: clauses of concession, condition, cause, and result.
Once again, the hypothesis collapses in confrontation with the facts.
Of all our writers, only Hemingway's great mentor Gertrude Stein
has a higher incidence of these kinds of adverbial subordination (see
Table 7.3 at the end of this chapter).

In the wake of these early discoveries, I was under a strong temptation to believe that what most critics have done heretofore is to take

Figure 7.4a SUBORDINATION
42+43

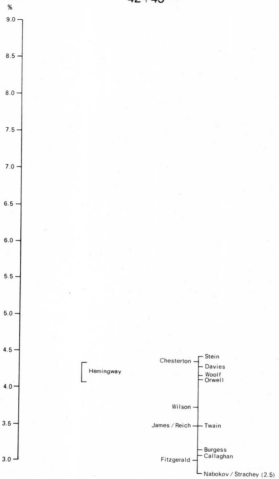

the famous paragraphs from *A Farewell to Arms*[18] and accept them
not only as a statement of aesthetic predisposition but as a typification of how Hemingway wrote all the time. It is chastening to return
to the text, both to the passages cited by Rovit and to sequences like
the one below:

> Joselito was admitted to be very good in the press, but it was pointed
> out that he was only able to place banderillas on one side, the right
> (the bulls of course were very small), he insisted on that; that he killed
> holding the sword so high that some said he pulled it out of his hat
> and others that he merely used it as a prolongation of his nose and,
> this is Christ's truth: he was hooted, whistled at and had cushions

Figure 7.4b RANK SHIFTING
42+43+05+06+07

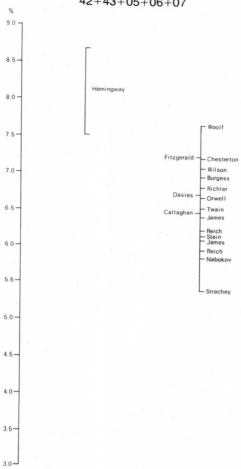

thrown at him the last day he fought in Madrid, the 15th of May, 1920, while he was working his second bull, after having cut the ear off his first, and was hit in the face by a cushion while the crowd shouted "que se vaya! que se vaya!" which can be translated "May he get the hell out of here and stay!"

(Hemingway, *Death in the Afternoon*, 242)

Whatever that is, it is not a simple or telegraphic style. Now, there are, to be sure, many passages in Hemingway like the ones below:

He acted as though it were not there. He did not favor it or avoid lifting the arm; he ignored it. He was a long way beyond pain. I never saw a man to whom time seemed so short as it did to him that season.

The next time I saw him he had been gored in the neck in Barcelona.

Figure 7.5 FIRST SUBORDINATION

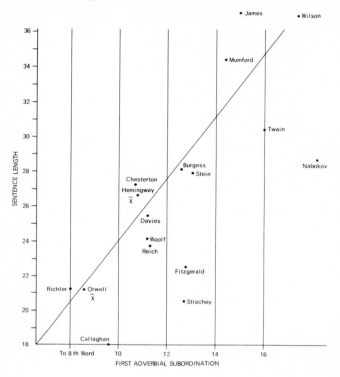

The wound was closed with eight stitches and he was fighting, his neck bandaged, the day after. His neck was stiff and he was furious. He was furious at the stiffness he could do nothing about and the fact that he had to wear a bandage that showed above his collar.

(Hemingway, 9301, *Death in the Afternoon*, 79)

Somehow, these latter are the ones that have stayed in the minds of the public. I can only suspect why: they are the passages that fulfill the stylistic ideals suggested by Hemingway himself and elevated to the status of representative fact by most of his commentators. Moreover, passages like those above contain one of his signal mannerisms, *verbatim* repetition (". . . and he was furious. He was furious . . ."). Impressive though the metaphysical impact of such passages may be (and there are many of them), they are not so representative of his entire set of expressive tools as we have been led to believe.

At the same time, one must concede that the commentary on Hemingway's style, now half a century in its growth, has not been the exclusive province of bloody fools. And, if only as an act of faith in other members of the critical profession, one must assume that there is in fact something in the overall quiddity of the style that has permitted Hemingway, with his gospel of plain talk, to con us into believing that he was talking plainly whilst he was often doing rather the opposite. Somewhere in his language there must be signals of plainness more substantial than Paganini's devil.

MORE STACCATO

There has been much discussion of Hemingway's use, indeed his overuse, of coordination. Gutwinski, who brings a good deal of rigor to his task, has established that connection within sentence boundaries is Hemingway's dominant technique of intrasentence cohesion. The traditional commentary has focused on his use of *and*, both the density and the eccentricity of that use, which has now become one of the staples of his reputation. Hemingway himself gave much encouragement to his admirers by cutting loose an occasional passage like the one below.

> The next day, the 16th of May, he was killed in Talavera de la Reina, gored through the lower abdomen so his intestines came out (and he was unable to hold them in with both hands, but died of traumatic shock from the force of the cornada while the doctors were working on the wound, and his face composed very peacefully on the operating table after he was dead, with his brother-in-law having his picture taken holding a handkershief to his eyes and a crowd of wailing gypsies outside with more coming and Gallo wandering around outside very pitiful, afraid to go in to see his brother dead, and Alamendro the banderillero saying, "If they can kill this man I tell you none of us is safe! None of us!") and at once became, in the press, and remains, the greatest bullfighter of all time.
>
> (Hemingway, *Death in the Afternoon*, 242)

Again, as with "he was furious-he was furious," the coordination is so mannered as to assume a disproportionate importance in a reader's response.[19] The overall use of *and* in our nineteen samples is given in Figure 7.6a. The figure suggests that the *and* passage quoted above is by no means typical. It also shows *Death in the Afternoon* to be high in its use of *and* but not startlingly so. Although Hemingway's mean would place him behind five, ahead of eleven, of the control writers, he is a long way from Miss Stein. Callaghan and Twain, writing fiction, exceed him in *ands* by a considerable amount.

Hemingway's overall use of the coordinator system is closer to his reputation, as Figure 7.6b suggests. Here, the mean for our two *Death in the Afternoon* samples is exceeded only by Miss Stein and by two fiction samples. In other words, he coordinates as much in non-fiction as other writers are likely to in fiction. On this evidence,

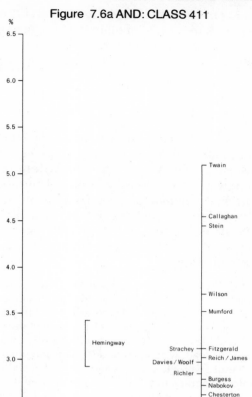

Figure 7.6a AND: CLASS 411

it seems that overall coordination is the one area of Hemingway's style that we have considered so far in which he practiced close to what has been written about him.

Before leaving the question of coordination, we should make the point (by no means an original one) that Hemingway often coordinates two clauses where it would be normal to interpose a sentence break, a semi-colon, or some other form of linkage. A classic case is given us in the following passage:

> There were always poppies in the wheat in the end of June and in July, and the mulberry trees were in full leaf and one could see the heat waves rise from the barrels of the guns where the sun struck them through the screens of leaves; the earth was turned a bright yellow at the edge of holes where mustard gas shells had been and the average broken house is finer to see than one that has never been shelled, but few travellers would take a good full breath of that early summer air and have any such thoughts as Mungo Park about those formed in His own image.
>
> (Hemingway, *Death in the Afternoon*, 138)

Figure 7.6b TOTAL COORDINATORS: CLASS 41

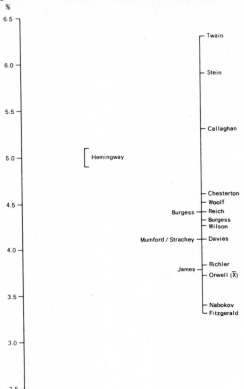

The last two clauses in the quotation, the first coordinated with *and*, the second coordinated with *but*, are introduced by usages that are unusual, arresting, and disproportionate in the critical memory.

Very nearly as mannered and distinctive as his coordination are his subject-verb clusters, especially the large number of pronoun subjects (with concomitant avoidance of nouns) and the frequency with which he places subject and verb (or subject and first auxiliary verb) together. Certainly our awareness of this fact, which buttresses the simplicitarian hypothesis, is much enhanced by passages such as the one quoted on page 147. Consider the sequence of subjects and verbs:

> He acted . . . it were not there . . . He did not favor . . . he ignored it . . . He was . . . I never saw . . . time seemed so short . . . it did . . .
> . . . I saw . . . he had been gored . . . The wound was closed . . . he was fighting . . . His neck was stiff . . . he was furious . . . He was furious . . . he could do . . . he had to wear.

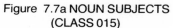

Figure 7.7a NOUN SUBJECTS
(CLASS 015)

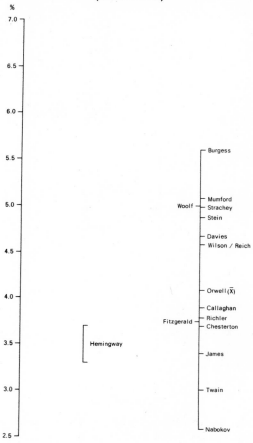

As we know, any carefully selected passage can support almost any hypothesis about a writer's style. In this case, however, the hypothesis is also supported by the total figures for both our random samples. Figures 7.7a and 7.7b give noun- and pronoun-subjects respectively. We should note that Hemingway ranks very low in noun-subjects, and rather high in pronoun-subjects, in accordance with expectations. This is more than a function of the fact that Hemingway writes an un-nominal but fairly pronominal style; it is rather a peculiar kind of distortion of the language that he shares with Callaghan (see Table 7.3). Among the controls, 19% of all nouns and 63% of all pronouns function as grammatical subjects; in Hemingway, under 17% of the nouns and over 67% of the pronouns are used in this way.

Figure 7.7b PRONOUN SUBJECTS
(CLASS 115)

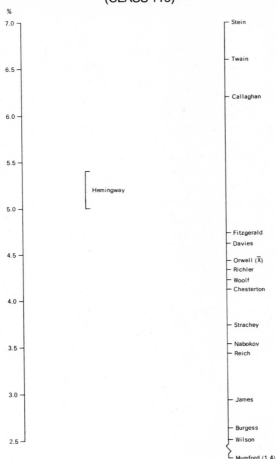

A propensity for placing subject and verb directly next to one another can be obliquely (although not precisely) tested through examination of the various patterns generated by the routine in our computer program that computes the "D" statistic and counts all the different three-class patterns in the text. Just as certain configurations are *prima facie* evidence of parallelism, so certain others are evidence of closely placed subject and verb. These, in Hemingway's case,[20] would be:

31–01–02   (Determiner-noun-verb: "The matador ducked," "The crowd roared," etc.)

31–01–21   (Determiner-noun-auxiliary/be verb: "The house is," "The time was," etc.)

11–21–21   (Determiner-auxiliary-auxiliary: "He has been," "They were being," etc.)

11–21–02   (Pronoun-auxiliary-verb: "They were running," "He has won," etc.)

The tabulation of these patterns, total per 3,500 words, is given in Figure 7.8. In this measure, Hemingway tops the non-fiction group, even Gertrude Stein; the only people who challenge or exceed him are Callaghan and Twain, both with samples of fiction. Concurring evidence of his frequent directness came from the section of our program that analyzes sentence openings: in the opening 11–21–02 (pronoun-auxiliary-verb), only Chesterton (with 14 uses) exceeded our man (with 8 and 7 uses in his two samples), and only Chesterton, Twain (7), and Richler (8)—with Hemingway—had that opening among their three favorites.

Before leaving Hemingway's overall syntactic strategy for other aspects of his style (noun clusters, modification, predication), we should examine one final possible support for the simplicitarian theory: density of the standard prepositional phrase (51–31–01, preposition-determiner-noun). We have already noted that this is the most common three-class cluster in the language.[21] Among the 19 samples of this chapter, it was the most common pattern for 17, with Reich and Mumford being the sole exceptions. Hemingway himself was not a highly prepositional writer. In Class 51 alone he ranked exactly midway between Miss Stein's (7.0%) and Mr. Mumford's (15.7%) propensities (Figure 7.9a). Nevertheless, he exceeded everyone but James in the 51–31–01 pattern (Figure 7.9b). Surprising in this connection is the fact that James had more nouns, more determiners, many more prepositions (Figure 7.9a), and prodigiously more strung prepositional phrases (by a margin of 149 to a mean of 84) than did Hemingway; in short, James exceeded him appreciably in all the measures that are associated with the pattern 51–31–01, yet his margin over Hemingway in density of that pattern is not large at all. We do not have to look far in *Death in the Afternoon* to find passages like the one below:

> I have seen bullfighters gored *in the chest*, have heard the rib crack, literally, *with the shock* and seen a man turn *on the horn with the horn* in him and out of sight, muleta and sword *in the air*, then *on the ground*, the bull thrusting head and man high and the man not leaving the horn when he is tossed to come off the next toss *into the air* and be caught by the other horn and come down, try to get up, put his hands where he was breathing *through his chest* and be carried *with his teeth* knocked out to die *within an hour in the infirmary* still *in his clothes*, the wound too big to do anything with. I have seen that man's, Isidoro Todo's, face while he was *in the air*, he being fully conscious all *of the time on the horn* and after and able to talk *in the infirmary* before he

Figure 7.8 DIRECT PREDICATION
31-01-21   11-21-21   11-21-02   31-01-02

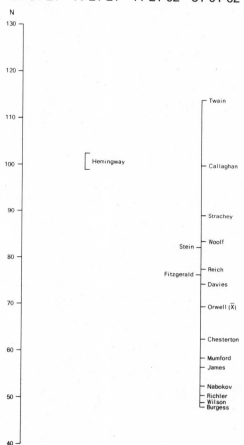

died, although the blood *in his mouth* made his words unintelligible, so I see the bullfighters' viewpoint about killing recibiendo when they know the cornada comes *in the chest.*

(Hemingway, *Death in the Afternoon,* 239)

Here, of course, we have an instance of two of Hemingway's tendencies mutually reinforcing one another: his propensity for the phrase 51–31–01 and his propensity for lexical repetition.

It is possible that these two characteristics, combined with one or two others dicussed below, are responsible for the epithet "biblical" that I heard from my high school English teachers. A high density of the phrase 51–31–01 can be associated with a variety of characteristics. In the case of Gibbon, it is associated partially with his Francophone mannerisms ("The clothing of the Emperor" instead of "The

Figure 7.9a PREPOSITONS (CLASS 51)

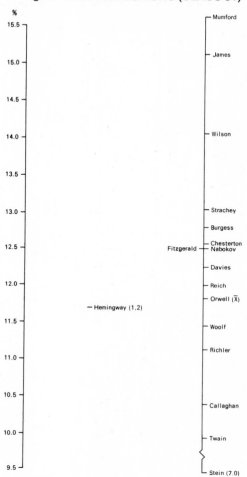

Emperor's clothes," etc.) and his persistent use of synecdoche and abstract personification, partially with his whole technique of sentence building. In the cases of Clarendon and James, our samples are very high in prepositional phrase strings. In the cases of the Bible,[22] Bunyan,[23] and possibly Hemingway, it works in combination with other characteristics to generate a metaphysics of plainness, a subject to which we shall return at the conclusion of this chapter.

NOUN CLUSTERS

For a twentieth-century writer, Hemingway writes a very un-nominal style. Of our controls, only Twain and Stein, each an acknowl-

Figure 7.9b PREPOSITIONAL PHRASES
51-31-01

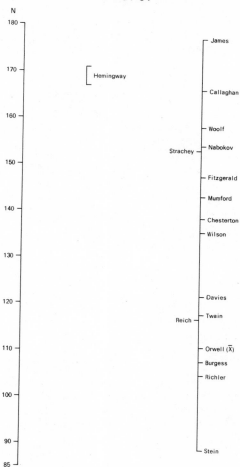

edged mentor-model, steered farther from the modern tendency in this regard. Figure 7.10a shows the density of nouns in our 19 samples.[24] Despite his low rank in nouns (14th of 17), he ranked third of the 17 in determiners (Figure 7.10b). James exceeds him here, as in the pattern 51–31–01,[25] and the prolifically nominal Mumford does likewise. Figure 7.11 shows nouns and determiners in a biaxial relationship for all our samples. Notice that Hemingway and James are isolated in the lower right portion of the graph.

Within this tendency to attach a determiner to each noun, Hemingway had the strongest propensity of all our writers to use definite determiners. The propensity has already been observed by Peterson, rightly I think, as an aspect of Hemingway's overuse of foreignism,

Figure 7.10a NOUNS
(CLASS 01)

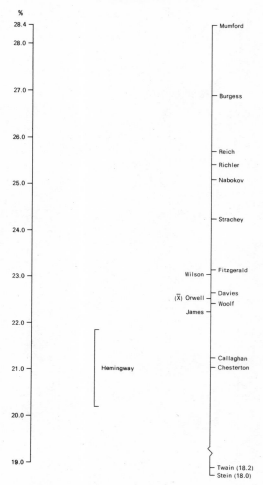

which reached a high point in *Death in the Afternoon*.[26] If we recur to page 154 and consider again the paragraph with 17 prepositional phrases (51–31–01) in it, we can note that of the 17 phrases, 12 contain definite determiners, four personal pronouns, and only one an indefinite determiner. It would in this way seem to be a representative passage from the work, for in our two samples something over 60% of Hemingway's determiners were of class 311, the definite/demonstrative category. Figure 7.12 shows all our writers, ranked by the density of definite/demonstrative determiners; interestingly, it is once again one of his acknowledged mentors, James, who is closest to him, and he is exceeded only by Mumford.

Figure 7.10b DETERMINERS
(CLASS 31)

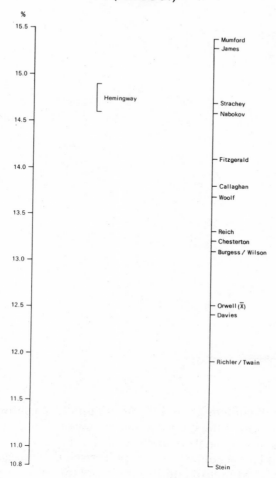

At the same time, in a surprising instance of living up to his reputation, Hemingway was inordinately sparing of adjectives. For example, Figure 7.13a shows him joining Twain and Stein as the most restrained of adjective users. This is, we might say, as it should be, since these three are the least nominal of all our writers. The correlation, however, is by no means infallible.[27] Neither is it infallible that a low incidence of adjectives will produce a low incidence of the modified noun cluster (31–03–01, determiner-adjective-noun). In the degree to which Hemingway suppresses or avoids this cluster, he is unique among all our writers, as Figure 7.13b suggests.

He is almost similar in his avoidance of attributive nouns, a prin-

Figure 7.11 NOUNS/DETERMINERS BIAXIAL

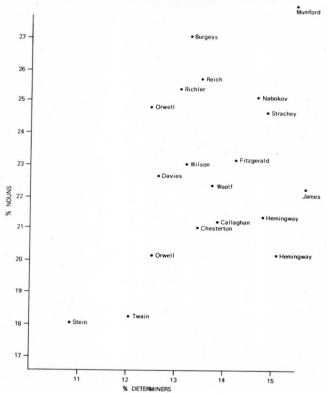

cipal feature of contemporary English. Figure 7.14a shows Hemingway at the bottom of the group, joined by Twain and three linguistic reactionaries. The data at the bottom of that Figure are not surprising, although I must confess to being surprised that our gas-powered society analysts Mumford and Reich did not top the group. This surprise drove me back to the texts of Fitzgerald, Burgess, Nabokov, and Richler, to discover things the sharing of which is irresistible. What accounts for the very high number of attributives in Burgess, Richler, and Nabokov? In Burgess it is story writers, myth makers, and tram drivers (all 012-011 clusters) who swell the attributive population. In Fitzgerald it is movie endings, football players, cavalry leaders, leather screens, summer hotels, and Wiener waltzes (all 012-011). In Richler—for whom the attributive pile is virtually a signature—we are introduced in succession to figures like the ten dollar-a-game amateur (811-012-313-011-011), the security officer, with revolver and bullet belt (311-012-011-511-011-411-012-011), a girl who wore pearls and a cashmere twin set (313-011-431-021-011-411-

Figure 7.12 DEFINITE DETERMINERS AS % OF ALL DETERMINERS

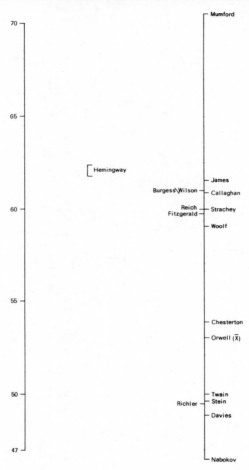

313-012-012-011), and the newspaper delivery boy (012-012-011). Nabokov (or his narrator Humbert) plays over the entire attributive range; we are introduced not only to blood-red sunsets, pearl-grey shirts, and wax-pale roads (all 012-031-011) but to baseball-playing sons and comic-reading nymphets (012-033-011). In fact, at one point in *Lolita*,[28] over the space of a sentence and a half, he cuts loose sheet-wrap, scissor work, newspaper clippings, ball player, and delicatessen store (all 012-011), all these parading through on the spiked heels of the baseball-playing son (012-033-011).

Moving to the right-hand side of the nouns, we can note that Hemingway is almost as sparing of appositives as he is of attributives. Indeed the free-standing property of Hemingway's nouns, signalled

Figure 7.13a ADJECTIVES AS % OF TEXT

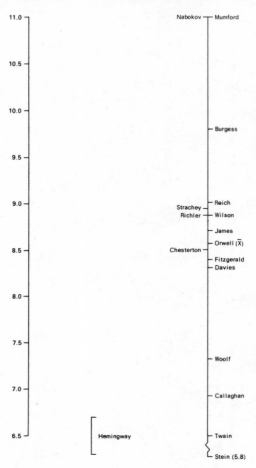

most often by the single definite determiner, has probably helped se-
duce commentators into finding the kind of simplicity he is alleged
to possess.[29] Figure 7.14b shows our 19 samples in their density of
apposition. Once again, the figure produces a surprise. My expectation was that James would be top man, and I was surprised by Burgess and Richler. Again, the texts were revealing. I discovered that
Richler's girl in the cashmere twin set is not just any old girl but is
specified appositionally (Joan Fontaine, Dorothy McGuire) (017-
017). With Burgess, apposition is simply an habitual device for con-
veying parenthetically: "The period we're concerned with in this
book—the twenty-five *years* since the Second World War—"; "If we
lay down conditions—the *need* for plot, dialogue, characters—";

Figure 7.13b INCIDENCE OF 31-03-01

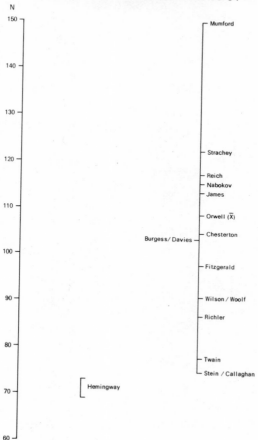

"John Horne Burns, whose first novel—*The Gallery*—is . . . "
These discoveries led me to compile all the prima facie evidences of
interruption, which is done in Table 7.2.

We should note that what is spoken of here is *indices* of interruption. The postmodifiers and passive participles, undeniably interruptive in James, are unlikely to be so in Hemingway, who will write
of the matador being carried off "with his teeth *knocked* out. . . ."
With Hemingway the passive participle is different, used most often
as a means of terminal elaboration of a sentence. In any case, it is interesting to see that in the full tabulation of these afterthoughts and
interruptors, Hemingway, although in the middle of the group, is in
the bottom quarter of the range (30–46), a fact that reinforces our earlier conclusion that he liked his nouns freestanding. Those of us
who cherish the memory of Mr. James as king of the interruptors can

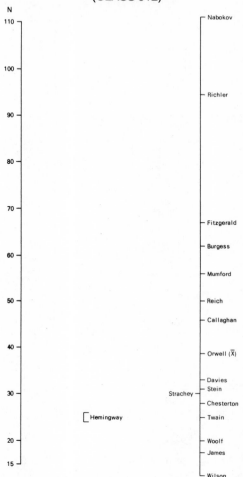

Figure 7.14a ATTRIBUTIVE NOUNS
(CLASS 012)

take heart from the prospect of new samples and a rematch between his phrases, measured and tuned to a pitch of exqusiteness, and those of M. Richler, the St. Urbain Street Noun Piler.

VERBS AND MODIFIERS

A corollary to the conventional wisdom about Hemingway's style, the wisdom that speaks of his staccato sentences, his insistent parataxis, his strings of short clauses, is that he must be a highly predicative writer who uses a minimum of modification. After all, each of those staccato clauses has to have a verb in it and to be truly staccato

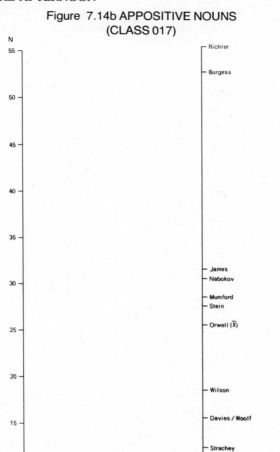

Figure 7.14b APPOSITIVE NOUNS (CLASS 017)

it can't have much other furniture except for a couple of unuphol-stered nouns. Thus far in our study, the conventional wisdom has been inconsistent in its accuracy—almost completely random. We would therefore be prudent to test it again, on this particular point.

Looking at the total of main verbs in Table 7.3, we can see that Hemingway is nothing unusual; he is well above the relatively pon-derous styles of Wilson, James, and Mumford, but at the same time he is well below Callaghan, Twain, and Miss Stein. Similarly, in to-tal predication (main verbs, 02, plus "be" main verbs, 213), a mea-sure that militates in his favor because of his high number of main verb be's,[30] he is not truly exceptional. These totals are given in Fig-

Table 7.2 INDICES OF INTERRUPTION: PARTICIPLES (062), AP-
POSITIVE NOUNS (017), AND POSTMODIFYING ADJECTIVES (035)

	062	017	035	TOTAL
Richler	22	54	20	96
James	22	32	34	88
Burgess	23	53	14	88
Mumford	21	29	8	63
Nabokov	19	32	11	62
Stein	9	28	18	55
Wilson	15	19	17	51
Davies	18	16	13	47
Hemingway ($\bar{x}$)	15	8	21	44
Woolf	18	16	7	41
Orwell ($\bar{x}$)	10	26	5	41
Reich	16	18	6	40
Twain	11	5	23	39
Fitzgerald	25	5	7	37
Chesterton	11	14	11	36
Callaghan	11	6	14	31
Strachey	13	13	4	30

ure 7.15a. When we add the verbals to these, Hemingway's station
changes (Figure 7.15b). He moves from the middle of the range to
near the top, where he joins his models Twain and Stein and sits not
far below the most verb-rich writer of our group, Callaghan. We
should note that he is propelled into this prominence by his frequent
recourse to the verbals, particularly the participles: in total verbals
he is exceeded only by Callaghan and Fitzgerald (4.5% and 4.3% respectively, to Hemingway's mean of 3.9%), and in participles his
mean of 1.6% is exceeded only by Callaghan (2.9%) and Nabokov
(1.8%). All the participles and many of the other verbals represent a
rank shift, represent in other words an opting for hierarchial rather
than paratactic arrangement of structures. For example:

Paratactic	*Rank shifted*
José turned and stepped to the side and avoided the bull.	José turned, *stepping* (06) to the side *to avoid* (05) the bull.
Juan made a bad pass and let himself be gored.	By *making* (07) a bad pass, Juan let himself be gored.

Hemingway's richness in verbals is a kind of corroboration of what we discovered about subordinators and relatives earlier in the chapter (Figure 7.4).

We attempted a variety of other inspections of Hemingway's use of the verb system, particularly in the auxiliaries, and could find nothing unusual there. In most measures he sat close to the middle of the range. There was, however, one exception, a surprising one in view of the reputation of his style. That exception was the passive voice, in the use of which he ranked very high (cf. Table 7.3). No doubt the staccato vigor of Hemingway's prose was sapped by the density of passives. Passages like the following one are by no means hard to find:

> A bull that has gored a man becomes more liable to gore again. A great part of the matadors who have been gored and killed in the ring have been caught and tossed previously by the bull that finally killed them. Of course many times this repetition of the goring in the course of the same fight is due to the man being shocked into grogginess or deprived of his agility or judgment of distance by the first tossing, but it is also true that a bull which has found the man under the lure or after the placing of a pair of banderillas, will repeat the process by which he caught him.
>
> (Hemingway, 9319, *Death in the Afternoon*, 129)

I think that there is an explanation for at least some passivity in Hemingway's style, which I must admit I found surprising. It is this: Hemingway has a strong tendency to maintain one or two entities—the same one or two nouns or their pronouns—as grammatical subjects over a succession of clauses (see Figure 7.11). This tendency may be partly responsible for his reputation for simplicity. Moreover, it leads him into situations where in a series of clauses he must choose (often unconsciously) between a shift of subjects and a passive verb. Many of the passives that I found in *Death in the Afternoon* are used to avoid a subject shift. Notice in the passages that follow both the density of the passive voice and the persistent tendency to stay with one or two grammatical subjects.

> He gave emotion always and, finally, as he steadily improved his style, he was an artist. But all the last year he fought you could see he was going to die. He had galloping consumption and he expected to die before the year was out. In the meantime he was very *occupied*. He was *gored* badly twice but he paid no attention to it. . . . The next time I saw him he had been *gored* in the neck in Barcelona . . .
>
> (Hemingway, 9301, *Death in the Afternoon*, 79)

> Originally quites were *made*, preferably, by the use of largas. In these the cape was fully *extended* and one end offered to the bull, who was *drawn* away following the extended cape and then turned on himself to fix him in place by a movement made by the matador, who would

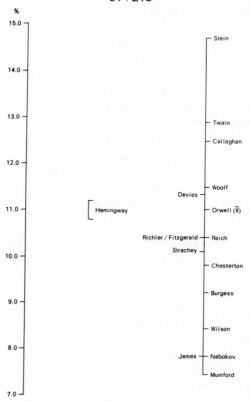

Figure 7.15a PREDICATION
01+213

swing the cape over his shoulder and walk away. These could be *executed* with great elegance . . .

(Hemingway, 9301, *Death in the Afternoon*, 177)

In bullfights now a good pic is not one in which the picador, pivoting, protects his horse completely. That is what it should be, but you might go a long time and never see one. . . . A bad pic is one that is *placed* anywhere else but in the morillo, one which rips or opens a big wound, or one in which the picador lets the bull reach the horse. . . .

(Hemingway, *Death in the Afternoon*, 188–189)

We have already noted that Hemingway was sparing of nouns and extremely sparing of adjectives. The case is similar with the adverbial modifiers, despite the great number of verbs and verbals in his prose. Figure 7.16a takes, together, all the adverb types: true adverbs (04), intensifiers (33), and function adverbs (34). To be sure, he is less sparing of the adverbial modifiers than of the adjectival, but he

Figure 7.15b PREDICATION + VERBALS
02+213+05+06+07

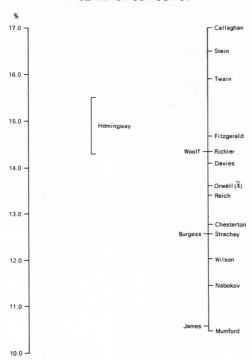

is still not generous. Interestingly, no one of the adverb types dominates Hemingway's adverbial usage in the way that the function adverb dominates Miss Stein's (5.1% of 8.0) or in the way that the descriptive adverb dominates Callaghan's (2.4%—very high—of 5.9).

A final point of examination can bring us home on a note of fulfilled expectation: the "M" statistic. Of all our writers for this chapter, Hemingway is the only one with an "M" under 400, and he produced that low "M" on two equally random samples. If we are to have any faith at all in the simplicitarian description of Hemingway's style, he would have to be—like Bunyan and the Bible—low in this measure in comparison to other writings of his time, and he is. Figure 7.16b gives the "M" statistics of our 19 samples.

CONCLUSIONS

There are many qualities in the style of *Death in the Afternoon* that can be seen, given imaginative handling, to provide some kind of basis for the conventional wisdom about Hemingway's style. His gram-

Figure 7.16a ADVERBS OF ALL KINDS
04+33+34

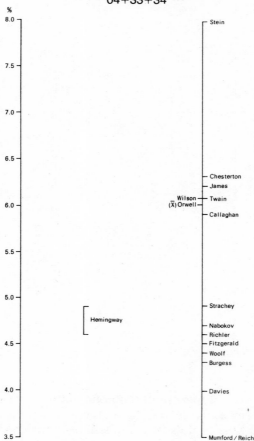

matical subjects (e.g., the high incidence of pronoun subjects), the proximity of much of his subject-verb placement, his persistent and repeated use of the most common cluster in the language (and the repetition of that pattern with repeated words), his penchant for definite determiners (suggestive of specificity and concreteness), his high ratio of determiners to nouns, and his very sparing use of modifiers—all these things can be seen as factors in the metaphysics of plainness, which has been the principal support of his stylistic reputation. We might call them the tricks of seeming simplicity.

Underneath the mannered and heavily-marked tricks, however, there is a lot going on in *Death in the Afternoon* that Hemingway's reputation invites us to be blind to. Beneath the inordinate repetition of the 51-31-01 phrase, the syntax of *Death in the Afternoon* is sur-

Figure 7.16b "M" STATISTIC
03+ 04+33+34

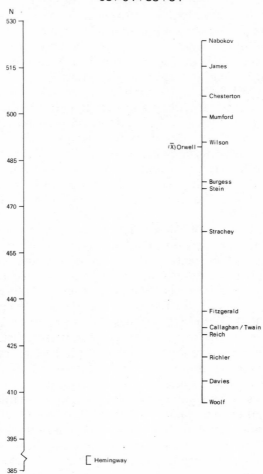

prisingly varied, much as Burton's is seen to be beneath his exhaustive and repetitive seriation.[31] Despite his tendency to put subject and verb close to one another, Hemingway seems more likely than his contemporaries to suspend his sentences frontally; in fact, the second *Death in the Afternoon* sample was the only one of all our samples that offered as a most frequent sentence opening a cluster that begins with a subordinator.[32] Underneath the tricks he is rank shifting far more than is commonly suspected, frequently (in the relative clauses) with passive verbs.

The "authorship" hypothesis—that a mature professional writer will show strong consistencies in his style over his lifetime, even in a variety of genres—has a widespread following. Mosteller and Wallace, Wachal, Milic, Wimsatt, Vickers, Gutwinski, and others have with varying degrees of explicitness subscribed to it. As a subscriber to the hypothesis, I must assume that when we move this investigation into Hemingway's other works, we shall find many if not all of the stylistic properties of *Death in the Afternoon.* To be sure, there will be some impact of genre: in the fiction the sentences will be shorter; there will be a higher verb-auxiliary ratio and a higher pronoun-noun ratio; there will be a bit less hypotaxis, although for the genre Hemingway might well remain a relatively hypotactic writer, and it seems probable that there will be no consequential difference from *Death in the Afternoon* in overall rank shifting, at least in the narrative and descriptive passages. I am buttressed in these beliefs by the citations selected by other critics, especially by the more perspicacious of them. For instance, Gutwinski selects a passage from *For Whom the Bell Tolls* as "a perfect example" of Hemingway's own mode of lexical cohesion.[33] The passage, 500 words in length, with only a slight reduction in subordination, exhibits virtually all the distinctive stylistic features discussed in this chapter.

The possibility remains, of course, that the early Hemingway manner cleaves closer to his reputation than what he wrote between 1932 and the publication of *The Old Man and the Sea.*[34] The possibility also remains that *Death in the Afternoon* is truly atypical of Hemingway's total corpus. We must certainly leave these possibilities open, for Peterson has already demonstrated at the lexical level some differences between Hemingway early and late, and talk of such differences has been extant among critics for a long time. Nevertheless, major elements of consistency are what we expect to find, consistency of a sort rather at variance with the critical stereotypes that have been heretofore accepted. But that, as Colonel Cantwell said, was another war, and I can only regret that there is not space in this book to pursue it to its conclusion.

Table 7.3 STATISTICS FOR CHAPTER 7

CATEGORY	9313 Twain	9301 Hemingway	9319 Hemingway	9318 Stein	9611 Callaghan	9323 Fitzgerald	9327 Wilson	9401 Orwell	9196 Orwell
01	18.2	20.1	21.8	18.0	21.2	23.1	23.0	20.2	24.8
31	11.9	14.9	14.6	10.8	13.8	14.1	13.1	12.4	12.6
02	10.5	8.1	7.7	10.4	11.1	8.1	6.0	7.1	7.3
21	6.9	7.5	7.3	9.8	5.0	5.9	6.8	8.8	7.9
213	2.4	3.1	3.1	4.3	1.4	2.2	2.4	4.2	3.5
311	6.0	9.3	9.0	5.3	8.4	8.4	8.0	7.1	6.2
312	2.0	1.8	1.7	1.5	2.7	1.4	2.0	1.7	2.0
313	3.2	2.6	2.8	3.5	2.2	3.7	2.1	3.1	3.8
032	1.1	1.3	1.2	1.6	1.6	1.1	1.6	1.8	1.4
014	.7	.9	.8	1.3	.2	.6	.8	1.5	1.5
03	6.5	6.7	6.3	5.8	6.9	8.4	8.8	8.8	8.3
04	1.5	1.5	1.4	2.2	2.4	1.1	2.1	2.5	2.0
33	.2	.9	.6	.7	.7	.6	1.0	.6	.7
34	4.3	2.2	2.9	5.1	2.8	2.8	2.9	3.3	2.8
35	1.2	.8	.7	1.6	.6	.6	.5	1.1	1.1
32	1.2	.6	.5	.8	1.5	.9	.5	.7	.4
43	.8	1.5	1.4	1.5	.4	1.0	1.8	1.7	1.5
42	2.7	2.7	2.7	2.9	1.5	1.8	1.9	2.6	2.3
99	115	131	121	121	192	145	90	168	150
05	1.8	1.9	1.6	.8	1.0	1.4	1.7	1.7	.8
06	.6	2.0	1.2	.7	2.9	1.5	.6	.5	.9
07	.6	.5	.6	.3	.6	1.4	1.1	.3	.6
062	11	14	17	9	11	25	15	7	12
61	14	25	26	57	10	29	19	28	14
62	1.6	1.7	1.6	1.3	1.0	1.4	2.0	1.9	1.4
11	10.4	8.0	7.4	10.7	9.1	7.1	4.9	7.2	5.5
M	430	386	388	476	430	436	491	516	463
41	6.3	4.3	5.0	5.9	5.3	3.3	4.4	3.9	3.7
51	9.8	11.7	11.7	7.0	10.4	12.4	14.1	11.1	12.5

9402 Reich	9336 Nabokov	9192 Strachey	9179 James	9614 Davies	9187 Woolf	9166 Chesterton	9194 Burgess	9617 Richler	9329 Mumford	CATEGORY
25.7	25.1	24.2	22.2	22.6	22.4	21.0	26.9	25.4	28.4	01
13.3	14.6	14.7	15.3	12.4	13.7	13.2	13.1	11.9	15.4	31
7.6	6.9	7.5	5.4	8.0	8.4	6.9	6.0	7.9	5.6	02
7.6	4.6	6.8	6.0	8.8	7.4	8.4	6.8	6.0	5.2	21
2.7	.9	2.7	2.4	3.5	3.2	2.9	3.2	2.4	1.8	213
8.0	6.7	8.9	9.4	6.1	8.0	7.1	8.3	5.9	10.9	311
1.7	3.0	3.0	2.6	1.9	2.7	1.3	1.3	1.6	1.2	312
2.9	4.0	2.3	2.6	3.5	2.2	3.6	3.0	3.9	2.9	313
.8	.6	1.5	.8	1.3	1.7	1.4	1.7	1.4	.8	032
1.5	.1	.6	.8	1.5	.8	.7	1.1	.9	.7	014
9.0	10.9	8.9	8.7	8.3	7.3	8.5	9.8	8.8	10.9	03
1.7	1.7	1.5	2.4	1.7	1.5	1.4	1.5	1.5	1.4	04
.2	.5	.7	.7	.3	.9	.9	.9	.4	.5	33
1.6	2.5	2.7	3.1	2.0	2.0	4.0	1.9	2.7	1.6	34
1.0	.5	.7	.5	1.0	.7	.9	.7	.9	.3	35
.7	.6	.4	.4	.3	.7	.7	.5	.9	.4	32
1.8	.8	.9	1.6	2.2	1.6	1.4	1.4	1.1	1.0	43
1.7	1.7	1.6	1.9	2.2	2.7	3.0	1.5	1.8	1.4	42
151	119	172	92	137	150	131	118	160	101	99
1.5	1.1	1.0	.9	1.2	1.9	.9	1.5	1.6	.8	05
.7	1.8	1.2	1.1	.6	1.1	1.3	1.0	1.5	.9	06
.5	.5	.2	.8	.5	.5	.7	.9	.7	1.0	07
16	19	13	22	11	18	11	23	20	26	062
23	12	21	15	20	33	38	29	22	11	61
1.6	1.3	1.5	1.3	1.7	1.9	1.4	1.8	1.4	.9	62
5.3	5.3	5.8	6.0	6.7	6.4	5.9	4.4	6.4	2.4	11
428	522	462	516	413	401	506	478	421	499	M
4.4	3.3	4.1	3.9	4.1	4.5	4.6	4.4	4.0	4.1	41
11.9	12.4	12.9	15.2	12.2	11.3	12.5	12.8	11.0	15.7	51

Table 7.3 (continued)

CATEGORY	9313 Twain	9301 Hemingway	9319 Hemingway	9318 Stein	9611 Callaghan	9323 Fitzgerald	9327 Wilson	9401 Orwell	9196 Orwell
Strings	56	81	87	33	46	74	129	73	73
513101:	117	171	167	88	166	147	135	107	113
310301:	75	71	66	72	72	97	90	110	106
112102:	51	33	37	27	28	30	18	31	24
115	6.6	5.4	5.0	7.0	6.2	4.7	2.5	4.5	4.0
015	3.0	3.4	3.7	4.9	3.9	3.8	4.6	3.9	5.0
017	5	7	9	28	6	5	19	27	25
012	26	24	25	32	47	68	13	28	52
033	25	25	16	11	12	49	16	25	32
023	8	15	8	12	29	10	17	8	9
022	31	45	39	40	22	24	26	36	32
427	29	18	6	25	16	16	21	46	25
416	12	18	25	14	4	15	21	10	20
421	27	25	27	26	25	14	9	13	16
422+423+ 424+425	26	31	35	35	11	12	12	18	15
"D"	949	898	882	1000/ 3257	800	804	912	913	938
411	5.1	3.0	3.4	4.5	4.5	3.2	3.8	2.6	2.4

9402 Reich	9336 Nabokov	9192 Strachey	9179 James	9614 Davies	9187 Woolf	9166 Chesterton	9194 Burgess	9617 Richler	9329 Mumford	CATEGORY
84	91	115	149	83	85	112	94	60	153	Strings
116	154	153	177	121	158	138	107	104	143	513101:
117	115	122	113	103	90	104	103	86	150	310301:
22	20	27	13	28	18	30	14	26	15	112102:
3.3	3.4	3.7	3.0	4.5	4.2	4.1	2.5	4.2	1.4	115
4.6	2.6	5.0	3.4	4.6	5.0	3.8	5.6	3.9	5.0	015
1	32	13	32	16	16	1	53	56	29	017
51	111	30	19	34	21	29	63	95	57	012
34	59	37	38	26	20	12	26	41	29	033
9	11	3	4	7	10	6	1	27	4	023
53	14	37	25	57	36	37	41	29	43	022
33	16	24	28	31	38	54	23	26	17	427
9	18	10	15	16	20	8	9	4	7	416
5	16	10	6	10	15	15	5	14	17	421
12	8	8	15	18	18	24	12	13	9	422+423+424+425
773	876	748	950	846	918	843	904	992	659	"D"
3.0	2.7	3.2	3.0	2.9	2.9	2.6	2.8	2.8	3.5	411

. . . Not a May-game is this man's life; but a battle and a march, a warfare with principalities and powers. No idle promenade through fragrant orange-groves and green flowery spaces, waited on by the choral Muses and the rosy Hours: it is a stern pilgrimage through burning sandy solitudes, through regions of thick-ribbed ice. He walks among men; loves men, with inexpressible soft pity—as they cannot *love him: but his soul dwells in solitude, in the uttermost parts of Creation. In green oases by the palm-tree well, he rests a space; but anon he has to journey forward, escorted by the Terrors and the Splendours, the Archdemons and Archangels. All Heaven, all Pandemonium are his escort.*

Thomas Carlyle, Past and Present

Chapter 8

VICTORIA RESARTA: Carlyle among his Contemporaries

THAN Thomas Carlyle, the dyspeptic Craigenputtock sage, no man—not even you, Prince Albert!—has written English awkwardlier.

Indeed, his awkwardness has served as a magnet unto critics and parodists alike; he is nearly irresistible. He commended himself unto this book, however, for a variety of reasons, the least of which is his distinctiveness. First, he offers us a nineteenth-century figure, a Scottish crag from which to view the stylistic landscape of a period that we have not otherwise considered in this book. Second, because of changes perceived by other commentators in his post-*Schiller* style, he offers us a chance to test, under the York Inventory's conventions, the hypothesis that changes took place—to test as well the larger hypothesis that a writer *can* change his style. Third, because two very thorough quantitative studies have been done on Carlyle within the last decade (within different conventions from ours), he can offer a glimpse of the compatibility of differing quantitative approaches. Fourth, because both these studies dealt with late Carlyle vs. early, without reference to other writers, they left unanswered questions, which the York Inventory might answer, about whether certain elements of constant form in his prose were properties of Carlyle himself or of the literary language of his time. After looking at Carlyle's reputation, we will compare him with a number of his contemporaries to find both his lifelong and his late distinguishing habits, after which we shall consider the question of changes in his style after the *Life of Schiller.*

CARLYLE'S REPUTATION

Thomas Carlyle is one of those rare figures in literary history whose style has a reputation very close to what it deserves. Like Hemingway's, it is a style that early on was recognized to possess qualities both distinctive and radical. In the nineteenth century the style was praised by Emerson and Thoreau, patronized by James Russell Lowell, and depicted with ambivalent wonder by James in his oft-quoted remark that

> It is not defensible, but it is victorious; and if it is neither homogeneous, nor, at times, coherent, it bristles with all manner of felicities.[1]

The style was also praised by the eminent Carlylean, James Froude, in whose biography of Carlyle was joined one of the main historical issues surrounding the dialect known as Carlylese: How much did Carlyle's mature style owe to Jean-Paul Richter? A lot, seems to have been the conventional Victorian answer, for Froude is at some pains to develop his own thesis that Carlyle's sources lay not in Richter but in family and education.

Thus the three main issues in the study of Carlyle's style today were defined nearly a hundred years ago: its distinctiveness, its development, its sources. Holloway reflects some kind of consensus when he speaks of Carlyle's "wild, passionate energy . . . disorderly and even chaotic, but leaving an indelible impression of life,"[2] a judgment that can be said to overlap with Levine's appraisal of late Carlylese as "so violently mannered and extravagant that it seems unjustifiable on any grounds."[3] One central question for scholarship has been that of exactly wherein this pyrotechnic extravagance consists. G.B. Tennyson found in 1965 that the manifestations begin early and grow in development to their fruition in 1831 in the style of *Sartor.* In short they consist of rhetorical questions, capitalization, apposition, repetition, parenthesis, odd punctuation, unusual syntax (loose, inverted, unbalanced), and unusual sentence modes (exclamations and interrogations).[4] Grace Calder, working 15 years earlier than G.B. Tennyson, found in the revisions of *Past and Present* an unremitting drive on Carlyle's part to expand and complicate things as he revised, to add modifiers, and to accentuate deviant uses of punctuation.[5] Both these appraisals accord with the consensus reflected by Holloway and Levine.

A second question—when did the extravagance begin and how did it grow old—has been approached by numerous scholars, notably Wellek, Roellinger, Levine, Burwick, and Oakman, the last four of whom have published analyses of Carlyle within the last two decades. Wellek perceived in Carlyle two separate styles, a wild baroque germanic one *(Richter)*, and a "tame, Augustan, rhetoric-book" one *(Schiller)*. The wild style Wellek found most intensely in *Sartor*, but as well in highly rhetorical passages throughout the remainder of Carlyle's writing career.[6] Roellinger, testing Wellek's theory, saw a major difference between the early writings through *Schiller*, and *Sartor*, with Carlyle's essays in 1828 and 1829 forming a transition between these two styles. The changes that he elucidated were primarily in the direction of irregularity, asymmetry, and emphasis (rhetorical questions).[7] Levine thought he saw something different in late Carlyle, but little that is different in style; he concluded, however, that the substance carried by the style is no longer either persuasive or morally affecting.[8] Burwick noted, like Tennyson, a continuity in Carlyle's style—a "general uniformity of Carlyle's syntactic predilections . . . the patterns favored by Carlyle in 1821 continue to dominate in the prose of 1875."[9] Nevertheless,

> The style of the *Life of Schiller,* in contrast to the rhetorical pyrotechnics of Carlyle's later polemical prose, seems bland and conservative; formal and fluent, not stiff but not vibrant either. The syntax is not often varied, and the clausal patterns do not alternate as often as in the later texts. . . . Many of the figures frequent in the later prose are used, but less exuberantly. . . .[10]

Burwick also noted that Carlyle "frequently ignores terminal boundaries" and that he uses various kinds of punctuation "as rhetorical rather than grammatical devices."[11] He apprehended a consistent, and with time a growing, disposition to use seriation and other forms of repetition, saying that Carlyle "frequently catalogs noun after noun, verb after verb, modifier after modifier, a whole series of appositions. . . ."[12]

Building on the work of Burwick and others, Oakman saw in Carlyle "a strong preference for nominal syntactic constructions,"[13] together with an "overwhelming choice of the active verbal vocabulary—61.5% of all verbs in the sample," which he interpreted as "one indication of that concrete particularity and fascination with the vibrantly alive universe which have long been noted in Carlyle."[14] Oakman also catalogued "an increasing reliance on expressive punctuation as his writing career progressed,"[15] and after

Sartor "a marked increase in the frequency of emphatic marks."[16] He saw "a tendency for the syntax to become more fragmented and disconnected in later years,"[17] although throughout his prose there seemed to be a habit of accumulation through parallelism, repetition, apposition, and other devices. He saw Carlyle's career as unfolding in five stages, even while perceiving "Carlyle's stylistic career as a logical growth of certain tendencies, present from the beginning," including apposition and accumulation.[18]

A third question, that of sources and influences, remains open, even though Smeed has made a strong case for certain intermittent, certain consistent, influences on Carlyle from Richter.[19] This question we must treat with diffidence, there being insufficient data in our hands to attempt to answer it fully. The first two questions, however, receive interesting answers from the materials of the York Inventory. The answers suggest that Carlyle's critics have been both detached and careful in their examination of him, even though their findings can be much enriched by a comparison of Carlyle samples with samples from several of his contemporaries. The Inventory samples to be used in this chapter are given in Table 8.1.

CARLYLE vs. HIS CENTURY

When reading Carlyle, I find it difficult to resist the temptation to feel that his style, so distinct and so heavily foregrounded, must be in every way unique. Alas, distinctive as he seems, it is not so. For example, his sentence length in words is on the low side of the average for his time, with four of the control samples falling within his range for sentence length, one below and eight above, but there is no evidence of the kind of quirkiness that we might well expect. The sentence length statistics are given in Figure 8.1.

This low to middling length sentence is not distinguished by any special introductory features.[20] Carlyle falls within the normal range for every major introductory word-class category, as an examination of Table 8.2 will reveal. The one unusual feature of his sentence openings is their great variety in the works from *Sartor* on; in each of the four mature works, the number of different sentence openings is between 75% and 80% of the number of sentences, percentages exceeded only by Coleridge and DeQuincey. To be sure, Ruskin, Newman, and Pater come close to Carlyle, but we should note that *all five* of these control writers wrote between 20% and 35% fewer sentences per sample than did Carlyle. The greater the number of sentences in a sample, the higher the likelihood of repetition of an initial pattern. It is obvious from the figures that over a given number of sentences (50, 75, 150) Carlyle's openings will be more varied than

Table 8.1 SAMPLES FOR CHAPTER 8[a]

9216	Carlyle	Life of Schiller
9110	Carlyle	Sartor Resartus
9703	Carlyle	French Revolution
9701	Carlyle	Past and Present
9140	Carlyle	Frederick The Great
9103	Ruskin	Seven Lamps
9104	Pater	Appreciations
9105	Arnold	Essays in Criticism (II)
9111	Macaulay	Critical and Historical Essays
9201	DeQuincey	Confessions
9204	Hazlitt	Selected Essays
9205	Coleridge	Biographia Literaria
9207	Mill	On The Subjection of Women
9209	Newman	Idea of a University
9211	Hogg	Life of Shelley
9139	Froude	Life of Carlyle
9141	Spencer	Principles of Sociology
9137	Darwin	Voyage of the Beagle

[a]All references to primary text are by author, sample number, work, and page. A full catalog of the samples is given in Appendix B.

those of any of the controls. In the sentence endings, too, the Carlyle works from *Sartor* on are the most various of our 18 samples.

The great increase in variety of both sentence beginnings and endings (*Sartor* ff.) is parallel to a general enrichment of syntactic range that occurred all through Carlyle's style some time near 1830. Of this we shall speak presently; both richness and ingenuity in the exploitation of syntactic possibilities are features of his reputation, and a reading of any considerable block of his post-1830 prose will reaffirm the impression with which the literary historians have left us. Surprising in this regard is that, despite his renowned propensity for inversion and Germanic word ordering, he does not write a highly complex sentence. The incidence of unsubordinated sentences is high, compared with the controls (Figure 8.2a), and the density both of subordinators and of subordinators and relatives combined is low (Figure 8.2b and 8.3), but the odd word orders, especially the long interruptions that Carlyle is inclined to put between subject and verb, create a spurious impression of complexity. A few samples of mature Carlylese are instructive. In the six sentences below, all from

Figure 8.1 PERIOD LENGTH IN WORDS

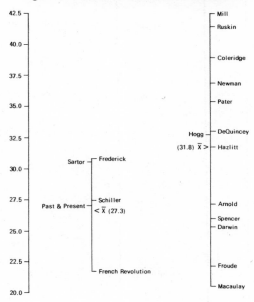

Past and Present, most of the subjects and verbs are italicized, subordinators and relatives placed in parentheses:

> Amid all violent stupidity of speech, a right noble *instinct* of (what) is doable and (what) is not doable never *forsakes* them: the strong inarticulate men and workers (whom) Fact patronises; of (whom), in all difficulty and work whatsoever, there *is* good *augury!*
>
> (Carlyle, 9701, *Past and Present,* 23)

> And truly this first practical *form* of the Sphinx-question, inarticulately and so audibly put there, *is* one of the most impressive ever asked in the world.
>
> (Carlyle, 9701, *Past and Present,* 23)

> In this way, not without troubles, but still in an erect clearstanding manner, *has* Brother *Samson reached* his forty-seventh year; and his ruddy beard is getting slightly grizzled.
>
> (Carlyle, 9701, *Past and Present,* 77)

> True, it must be owned, *we* for the present, with our Mammon-Gospel, *have come* to strange conclusions.
>
> (Carlyle, 9701, *Past and Present,* 148)

The *theories and speculations* of both these parties, and, we may say,

Table 8.2 DIFFERENT INITIAL THREE-CLASS CLUSTERS AS PERCENTAGE OF SENTENCES: CARLYLE VS. CONTROLS

Class of Initial Word	CARLYLE					CONTROLS												
	Schiller 1824	Sartor 1830	Fr. Rev. 1837	Past & Pres. 1838	Frederick 1851	Ruskin	Pater	Arnold	Macaulay	DeQuincey	Hazlitt	Coleridge	Mill	Newman	Hogg	Froude	Spencer	Darwin
41	5	8	6	4	14	13	14	14	7	8	1	9	7	11	10	4	10	1
41-42-91	8	17	9	9	17	20	17	20	14	22	8	17	30	22	13	8	22	7
51	19	15	10	8	9	5	12	13	11	13	3	16	9	4	16	7	23	17
31	27	15	12	21	20	24	21	16	31	17	22	23	18	13	22	19	19	41
01	14	3	16	7	20	2	5	8	17	4	10	0	5	13	5	12	19	2
11	11	9	7	17	6	3	14	16	12	19	43	19	28	23	32	30	5	19
DSO	78	87	113	95	84	59	70	85	92	83	61	67	57	67	58	90	87	65
N	124	109	149	125	108	82	96	117	168	103	107	87	80	90	104	147	133	137
DSO as %	62.5	79	76	76	77	73	73	71	55	81	57	77	71	74	56	61	65	49

of all intermediate parties and persons, *prove* to be things (which) the Eternal Veracity did not accept; things superficial, ephemeral, (which) already a near Posterity, finding them already dead and brown-leafed, is about to suppress and forget.

(Carlyle, 9701, *Past and Present,* 169)

This, speaking in the language of Eastcheap, *is* not correct.

(Carlyle, 9701, *Past and Present,* 177)

Of the six sentences, only two (the first and the fifth) include clausal subordination, but the initial and interruptive phrases, combined sometimes with peculiar ordering or placement of subject and verb, make the syntax complicated, although the sentences technically speaking are less complex than one would expect from their complications.

Turning our attention to other aspects of Carlyle's subordination, we can note that his placement of first subordinator does not, *prima facie,* suggest a frontally subordinated style (i.e., a "periodic" style with the periodicity attained through subordinate clauses). Figure 8.4 shows him earlier in his subordination than Newman, Ruskin, Pater, and Arnold, but it also shows him as far less early than either Coleridge or Mill. We should remind ourselves here that the initial average point of subordination tends to be strongly related to sentence length, and that Carlyle, having shorter sentences than all six of these controls, could be expected to subordinate earlier than not just four but all six of them. He seems, for his time, an average frontal-suspender. This finding, I should note, does not run necessarily counter to Oakman's discovery of considerable "periodicity"[21] in Carlyle, for periodicity, as in the six examples above, can be obtained by frontal and interruptive phrases and by inverted word orders. We cannot enumerate Carlyle's many inversions within the limitations of the York Inventory; his inordinate propensity, however, so often noted, remains only to be counted and normed against some of his contemporaries. The question is one not of whether Carlyle was deviant in this but of how grossly deviant he was. Moreover, his tendency to interrupt the flow of subject and verb (as strong in its way as Hemingway's opposite tendency) manifests itself insistently on every page. The interruptions come not just as subordinations but as appositives, postmodifying adjectives, prepositional phrases, and a variety of other parenthetical devices. Take for example the interruptions from just one page from our *Past and Present* sample:

work, much more than fighting, is henceforth the necessity of these new ages.

But mean governments, as mean-limited individuals do, have stood by the physically indispensable . . .

Figure 8.2a UNSUBORDINATED SENTENCES PER SAMPLE

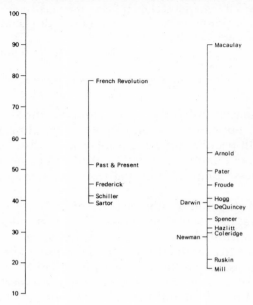

. . . but Governments, had they not realized him, could not have existed.

Thou thyself, cultivated reader, has done something in that alone true warfare . . .

Thee no beneficent drill-sergeant, with any effectiveness, would rank in line beside thy fellows . . .

Forethought, even as of a pipe-clayed drill-sergeant, did not preside over thee.

Forty soldiers, I am told, will disperse the largest Spitalfields mob.

(Carlyle, 9701, *Past and Present*, 141)

Some interruptions (appositions and postmodifying adjectives) are picked up by the York Inventory program, and others could be, but by no means all.

Carlyle's unusual nominality has been noted before (by Oakman) and would seem to be affirmed by the 18 samples we are using for this chapter. Carlyle's mean of 23.5% nouns[22] is above the mean of 22.2% for the controls, and only three of the 13 control samples come in above his mean. This machine-derived nominality is probably given heightened emphasis in the minds of his readers by two reinforcing habits: first, his Germanic tendency to capitalize nouns, and second, his dense use of noun subjects. Carlyle's mean of 158.6 noun subjects per sample exceeds the mean for the controls (128.6)

Figure 8.2b SUBORDINATORS
(CLASS 42)

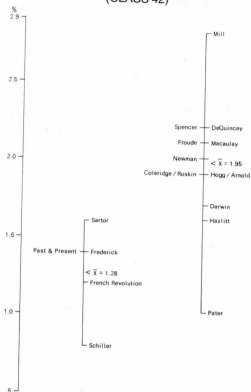

by nearly 25%. There is a converse scarcity of pronoun subjects in Carlyle (89.0 vs. 138.4 for the controls). Figure 8.5 compares Carlyle with the controls in these two respects.

Adjectives being somewhat correlated with nouns, we should not be surprised to find that the Carlyle samples contain on the average a greater density of adjectives than do those of the controls (9.9% for Carlyle vs. a mean of 9.2%). The ranking of the controls, however, provides some surprises, once we get below Pater, who is both the most adjectival and the most nominal of all the writers in this chapter. Spencer, rather a nominal writer, is equal to Carlyle in adjectives; on the other hand, Macaulay, second in nominality, is last in adjectives, whereas Hogg, last in nouns, ranks at the top in adjectival density (see Figure 8.6b).

Alongside his affection for adjectives was a liking—indeed a lust—for the other modifiers. For none of Carlyle's samples did the "M" statistic come in under 500, and his mean of 534 is the all-time record in the Inventory for a multi-work author. To be sure, when

Figure 8.3 SUBORDINATORS + RELATIVES
42+43

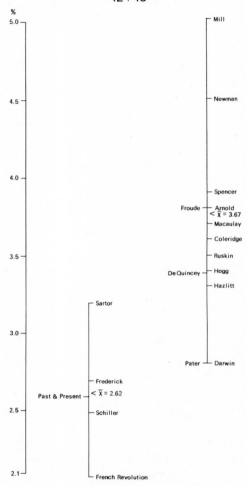

further works of Pater are sampled and when extensive samples from the twentieth century have been taken, Carlyle's record will probably be eclipsed, although it is possible that his "M" statistic of 611 in our sample of *Sartor Resartus* could remain the all-time high outside fiction and homiletic literature. An interesting feature of his use of modifiers is that beginning with *Sartor* he became the most lavish user of function adverbs (Class 34) that we have yet uncovered. Figure 8.7 shows Carlyle and the controls compared in their uses of total modifiers and of function adverbs. Before looking at the Figure, we should perhaps renew our acquaintance with this particular Carlylean abnormality, i.e., his use of adjectives and adverbs:

Figure 8.4 FIRST SUBORDINATION

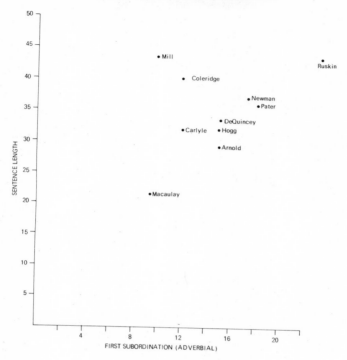

Strange enough how creatures of the human-kind shut their eyes to *plainest* facts; and by the *mere* inertia of Oblivion and Stupidity, live at ease in the midst of Wonders and Terrors. But *indeed* man is, and was *always*, a blockhead and dullard; *much readier* to feel and digest, than to think and consider. Prejudice, which he pretends to hate, is his *absolute* lawgiver; *mere* use-and-wont *everywhere* leads him by the nose; *thus* let *but* a Rising of the Sun, let *but* a Creation of the World happen *twice*, and it ceases to be *marvellous*, to be *noteworthy*, or *noticeable*. Perhaps not *once* in a lifetime does it occur to your *ordinary* biped, or any country or generation, be he gold-*mantled* Prince or russet-*jerkined* Peasant, that his Vestments and his Self are not one and *indivisible*. . . .

(Carlyle, 9111, *Sartor*, 141)

A signal feature of Carlyle's prose both early and late is his avoidance of prepositional phrase strings, constructions in which one prepositional phrase is linked to another in sequence ("at the home of my uncle"). Twelve of these strings[23] are picked up by the York Inventory program. Although substantially less for other periods, the normal range for such strings in the nineteenth century seems to be between 110 and 135 with a mean of 124.7 per sample. The range

Figure 8.5a NOUN SUBJECTS
(CLASS 015)

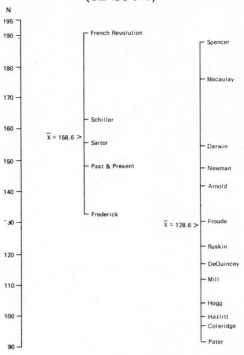

for the Carlyle samples was 74 to 96, with a mean of 84; only one of the control samples, that of his avowed disciple Froude, fell within Carlyle's range. His abnormality in this regard is both pronounced and life-long. It is a kind of abnormality that is hard to illustrate, since it is absence of something, but not an absence so extreme or so obvious as, say, the tendency of the *Psalms* to avoid subordination; perhaps the best way to illustrate it is by contrast with Ruskin, whose sample, at 133 strings per sample, is slightly high but not so exceptional as Carlyle's. Take Ruskin:

> Now I call that Living Architecture. There is sensation in every inch of it, and an accommodation to every architectural necessity, with a determined variation in arrangement, which is exactly like the related proportions and provisions in the structure of organic form. I have not space to examine the still lovelier proportioning of the external shafts of the apse of this marvelous building.
>
> (Ruskin, 9103, *Seven Lamps,* 204)

Notice the dependence on strings, especially for sentence endings: "in every inch of it" (51-31-01-51-11), "with a determined variation in arrangement" (51-31-03-01-51-01), "in the structure of organic form" (51-31-01-51-03-01), "of the external shafts of the apse"

Figure 8.5b PRONOUN SUBJECTS
(CLASS 115)

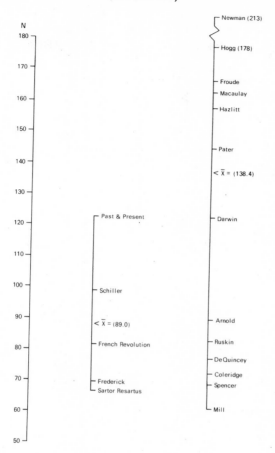

(51-31-03-01-51-31-01), "of the apse of this marvelous building" (51-31-01-51-31-03-01).

Some of the difference between this kind of prose and what Carlyle writes can be explained on the ground that Carlyle is likely to place his prepositional phrases interruptively rather than terminally, with the result that fewer opportunities for strings are generated, or, rather perhaps, the normal English language tendency toward stringing is frustrated. His inverted and Germanophilic word orders have a similar effect. Even as early as *Schiller* the twin tendencies show themselves: first toward interruptive techniques of sentence building, second toward syntactic arrangements that frustrate the generation of strings. Consider the following sentences from *Schiller* with possible (Ruskinian?) alternatives:

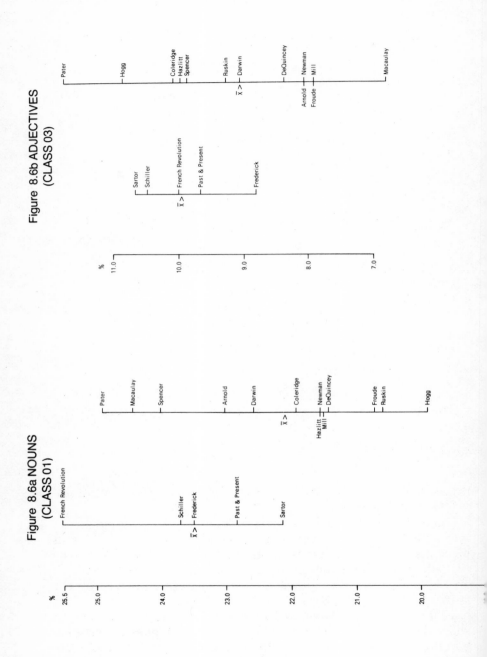

Figure 8.6a NOUNS (CLASS 01)

Figure 8.6b ADJECTIVES (CLASS 03)

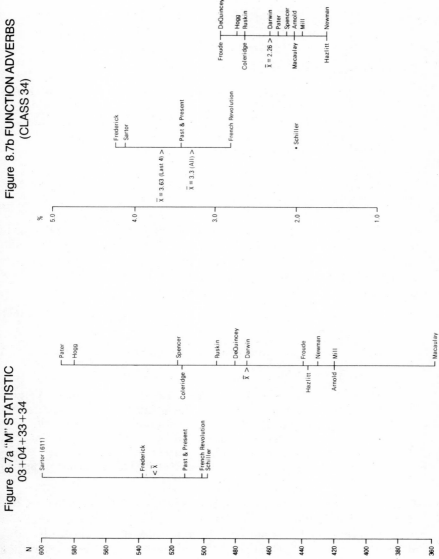

Figure 8.7b FUNCTION ADVERBS
(CLASS 34)

Figure 8.7a "M" STATISTIC
03+04+33+34

Carlyle	*Possible Alternative*
What effect this happy aspect of his circumstances must have produced upon him may be easily conjectured.[24]	We may easily conjecture what effect must have been produced *upon him by this happy aspect of his circumstances.*
On such subjects they often corresponded when absent and conversed when together.[25]	They often talked or wrote *to each other about these things.*

The habit persists through *Frederick the Great:*

Not till Henry's return (February 18th, 1771) could he entirely believe that the Czarina was serious;—and then, sure enough, he did, with his whole heart, go into it.[26]	He could not fully believe *in the seriousness of the Czarina until the return of Henry;*—and then, sure enough, he went *into it with his whole heart.*

The comparison of Carlyle with all the controls in this measure is given in Figure 8.8.

A further inhibitor of strings in our man's style is his often-noted tendency toward accumulation, an accumulation, we might add, that was augmented by additive revision.[27] Not far into any chapter need we read before encountering noun-cairns, adjective-cairns, and veritable haggises of multiplied verbs! From one page alone of *Past and Present* can we extract the following series:[28]

> an ingenious and ingenuous, a cheery-hearted, innocent, yet withal shrewd, noticing, quick-witted man . . .

> not in any simial, canine, ovine, or otherwise inhuman manner . . .

> of patient, peaceable, loving, clear-smiling nature . . .

> Our Jocelin, for the rest, has read his classical manuscripts, his Vergilius, his Flaccus, Ovidius Naso; of course still more, his Homilies and Breviaries, and if not the Bible, considerable extracts of the Bible.

> . . . whereby it failed not to be copied, to be multiplied, to be inserted in the Liger Albus; and so surviving Henry the Eighth, Putney Cromwell, the Dissolution of the Monasteries, and all accidents of malice and neglect . . .

Although Carlyle does not stand utterly alone in this measure, his mean for simple word parallelism (at 107.4 series per sample) is 25 series more than the mean for the controls (82.4), and only three (Coleridge, Newman, Hazlitt) of the thirteen control samples exceed his mean. The totals are registered in Figure 8.9a. The difference be-

Figure 8.8 PREPOSITIONAL PHRASE STRINGS

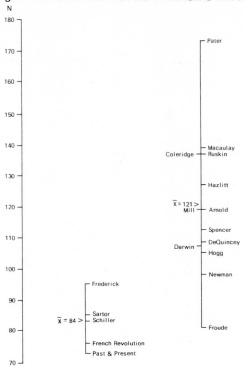

tween Carlyle and the mean for the controls amounts to a series every fourth sentence, which is a substantial difference.[29]

No doubt Carlyle's excessive tendency to seriate produces in him an abnormally high total of coordinators. Even including *The French Revolution,* in which he seems to have cut up his sentences, anaphorizing where he previously and subsequently coordinated, the mean for our five Carlyle samples is exceeded in coordinators by only three control samples, coincidentally the three who exceed him in number of series (Figure 8.9b).

In sum, the common elements throughout the five samples taken here consist, among other things, of a relatively short sentence with not much clausal subordination in it. The word-class distributions show rather high nominality and a somewhat dense usage of adjectives. Combined with the adjectives is a very high "M" statistic and a fondness for the function adverb group that became unique with the composition of *Sartor Resartus,* the work generally cited as the first

Figure 8.9a WORD SERIATION

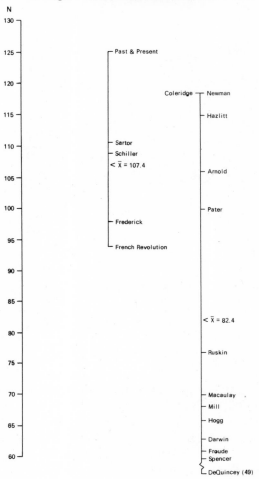

volume written in mature Carlylese. His unusual word orders tend to suppress prepositional phrase strings; his tendency toward seriation (and with it, his penchant for coordinators) was strong but not unique. In two aspects we have found him consistently and almost entirely distinctive: the absence of subordination with clauses, and the absence of phrasal strings. There are, of course, other utterly distinctive items to be discussed—his use of both appositive and attributive nouns—and beyond the function adverbs there are other parameters wherein he seemed "normal" in *Schiller,* in which he

Figure 8.9b COORDINATORS
(CLASS 41)

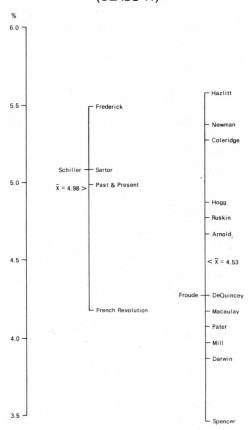

later turned into the sado-masochistic Attila of syntax, against whom we were warned by our schoolteachers. These measures include his use of postmodifiers, his syntactic variety, his punctuation, and his exploitation of prepositional phrases. To these we can now turn.

CARLYLE vs. CARLYLE

Most of what we have thus far dealt with has indicated properties both stable and lifelong in Carlyle's style. Two areas at least, however, have suggested a radical departure in the post-*Schiller* style from his earlier practice (class 34, function adverbs, and "D" and other aspects of syntactic variety). This departure can be seen in a number of other measures as well. In some of these, Carlyle started "normal," i.e., in the middle of the range established by the control writers; in others, he started with an already deviant tendency that magnified itself with the years. In any case, two things are obvious from our data: first, despite the persistence of a set of clear tendencies, the style of *Schiller* is radically different from the four later works chosen for this chapter; second, the style of *Frederick the Great* does show a few symptoms of decadent old age that some critics have noticed, although it is clearly of a piece with other works written in mature Carlylese.

The most dramatic changes from *Schiller* to *Sartor* and beyond were changes in syntax and punctuation. Burwick's conclusion that *Schiller* seems "bland and conservative" next to the later works can be easily illustrated. Not immediately identifiable as Carlylean are *Schiller* sentences like the following:

> After this severe attack, and the kind provision which he had received from Denmark, Schiller seems to have relaxed his connexion with the University of Jena: the weightiest duties of his class appear to have been discharged by proxy, and his historical studies to have been forsaken.
>
> (Carlyle, 9216, *Schiller*, 125)

> This tragedy of Carlos was received with immediate and universal approbation. In the closet and on the stage, it excited the warmest applauses equally among the learned and unlearned.
>
> (Carlyle, 9216, *Schiller*, 63)

> The cavilling of these people, awkwardly contrasted with their personal absurdity and insipidity, at length provoked the serious notice of two illustrious associates; the result was this German Dunciad; a production of which the plan was that it should comprise an immense multitude of detached couplets, each conveying a thought within itself, and furnished by one of the joint operators.
>
> (Carlyle, 9216, *Schiller*, 124)

Between these and the sentences of *Sartor* something radical happens. One sentence from the latter work will suffice to illustrate:

> Towards these dim infinitely-expanded regions, close-bordering on the impalpable Inane, it is not without apprehension and perpetual difficulties, that the Editor sees himself journeying and struggling.
>
> (Carlyle, 9110, *Sartor*, 186)

Interesting to note: in both the *before* and the *after* pictures, certain lifelong tendencies appear, namely Carlyle's tendency to multiply and seriate things and his avoidance of prepositional phrase strings. The doubling of elements is obvious, and the shortage of strings can be enumerated: in the *Schiller* sentences (135 words) there are only two strings (third line of sentence one; last line of sentence three), against a normal expectation for the controls of five or more strings (one string every 26 words). Nevertheless there are startling differences; the "tame Augustan rhetoric-book"[30] has gone out the window and with it several things: notably syntactic regularity and the extensive use of single prepositional phrases. Notice the almost Gibbonesque prepositional uses in the *Schiller* quotations: "the weightiest duties of his class," "This tragedy of Carlos," "In the closet and on the stage," "The cavilling of these people," and "the serious notice of two illustrious associates." These disappear from Carlyle's subsequent style; both prepositions and determiners drop dramatically. Moreover, as we can see in the *Sartor* sentence, we have the manifestations of two key features of mature Carlylese: unusual conjoining, frequently with hyphens (infinitely-expanded, close-bordering), and postmodification, both of which introduced a degree of syntactic eccentricity into his style unmatched by any other English writer of the nineteenth century that we have thus far come across.

Startling differences, we have noted before, are easily illustrated by carefully selected sentences. They are less easy to come by with the total data of random samples. Figure 8.10 shows the change in Carlyle's "D" value from Schiller to the mature works; it also shows the increase in exclamation points and question marks.[31] The latter of these changes, visible on any page of post-1830 Carlyle, is both visually and quantitatively dramatic; it is, however, the kind of change that is not difficult to impose on one's style; one can even edit such a change into the text after a first draft. No such cautions, however, apply to the change in Carlyle's "D" value, which covers the largest range of any multisample author in the Inventory to date. It contains, moreover, the only 1,000-plus figures, other than Gertrude Stein, after 1720.

I would not be surprised if the change in Carlyle's "D" figure represents the largest syntactic change ever made by a writer of the English language over the age of 30. A full account of all the sources of such a change is impossible. As we have noted, however, his sentence building grew increasingly interruptive, and he moved away from normal English word orders. Evidence of this can be seen in his overall use both of prepositions and of the standard prepositional phrase, 51-31-01 (preposition-determiner-noun). These statistics are given in Figure 8.11. In addition, Carlyle moved toward increasing variety of sentence ending: in *Schiller* his sentence endings are

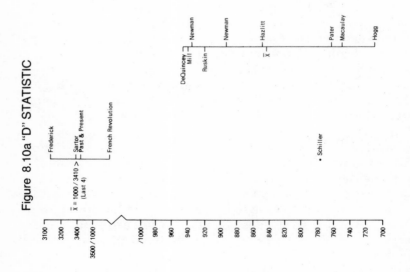

Figure 8.10b EXCLAMATION POINTS + ?S PER SAMPLE

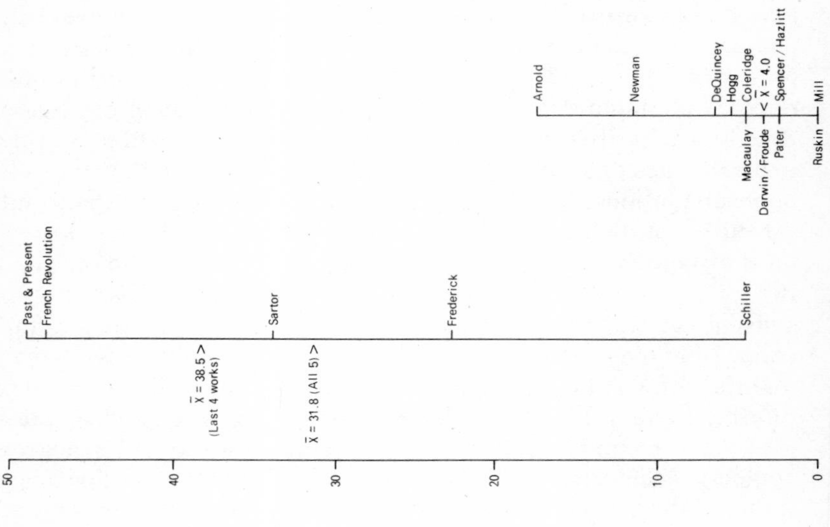

Figure 8.10a "D" STATISTIC

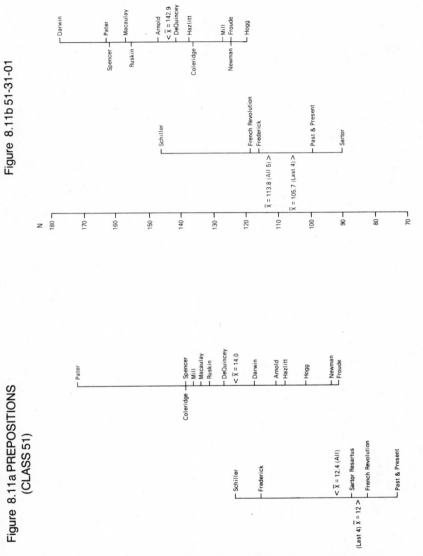

Figure 8.11b 51-31-01

Figure 8.11a PREPOSITIONS
(CLASS 51)

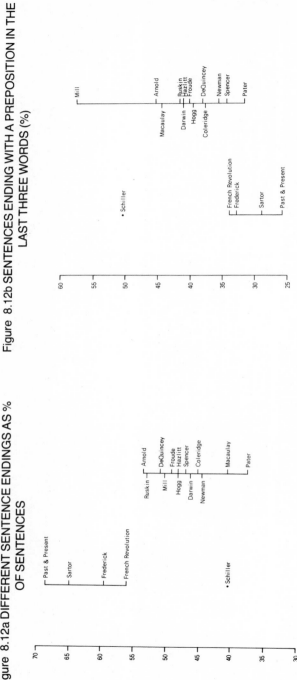

Figure 8.12a DIFFERENT SENTENCE ENDINGS AS % OF SENTENCES

Figure 8.12b SENTENCES ENDING WITH A PREPOSITION IN THE LAST THREE WORDS (%)

among the least varied of our group; after *Sartor* they are more varied than the endings of nearly all the other writers. Moreover, after *Sartor,* the prepositional endings (sentence endings with a preposition occurring in the last three words) drop from over half of Carlyle's endings to less than a third (30.75%) in the last four works; none of the 13 controls falls below Carlyle's mean for the last four works. These statistics are given in Figure 8.12.

A similar shift away from normal nineteenth-century English can be observed in his movement away from the noun/preposition/noun configuration and toward a pattern of attributive noun/noun; for example, "unity of aim," "vigour of character," "conduct of life," "vices of mankind," and other similar prepositional constructions dot the text of *Schiller.* These give way in the later works to noun-fusions like Charlemagne-Mantles, Gypsy-blankets, State papers, Arkwright looms, night constable, Bank papers, pudding-cheeks, logic-mortar, etc., etc. There is undoubtedly a lexical change here that is not entirely amenable to the kind of quantitative treatment to which we are submitting text. Nevertheless, the statistics in Figure 8.13a are a considerable indication of how that lexical shift was reinforced by the Germanic tortures to which Carlyle was subjecting English syntax after 1830. We can see in Figure 8.13 that already in the writing of *Schiller* he was disposed toward the use of attributive nouns, a measure in which his early sample was exceeded by only three of the controls. But five years later our gas-bloated hero-worshipper was rising Hindenberg-like from his native soil, born aloft—statelier even perhaps than Nietzsche himself!—on cube-footages of noun-attribution-hyphenation.

Related to other aspects of his movement away from normal English word orders is his growing disuse of determiners. Surprising in this connection is the fact that, although Carlyle remains in the late works one of the more nominal of the stylists that we are considering, he becomes consistently the most sparing of our 14 writers in the use of determiners (Figure 8.14). Concomitantly Carlyle indulged increasingly in two *post* constructions related to noun clusters: the appositive and the postmodifying adjective. In both of these uses he was already clear of the control samples in *Schiller,* but what began as uses that were modestly extreme became after 1830 egregiously so, as we can see in Figure 8.15. The means for the five Carlyle samples are 30.8 postmodifying adjectives (vs. 12.8 for the available controls)* and 30.4 appositive nouns (vs. 10.3 for the available

---

*In May 1973, eight new classes, including postmodifier (035) and appositive (017), were added to the code. At present writing, not all the old samples have been edited; Coleridge, DeQuincey, Mill, Hogg, and Newman have not been fully edited for the new code slots.

Figure 8.13a 01+51+01 PER SAMPLE

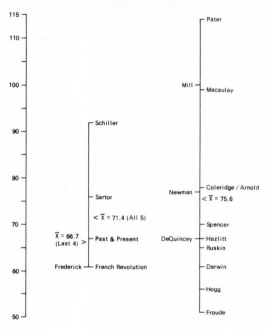

controls), an aggregate of almost 40 more *post* constructions per sample in Carlyle than in the controls, one every 55 words, one every second sentence.

A final aspect of his development to consider is verb voice. In his samples, Oakman noted an "overwhelming choice of active verbal vocabulary—61.5% of all verbs. . . ."[32] This is very close to our finding of 62.7% active verbs in our five samples, difference in the makeup of the samples possibly accounting for the slight difference in percentage. Oakman found fewer active verbs in *Schiller* (49%) than in any other work; although our sample of *Schiller* was nearly twice the size of his, we had a similar finding—that *Schiller* is the most passive of the works under consideration, although in our case the active percentage was 56.5. Comparison of Carlyle's use of the verb system with that of his contemporaries, however, does not reveal any distinctive "concrete particularity and fascination with the vibrantly alive universe."[33] Figure 8.16, which shows percentages of active and passive verbs, suggests that after *Schiller* he is slightly but not substantially above normal in his active use of verbs. As one

Figure 8.13b ATTRIBUTIVE NOUNS
(CLASS 012)

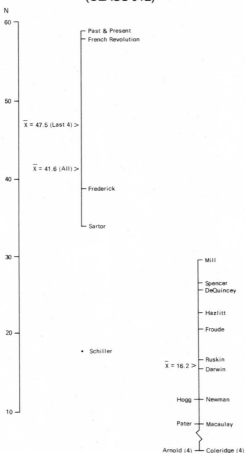

might expect, his use of passives declined as his use of actives increased. It may be, of course, that most Victorians were possessed of a "fascination with the vibrantly alive universe"; it would not be difficult to demonstrate that they were more so than a number of our own contemporaries. Carlyle's active preference grew as he grew older.

The third question of Carlyle scholarship—the ineffable one of his influences—cannot be answered here. However, many of the changes in syntax that occurred in his style after 1830 had an undeniably Germanic direction. This fact would seem to strengthen the

Figure 8.14 DETERMINERS
(CLASS 31)

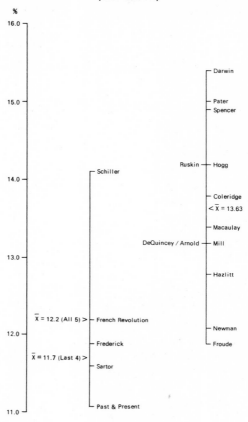

case of Smeed and others who believe that his long study (in German) of Richter left an indelible imprint on the way in which Carlyle used the English language after 1830.

QUANTA vs. QUANTA

This study is in the unusual position of being not the first but the third to venture into Carlyle's style armed with the two-edged sword of computer and syntactic analysis. It might be expected that among Burwick, Oakman, and the York Inventory several findings about Carlyle might differ. Not only are the grammars and data-processing techniques different in important respects, but there are great differ-

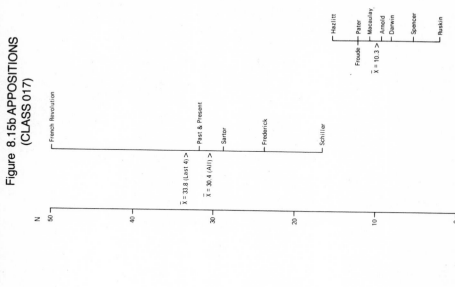

Figure 8.15b APPOSITIONS
(CLASS 017)

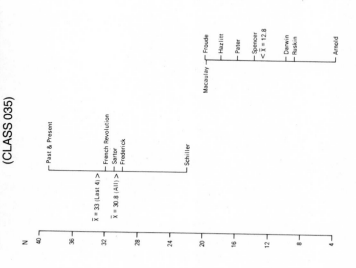

Figure 8.15a POSTMODIFYING ADJECTIVES
(CLASS 035)

Figure 8.16a ACTIVE VERBS AS % OF ALL VERBS
(CLASS 021)

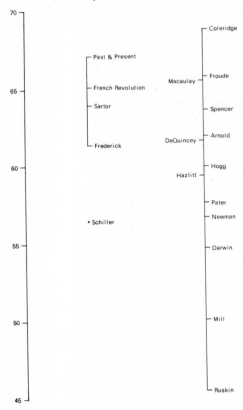

ences in the makeup of samples, in sampling procedure, and in sample size. For example, Oakman sampled all the words in 15 random samples ranging from 1,100 to 5,400 words each; all but three of his samples (numbers 5, 7, and 14) were smaller than the standard York Inventory sample. Burwick sampled six works, including four of those in the present study, using 10,000-word continuous texts. It is interesting that there are no fundamental disharmonies among the findings of the studies despite these substantial differences in technique. *En passant,* we have already noted a number of findings in common between this study and the others. Three other points are

Figure 8.16b PASSIVE VERBS AS % OF ALL VERBS
(CLASS 022)

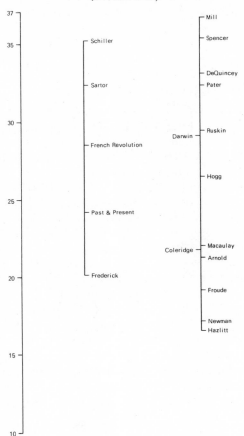

worth touching on: Oakman's findings about sentence length and two of Burwick's findings about Carlyle's syntax.

Of Oakman's 15 bodies of text, the York Inventory has sampled five. One measure used in common (besides active/passive verbs) is length of sentence. Table 8.3 compares the two studies in this respect. Despite the sampling differences, the correspondence is close, closer overall than the correspondence between the two studies in the density of active verbs.

Burwick displays a number of typical Carlylean syntactic con-figurations. Not all of them are susceptible of verification in the York Inventory output, but at least one of them is, the one he denominates by the sequence 52872[34] and illustrates with the following two clus-ters:

> gaining money and more folly
>
> drawing sword and popular contempt

Such configurations would appear in the York printouts under the listing of three-class patterns that follows the "D" statistic, at least the three center words of each would ("money and more" and "sword and popular"). Their appearance would be indicated respec-tively by 01-41-31 (noun-coordinator-determiner) and 01-41-03 (noun-coordinator-adjective). Figure 8.17 suggests that Carlyle's penchant for these patterns was indeed strong when measured against his contemporaries; Newman was the only control writer to make a major penetration of Carlyle's range in these measures.

Another assertion of Burwick's can be directly checked by the York Inventory data: "As Carlyle comes to rely more and more on the rhetorical patterns of omission, the verbal phrases often stand in place of predication."[35] The suggestion here is that Carlyle increas-ingly relied on verbals as he grew older, which is exactly what the York samples show. Table 8.4 shows a steady growth in verbals over the time covered by our five samples. An interesting note here is that our *Schiller* sample had fewer verbals than any of the controls ex-cept three; none of the other 17 samples examined in this chapter had more verbals than the *Frederick* sample.

The York Inventory has managed to add a few things to the store of

Table 8.3 SENTENCE LENGTH, OAKMAN VS. YORK INVENTORY

| | OAKMAN | | YORK | |
	Length	N	Length	N
Schiller	27.9	68	27.6	124
Sartor	31.7	37	31.7	109
French Revolution	21.7	181	22.9	149
Past and Present	26.5	64	27.4	125
Frederick the Great	30.1	182	31.9	108

Figure 8.17 PATTERNS 01-41-03 + 01-41-31

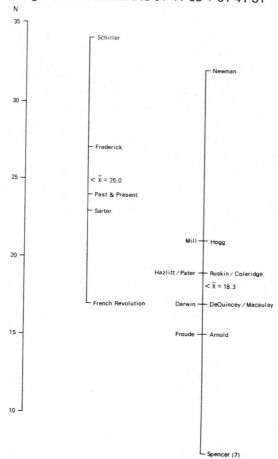

Table 8.4 CARLYLE'S VERBALS (05+06+07)

1824 Schiller 2.9%	1830 Sartor 3.7%	1837 French Revolution 3.6%	1838 Past and Present 3.8%	1851 Frederick 4.2%

Carlyle: mean ($\overline{X}$) = 3.5   range = 2.9 − 4.2

Controls: mean ($\overline{X}$) = 3.12   range = 2.0 − ,4.2

knowledge concerning Carlyle's syntax—notably information about syntactic variety, subordination, subject choice, and phrase sequences, plus whatever is gained from projecting Carlyle data against data from other nineteenth-century writers. The consonance of our study with previous quantitative studies is heartening. We may be a long way from a "science of literature";[36] many of us, myself included, hope that such a science does not come to dominate literary studies. Even so, it is useful and encouraging to know that a sample objectively taken from a work and treated rigorously is likely to reveal important formal features of that work that are susceptible of verification by a variety of other quantitative techniques. This may be fact at which the antiscientific Carlyle might have taken umbrage, but it is a fact nevertheless.

Table 8.5 STATISTICS FOR CHAPTER 8

CATEGORY	CARLYLE					CONTROLS												
	Schiller	Sartor	Fred'k the Gt.	Past & Present	French Revolution	Froude	Darwin	Spencer	Pater	Hazlitt	Coleridge	DeQuincey	Macaulay	Mill	Ruskin	Hogg	Arnold	Newman
01	23.7	22.1	23.5	22.8	25.5	20.7	22.6	24.0	24.9	21.6	21.9	21.4	24.4	21.5	20.6	19.9	23.0	21.6
02	6.5	7.6	6.5	7.2	7.7	8.0	7.6	7.7	4.4	6.5	6.1	6.5	8.7	6.9	6.2	7.2	7.7	7.4
21	6.1	6.2	6.0	6.4	6.1	8.3	6.6	5.3	4.2	6.6	5.6	6.5	6.5	7.7	7.2	6.7	6.4	8.2
05	1.3	1.6	1.4	1.3	.7	1.7	1.0	.6	.6	2.2	1.1	1.3	1.3	1.5	1.1	2.4	1.2	1.4
06	1.2	1.6	2.2	1.8	2.2	1.0	1.8	2.1	1.2	1.3	.7	1.7	.7	1.5	1.2	.5	1.0	.7
07	.4	.5	.6	.7	.7	.6	.5	.6	.5	.7	.2	.6	.9	.5	.6	.5	.4	.5
31	14.1	11.6	11.9	11.1	12.2	11.9	15.4	14.9	15.1	12.8	13.8	13.2	13.4	13.2	14.2	14.2	13.2	12.1
33	.8	.8	.5	.8	.8	.6	.8	1.1	1.1	.6	1.2	1.2	.6	1.1	.8	1.2	.7	.9
34	2.0	4.1	4.2	3.4	2.8	2.9	2.3	2.1	2.2	1.6	2.6	2.9	2.0	1.9	2.6	2.7	2.0	1.6
03	10.5	10.7	8.8	9.7	10.0	7.9	9.1	9.9	12.2	10.0	10.1	8.4	7.0	7.9	9.3	10.9	8.1	8.1
04	1.4	2.1	1.8	1.1	1.1	1.6	1.7	1.8	1.6	1.3	1.5	1.9	1.1	1.4	1.6	2.4	1.4	1.9
'M'	498	611	540	514	503	443	479	522	595	441	519	487	362	417	498	564	417	435
51	14.0	12.1	13.6	11.3	11.8	12.3	13.7	14.8	16.6	13.2	14.8	14.2	14.6	14.7	14.4	12.8	13.3	12.4
11	5.7	5.4	5.6	7.2	5.2	8.4	5.3	4.2	4.7	5.8	5.4	5.9	5.2	5.7	5.6	7.0	7.6	7.2
41	5.1	5.1	5.5	5.0	4.2	4.3	3.9	3.5	4.1	5.6	5.3	4.3	4.2	4.0	4.8	4.9	4.7	5.4
42	.8	1.6	1.4	1.4	1.2	2.1	1.7	2.2	1.0	1.6	1.9	2.2	2.1	2.8	1.9	1.9	1.9	2.0
43	1.7	1.6	1.3	1.2	.9	1.7	1.1	1.7	1.8	1.7	1.7	1.2	1.6	2.2	1.6	1.5	1.9	2.5

45	12	16	12	15	4	14	6	10	17	30	27	22	8	13	14	9	8	24
99	124	109	108	125	149	147	137	133	96	107	87	103	168	80	82	104	117	90
61	22	34	17	28	25	18	18	29	14	23	16	25	15	18	25	15	23	26
01-41-03	16	12	7	10	2	6	6	2	3	10	7	7	4	5	3	3	4	6
01-41-31	18	11	20	14	15	9	11	5	16	9	12	10	13	16	16	18	11	26
022+213+024	136	117	112	105	118	117	149	120	93	131	78	104	120	152	162	127	134	155
021	177	207	177	213	218	223	179	208	126	189	171	166	226	152	135	188	211	203
ACTIVE VB %	56.5	63.9	61.2	67.0	65.0	65.6	54.6	63.4	57.5	59.1	68.6	61.4	65.3	50.0	45.5	59.9	61.7	56.7
PASSIVE VB %	35.1	32.4	20.1	24.2	28.6	19.1	29.1	35.3	32.4	16.6	21.9	33.1	22.0	36.9	29.2	26.7	21.3	17.1
-71	2	10	5	20	28	3	0	2	3	1	0	9	0	0	1	0	9	1
-STRINGSx	84	88	96	74	77	82	108	113	173	128	138	109	140	120	138	106	120	98
-51-31-01	146	90	116	99	118	123	176	161	162	136	135	141	156	126	154	118	146	123
-'D'	778	3401	3150	3422	3600	884	833	824	762	854	874	906	740	905	921	711	904	896
-31-03-01	107	108	94	81	89	93	110	129	152	99	135	110	106	81	111	144	78	95
-015	163	156	134	149	191	130	153	187	91	99	97	116	175	111	122	104	141	147
115	100	68	71	123	83	168	124	69	146	159	71	79	164	61	83	178	90	213
014	31	28	16	34	34	33	11	7	39	27	20	23	16	29	22	14	26	76
032	43	29	31	29	29	43	45	31	22	54	26	26	37	25	37	72	54	27
992+993 +982+983	5	34	23	49	48	4	4	3	3	3	5	7	5	0	0	6	18	12
SERIATION	109	111	98	125	94	61	63	60	100	115	118	49	70	68	77	66	106	118
017	17	29	24	32	50	14	8	6	14	16	NA	NA	11	NA	3	NA	10	NA
035	22	31	30	39	32	20	10	13	16	18	NA	NA	20	NA	9	NA	4	NA
01-51-01	92	76	61	67	61	51	61	70	114	67	78	67	99	100	65	56	78	77
012	18	34	39	59	58	21	16	27	9	23	4	26	9	30	17	12	4	12

The language most likely to continue long without alteration, would be that of a nation raised a little, and but a little above barbarity, secluded from strangers, and totally employed in procuring the conveniencies of life; either without books, or, like some of the Mahometan countries, with very few: men thus busied and unlearned, having only such words as common use requires, would perhaps long continue to express the same notions by the same signs. But no such constancy can be expected in a people polished by arts, and classed by subordination, where one part of the community is sustained and accomodated by the labour of the other. Those who have much leisure to think, will always be enlarging the stock of ideas, and every increase of knowledge, whether real or fancied, will produce new words, or combinations of words.

Samuel Johnson, Preface to a Dictionary of the English Language

Chapter 9
HISTORICAL MATTERS:
Literary English
of the Modern Period

CAN there be a history of English prose style? The question is a difficult one for literary historians. By implication at least, it has been answered in the affirmative by a number of distinguished critics: Adolph, Croll, Jones, Williamson, Sutherland, and Corbett are merely six names among many on a long list.[1] At the same time, critics of the individualist school have implicitly rejected the concept of stylistic history, if only by avoiding the temporal and typological traps that such a concept is likely to involve. Not least of these traps is the notion of "period" styles: that literary style, like the styling of automobiles, undergoes periodic changeovers and that it therefore can be chronicled through the denomination of historical phases (the squareback/spokewheel era; the age of the tailfin, etc., etc.). Such a paradigm of stylistic history ignores the great number of historical and dialectal states of the language within a single era. As one individualist critic has pointed out,

The main tendency of writers in a given time is to be unlike rather than alike. The notion of period styles underrates this tendency and implies a uniformity of expression which is widely at variance with the facts.[2]

The individualist vision exists not so much in opposition as in tension with undeniable historical facts about the language and the development of its literary dialect. For example, we can readily see that literary English of the twentieth century is substantially more nominal than that of the seventeenth and that it has considerably less rank shifting of all kinds in it. Would a body of quantitative facts—if, say, we were able to get our hands on enough of them—constitute a history of literary style? My answer would be no. A body of such facts would offer us figures for the range, the mean, and the standard deviation of any parameters that we wanted to apply to given literary texts within a determined period of time. The range would give us what are presumably the possible extremes within that period; the mean would give us what is average; the figures one standard deviation either side of the mean would give us the admissible range of "normal" behavior.[3] There is no doubt that such figures over a variety of parameters would be most helpful to linguistic historians and to students of individual stylists who wish to quantify the conformity and the deviance of those whom they are studying. But a history of norms, possibilities, and expectations is not really the same as a history of style. What the norms and possibilities give us are a set of abstractions drawn from many different texts; there is no text written in the language that is defined by the norms; what those norms represent, therefore, being textless, is a mythical entity rather than a style, for style, although abstract, by definition has to be derived from real artifacts in real discourse.

The data to be offered in the tables and figures that follow are not intended as even a fragment of a history of English prose style. Even if such a history were possible, it would require a far larger data base than the 175,000 words of the 50 samples selected for this chapter. What they do offer is some hypotheses about the historical development of the norms for the literary dialect of the language. If within the conventions of our grammar we wish to make firm, conclusive statements about that dialect, we must await the completion of the York Inventory, some time in the second half of this decade, to a total of 800 to 1,000 samples. Nevertheless, the data of these 50 samples are of sufficient interest to display here, for they corroborate the conclusions of a number of writers on the history of the English language, and they suggest a few developments that might heretofore have been underestimated. The samples under scrutiny are listed in Table 9.1.

There are two possible objections to the selection of these 50 sam-

Table 9.1 SAMPLES FOR CHAPTER 9[a]

9000	Ascham	Scholemaster
9004	Sidney	**Defence of Poesie**
9021	Bacon	Advancement of Learning
9015	Donne	Sermons
9024	Jonson	Timber
9044	Browne	Religio Medici
9060	Milton	**Areopagitica**
9026	Hobbes	Leviathan
9075	Boyle	. . . Style of Holy Scriptures
9036	Taylor	Holy Dying
9043	Walton	Lives
9031	Clarendon	History of the Rebellion
9090	Wilkins	Sermons
9068	Sprat	History of the Royal Society
9085	Burnet	Life of Rochester
9096	Dryden	Essays
9078	Newton	Opticks
9108	Addison	Spectator
9109	Steele	Spectator
9101	Swift	Examiner
9107	Berkeley	Human Knowledge
9121	Defoe	A Journal of the Plague Year
9106	Johnson	Rambler
9102	Gibbon	Decline and Fall
9149	Austen	Letters
9205	Coleridge	Biographia Literaria
9201	DeQuincey	Confessions
9202	Hazlitt	Essays
9110	Carlyle	Sartor Resartus
9111	Macaulay	Critical and Historical Essays
9103	Ruskin	Seven Lamps of Architecture
9209	Newman	Idea of a University
9207	Mill	On The Subjection of Women
9211	Hogg	Life of Shelley
9105	Arnold	Essays in Criticism

[a]All references to primary text are by author, sample number, work, and page. A full catalog of the samples is given in Appendix B.

Table 9.1 (continued)

9104	Pater	Appreciations
9179	James	Notes on Novelists
9192	Strachey	Eminent Victorians
9187	Woolf	The Common Reader
9166	Chesterton	Essays
9318	Stein	Paris France
9319	Hemingway	Death in the Afternoon
9324	Fitzgerald	The Crack-up
9327	Wilson	Axel's Castle
9196	Orwell	Essays
9614	Davies	A Voice from the Attic
9617	Richler	Hunting Tigers under Glass
9194	Burgess	The Novel Now
9329	Mumford	Technics & Civilization
9402	Reich	The Greening of America

ples: First, that the samples have short-changed the eighteenth century by including only eight samples, of which five (Swift, Addison, Steele, Johnson, Defoe) are journalistic or quasi-journalistic in character; second, that the inclusion of writers so idiosyncratic as Gibbon, Stein, and Carlyle does violence to the averages within particular word-class categories. The first of these possible objections is really against the order in which the Inventory has been built, and that order is a byproduct of the facts of existing scholarship. Of all the periods of the last 400 years in English, the eighteenth century is the one whose most eminent writers have received, in Wimsatt's work on Johnson and in Milic's work on Swift, the greatest amount of sustained, rigorous, and intelligent attention. As such, it was the period that at the outset seemed least to need illumination from this kind of technique. Our initial focus had to be on places that we thought needed ventilation and light. Of our first 100 samples, only two (Burnet) were from the eighteenth century; of our second 100 there were the eight used in this chapter. Of the third 100 there will be 22; this will be the first group of samples to give the eighteenth century its due representation. With the present size of the Inventory, many statements of necessity have to be tentative, however promising and satisfying they seem to be. The proportion of journalism among our eighteenth-century samples thus far seems to me justified: the journalism of the eighteenth century was of a more literary character than we are accustomed to today, and the period's great stylists were likely to have been journalists of sorts. Gibbon, Berkeley, and Burke are probably exceptions to a general rule formed by people like Defoe, Addison, Steele, Swift, and Johnson.

As for the possible objection that the likes of Gibbon, Stein, and Carlyle are too idiosyncratic and kinky for inclusion, that can be raised against almost every single writer of the 50. Clear-headed perusal of Table 9.2 will show how. Just begin at the left: Ascham's unusual "M" statistic, Sidney's inordinate rank shifting, Donne's abnormal suppression of modifiers, Bacon's affection for word parallelism, Johnson's predicate nouns, Browne's overuse of *be* as a main verb, etc., etc. Distinctiveness is the rule rather than the exception, and there is no reason to exclude writers like Gibbon *et al.* simply because they *seem* more distinctive in a greater number of ways.

The historical patterns suggested by our 50 samples in Table 9.2 are of several kinds, most obvious of which are steady increase and steady decline of a particular word class or configuration. In some other features (such as the prepositions), the data indicate a steady rise to 1900, then a fall. In others (e.g., auxiliary verbs), we have a decline to 1900, then a resurgence. In some grammatical classes (participles, subordinators), the practice of the seventeenth and eighteenth centuries would seem to be clearly marked off from that of the nineteenth and twentieth. And finally, there are classes (like the verb) that show seemingly random fluctuation over the last 400 years.

The most evident long-term development in the written language of these 50 writers is the decline in length of the sentence, from a seventeenth-century mean of almost 50 words to a twentieth-century mean of barely half that (Figure 9.1, Table 9.2). Together with that development has come a simplification of the sentence that exceeds what we would arrive at simply by cutting periods in half. Over the centuries, the average occurrence of rank shifting among our samples[4] declines from 280 per 3,500 words to 220 (Figure 9.2). On a per-sentence basis, this moves us from 4+ rank shifts to fewer than 2. Naturally, as the simplification and shortening proceed, the number of unsubordinated sentences per 3,500 words shows a substantial increase (Figure 9.3), and the number of correlative conjunctions[5] (Figure 9.4) shows a concomitant decline. Obvious in this simplification is the fact that although it has been going on for a long time its greatest surge was in the early twentieth century. For example, Ruskin and Strachey are not much more than a generation apart, and they give a stark, perhaps exaggerated, sense of two great differences between the age of Victoria and the twentieth century: first, complexity, and second, the sense of sentence proportion.

It is a safe manner, *as* I think, to design all things at first in severe abstraction, and to be prepared, *if* need were, to carry them out in that

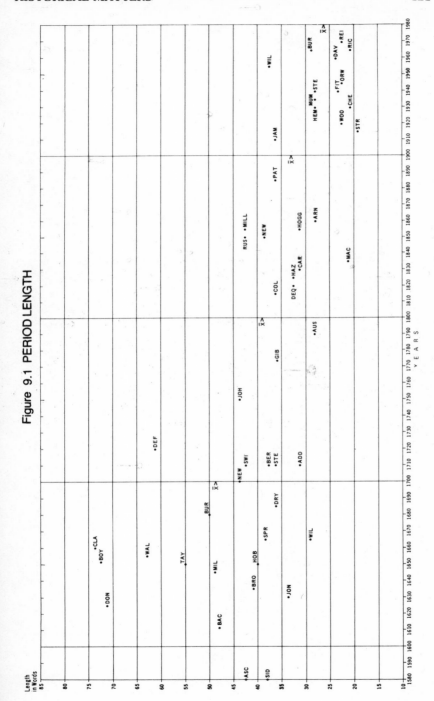

Figure 9.1 PERIOD LENGTH

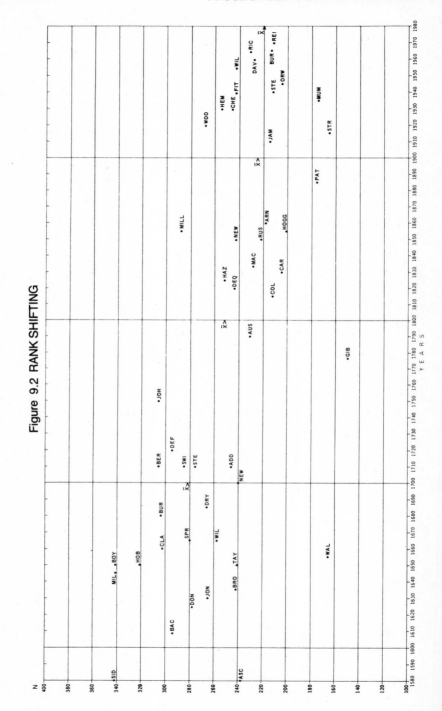

Figure 9.2 RANK SHIFTING

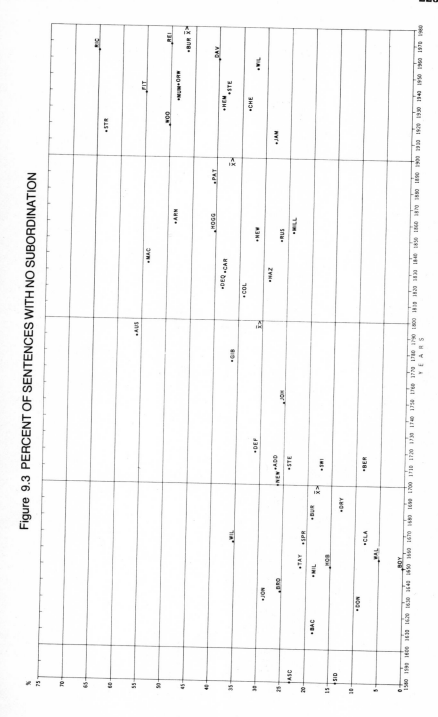

Figure 9.3 PERCENT OF SENTENCES WITH NO SUBORDINATION

Figure 9.4 CORRELATIVE CONJUNCTIONS
(CLASS 45)

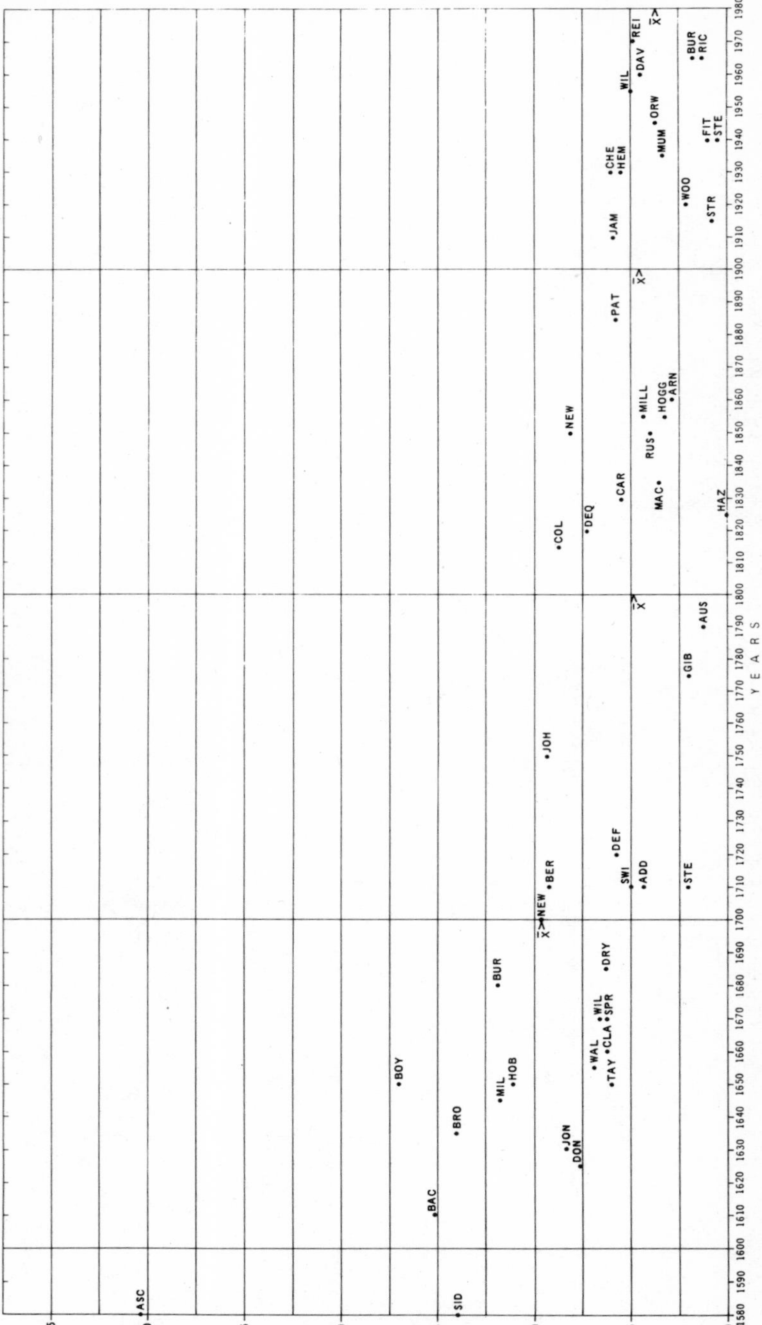

form; then to mark the parts *where* high finish would be admissible, to complete these always with stern reference to their general effect, and then connect them by a graduated scale of abstraction with the rest. And there is one safeguard against danger in this process on *which* I would finally insist. Never imitate anything but natural forms, and those the noblest, in the completed parts. The degradation of the cinque cento manner of decoration was not owing to its naturalism, to its faithfulness of imitation, but to its imitation of ugly, i.e. unnatural things. So long *as* it restrained itself to sculpture of animals and flowers, it remained noble. The balcony, on the opposite page (Plate XI.), from a house in the Campo St. Benedetto at Venice, shows one of the earliest occurrences of the cinque cento arabesque, and a fragment of the pattern is given in Plate XII. fig. 8. It is but the arresting upon the stone work of a stem or two of the living flowers, *which* are rarely wanting in the window above (and *which,* by the by, the French and Italian peasantry often trellis with exquisite taste about their casements).

(Ruskin, 9103, *Seven Lamps,* 175)

As for Aristophanes, owing to his strong moral disapprobation, he could not bring himself to read him *until* he was forty, *when,* it is true, he was much struck by the "Clouds." But Juvenal the Doctor could never bring himself to read at all.

Physical science was not taught at Rugby. *Since,* in Dr. Arnold's opinion, it was "too great a subject to be studied" obviously only two alternatives were possible:—it must either take the chief place in the school curriculum, or it must be left out altogether. Before such a choice, Dr. Arnold did not hesitate for a moment.

(Strachey, 9192, *Victorians,* 209)

The contrast, of course, is marked. In each case the five sentences give a reasonable typification of the authors' tendencies in sentence length, and the authors themselves are not atypical of their respective ages, although Strachey is one of the twentieth century's sparser users of clausal subordination.[6]

The gradual long-term shift, of which the sudden shift above was no more than a part, is perhaps best illustrated by two comparisons, one between two avowedly plain stylists (Sprat and Hemingway) and another between two who are, by use if not by self-description, ornate (Milton and Wilson). Thomas Sprat was the loudest of the plain talkers that emerged after the Restoration;[7] and Hemingway, though not loud, was perhaps the most audible and visible of the plain talkers of the first half of this century. Both men wrote, for their ages, a very middling-sized sentence, and both are somewhat above average in their use of subordinate clauses.

Let it only therefore be granted, *that* we are Men, and not Angels: Let it be confess'd, *that* there may be an excess, as well as defect, in mens opinions of holiness: And then I will make no scruple to say, *that* the Philosopher defiles not his mind *when* he labors in the works of Nature; *that* the Diversion (00) they give him, will stand with the greatest constancy, and the delight of pursuing them, with the truth and reality of Religion. But to say no more, How can it be imagin'd to be a sinful and carnal thing, to consider the objects of our senses; *when* God, the most Spiritual Being, did make them all? *Since* they first were conceiv'd in his unspotted mind, why may they not innocently enter into ours? For *if* there be any pollution *which* necessarily flows from thinking of them, it might as well be concluded to stick on the Author, as on the Souls of them *that* only observe them.

(Sprat, 9068, History, 369)

Of the thirty-four other full matadors in active service only a few are worth mentioning. One, Andres Merida, from Malaga is a tall, thin, vacant-faced gypsy who is a genius with cape and muleta and is the only bullfighter (00) I have ever seen *who* had a completely absent-minded air in the ring *as though* he were thinking of something very distant and very different. He is liable to attacks of fear so complete *that* there is no word for them, but *if* he becomes confident with a bull he can be wonderful. Of the three real gypsies, Cagancho, Gitanillo de Triana and Merida I like Merida the best.

(Hemingway, 9301, Death in the Afternoon, 223)

The two passages, four sentences in 161 words for Sprat and four sentences in 109 words for Hemingway, are almost exactly representative of the samples from which they are taken.[8]

The same long-term shift can as easily be illustrated by John Milton and Edmund Wilson:

And *as* it is a particular disesteem of every knowing person alive, and most injurious to the written labours and monuments of the dead, so to me it seems an undervaluing and vilifying of the whole nation. I cannot set so light by all the invention, the art, the wit, the grave and solid judgment *which* is in England, *as that* it can be comprehended in any twenty capacities how good soever; much less *that* it should not pass *except* their superintendence be over it, *except* it be sifted and strained with their strainers; *that* it should be uncurrent without their manual stamp.

(Milton, 9060, Areopagitica, 736)

Theodore Roosevelt, *as* these letters show, was fortunate in his early surroundings and the situation to *which* he was born. The first sections of the correspondence take us into a well-to-do family of the New York of the seventies and eighties, *where* the adored mother and father and sisters and brother, sheltered by the cozy shrubbery of a house at Sagamore Hill, embraced by its ample piazza, seem multiplied ad infinitum in the world beyond Oyster Bay by innumberable cousins and uncles and aunts. The children are taken abroad, climb Vesuvius and see Karnak in their teens and at home they learn to ride their ponies, collect ornithological specimens, and celebrate the Fourth of July with much popping of firecrackers.

(Wilson, 9328, *Essays,* 378)

Even though we have picked Milton's most sententious (i.e., most short-sentenced) work and have compared two typical sentences from it with three sentences from one of the least sententious writers of our age, the reduction in both size and complexity over the years is easy to see. As a kind of mathematical inevitability, the long-term reduction in size illustrated by both the Sprat/Hemingway and the Milton/Wilson comparisons leads to a far greater number of unsubordinated sentences in the more recent samples than in the earlier ones (Figure 9.3).

Several other changes accompany the reduction in sentence size. Most obvious of these is the decline both in formal parallelism and in the *copia* that is often associated with it. These are indicated by the decline in correlative conjunctions (Figure 9.4) and in total coordinators (Figure 9.5). The decline in correlatives we can illustrate by taking almost any sentence out of Ascham and comparing it with a sentence or two from a contemporary writer, even the relatively copious Mumford:

> And therefore if the Pope himself do *not only* grant pardons to further these wicked purposes abroad in Italy, *but also* (although this present Pope in the beginning made some show of misliking thereof) assign *both* meed *and* merit to the maintenance of stews and brothel houses at home in Rome, then let wise men think Italy a safe place for wholesome doctrine and godly manners and a fit school for young gentlemen of England to be brought up in.
>
> (Ascham, 9000, *Scholemaster,* 73)

> The signs of the change are the impregnation of capitalistic modes of existence with normative ideas: the displacement of the struggle for profit as the sole condition of orientation in industrial relations, the undermining of private competition through the principle of understandings, and the constitutional organization of industrial enterprise. These processes, which have actually begun under capitalism, have only to be pushed to their logical conclusions to carry us beyond the capitalist order.
>
> (Mumford, 9329, *Technics,* 422)

The decline in coordinators spans the entire 400-year period of our study, although as in the case of sentence length there seems to me to have been one fairly considerable break. That break occurred between Gibbon and Arnold. Before Gibbon it was common for writers to write prose containing coordinators as 6% of the entire word stock; prior to 1825, a writer with fewer than 5% coordinators in a

Figure 9.5 COORDINATORS
(CLASS 41)

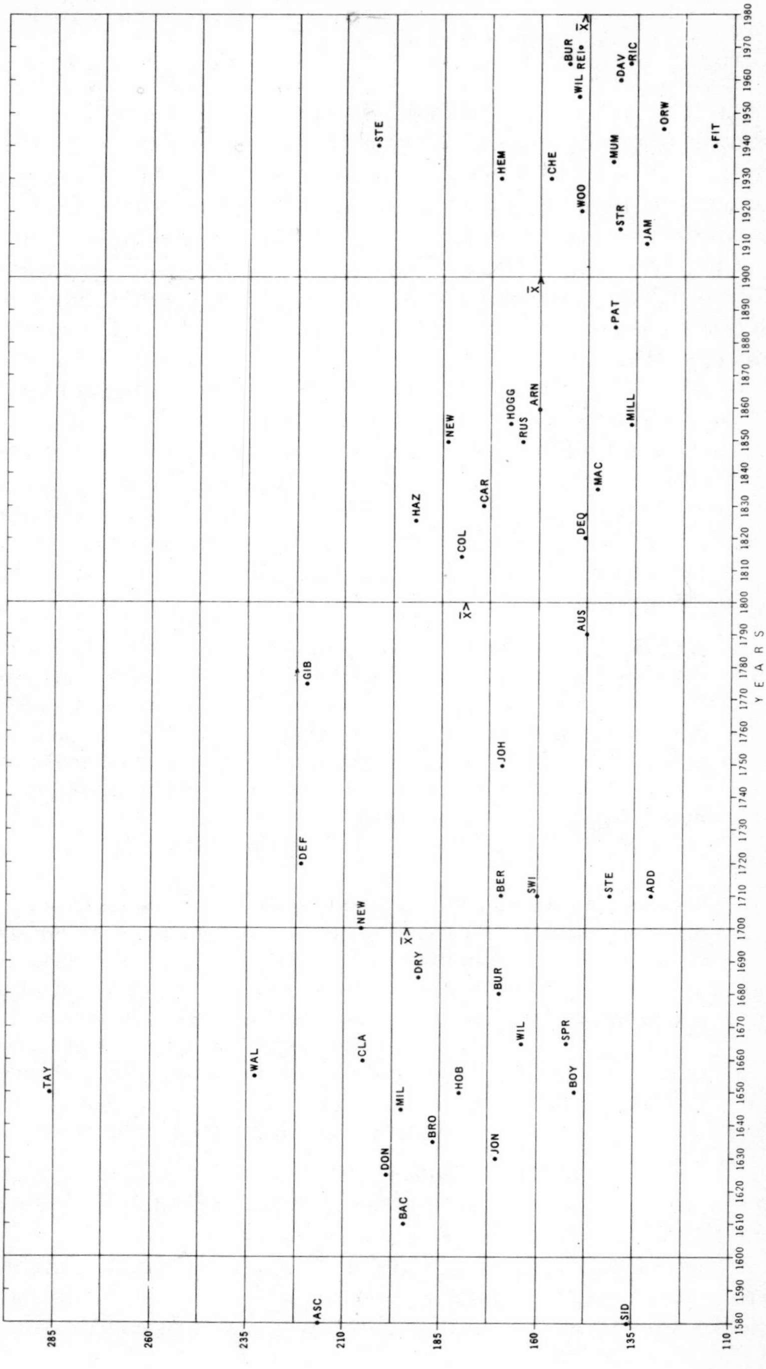

sample—a writer like Sprat, Swift, Addison, or Steele—was the exception. After Hazlitt, the only writers to rise above the 5% point are Carlyle, Cardinal Newman, and Gertrude Stein.[9] A comparison between Gibbon and Arnold, writing less than 100 years apart, will illustrate the extent of the decline:

> The naphtha was mingled, I know not by what methods *or* in what proportions, with sulphur *and* with the pitch that is extracted from evergreen firs. From this mixture, which produced a thick smoke *and* a loud explosion, proceeded a fierce *and* obstinate flame, which not only rose in perpendicular ascent, but likewise burned with equal vehemence in descent *or* lateral progress, instead of being extinguished, it was nourished *and* quickened by the element of water; *and* sand, urine, *or* vinegar were the only remedies that could damp the fury of this powerful agent, which was justly denominated by the Greeks the liquid, *or* the maritime, fire. For the annoyance of the enemy, it was employed with equal effect by sea *and* land, in battles *or* in sieges.
>
> (Gibbon, 9102, *Decline and Fall*, V, 417)

> Thus the tombs of Ali *and* of his son, the Meshed Ali *and* the Meshed Hussein, standing some thirty miles apart from one another in the plain of the Euphrates, had, when Gibbon wrote, their yearly pilgrims *and* their tribute of enthusiastic mourning. But Count Gobineau relates, in his book of which I have spoken, a development of these solemnities which was unknown to Gibbon. Within the present century there has arisen, on the basis of this story of the martyrs of Kerbela, a drama, a Persian national drama, which Count Gobineau, who has seen *and* heard it, is bold enough to rank with the Greek drama as a great *and* serious affair, engaging the heart *and* life of the people who have given birth to it; while the Latin, English, French, *and* German drama is, he says, in comparison a mere pastime *or* amusement, more *or* less intellectual *and* elegant.
>
> (Arnold, 9105, *Essays*, 233)

For both Gibbon (with 11 coordinators in 117 words) and Arnold (with 10 in 153 words), the passages are more coordinated than is their habit. But even when coordinating copiously for his time, Arnold cannot measure up to his great predecessor.

The long-term decline in sentence complexity, both rank shifting in general and use of dependent clauses, has already been illustrated. It is important to note that although both relative and adverbial subordinate clauses have dropped (Figures 9.6 and 9.7), the decline in relative clauses has been by far the more precipitous.* A comparison, this time between Milton and Richler, can be instructive.

---

*Indeed the twentieth century has seen, at least in our sample, a slight increase in adverbial subordination, although it remains lower in the measure than the period 1580 to 1820.

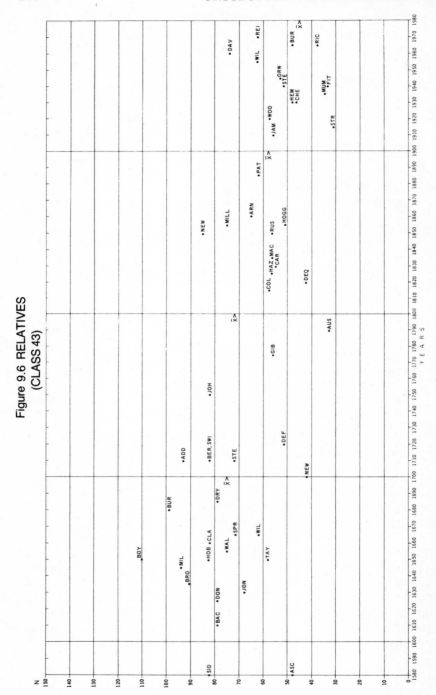

Figure 9.6 RELATIVES
(CLASS 43)

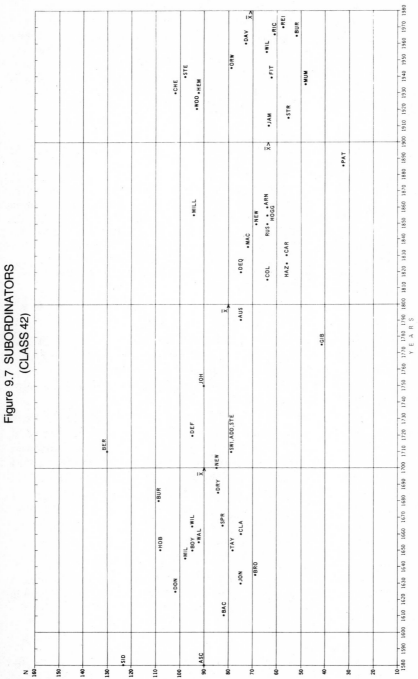

Figure 9.7 SUBORDINATORS
(CLASS 42)

Let her and Falsehood grapple; who ever knew Truth put to the worse, in a free and open encounter. Her *confuting* is the best and surest *suppressing*. He *who* hears what *praying* there is for light and clearer knowledge *to be sent down* among us, would think of other matters *to be constituted* beyond the discipline of Geneva, *framed* and *fabriced* already to our hands. Yet *when* the new light *which* we beg for shines in upon us, there be *who* envy and oppose, *if* it come not first in at their casements.

(Milton, 9060, Areopagitica, 746)

Nine storeys high with an enormous lobby, a sweep of red-carpeted stairway, and endless corridors leading here, there, and everywhere, the Concord can cope with 2,500 guests *who* can, I'm assured, consume 9,000 latkas and ten tons of meat a day. Ornate chandeliers drip from the ceiling of the main lobby. The largest of the hotel's three nightclubs, the Imperial Room, seats 2,500 people. But it is dangerous *to attempt* a physical description of the hotel. For even *as* I checked in, the main dining-room was making way for a still larger one, and it is just possible *that since* I left, the five interconnecting convention halls have been opened up and converted into an indoor spring training camp for the Mets. Nothing's impossible.

(Richler, 9617, Tigers, 138)

There are many "simpler" contemporary styles than Richler's, with its apposition and adverbial subordination, yet the illustration that he provides of the decline in relatives is dramatic—and in being so, it may also suggest recent developments in the clustering of nouns, of which more discussion below.[10] First, however, there is more to be said concerning the simplification of the sentence.

   The decline in relatives accounts for more than half the total decline in rank shifting from about 1620 to date. A portion of the rest of that decline is accounted for by the loss of adverbial subordination (class 42), but even more is accounted for by the diminishing use of infinitives (class 05, Figure 9.8). The Sprat/Hemingway comparison earlier was an exaggerated illustration; the Sprat passage contains five infinitives, the Hemingway none. More accurate in its reflection of the decline of infinitives over a period of time is a comparison among Jeremy Taylor, J.S. Mill, and Robertson Davies:

It is but a miserable remedy *to be beholden* to a sickness for our health: and though it be better *to suffer* the loss of a finger than that the arm and the whole body should putrify; yet even then also it is a trouble and an evil *to lose* a finger. He that mends with sickness pares the nails of the beast when they have already torn off part of the flesh: But he that would have a sickness become a clear and an entire blessing, a thing indeed *to be reckoned* among the good things of God, and the evil things of the world, must lead a holy life, and judge himself with an early sentence, and so order the noun of his Soul, that in the usual

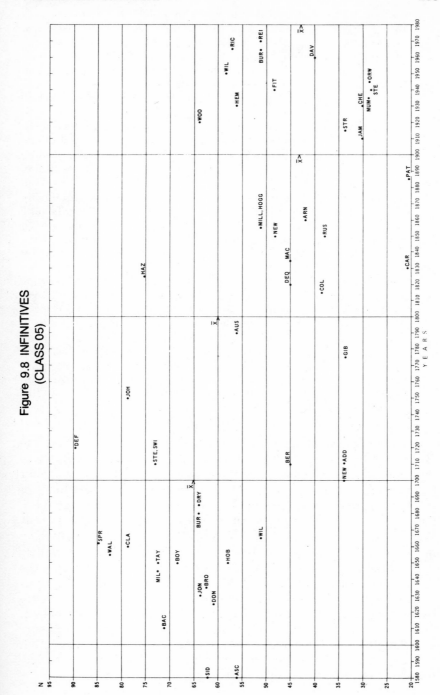

Figure 9.8 INFINITIVES (CLASS 05)

method of God's gerund use there may be nothing left *to be done,* but that such virtues should be exercised which God intends *to crown:* and then, as when the Athenians upon a day of battle with longing and uncertain souls sitting in their Common Hall, expecting what would be the sentence of the day, at last received a messenger who only had breath enough left him *to say:* (We are Conquerors,) and so died . . .

(Taylor, 9036, *Holy Dying,* 118-119)

The object of this Essay is *to assert* one very simple principle, as entitled *to govern* absolutely the dealings of society with the individual in the way of compulsion and control, whether the means used by physical force in the form of legal penalties, or the moral coercion of public opinion. That principle is, that the sole end for which mankind are warranted, individually or collectively, in interfering with the liberty of action of any of their number, is self-protection. That the only purpose for which power can be rightfully exercised over any member of a civilized community, against his will, is *to prevent* harm to others.

(Mill, 9207, *On Liberty,* 13)

It is, of course, very difficult *to draw* a portrait of a good and resolute virgin, and in evidence we may produce the dim creatures who serve as heroines in the novels of J.R.R. Tolkien, C.S. Lewis, and Charles Williams—three whom Mr. Fuller praises for their mastery of the demonic element in fiction. Demons these writers may understand: women, no. It is a common complaint against the novels of consciously moral writers—excellent as many of these are in other respects—that their heroines are wooden. Such characters are not women at all, but creatures embodying those qualities their authors would like women *to possess,* and no others.

(Davies, 9314, *Voice from the Attic,* 107)

Over the period spanned by these writers, and indeed during the 70 years before *Holy Dying,* the habit of initially connecting sentences with a coordinator, a subordinator, or a sentence connector (classes 41, 42, 91) steadily diminished; concurrently, the habit of initial coordination (41) also tended to fall out of use, although it has had a slight recovery in the twentieth century among such writers as Wilson, Chesterton, Stein, and Woolf (Figures 9.9 and 9.10). The most precipitous drop occurred after Newton, as the journalists nudged the divines and their audience out of the church and into the coffee-house: the habit of initially connecting a third or more of one's sentences, normal from 1580 through Newton, disappears entirely in the samples after him, except for Berkeley and Swift, both of whom were divines. A series of beginnings from Sprat, Addison, and Strachey can illustrate the overall decline of initial connection (41, 42, 91), together with our own century's stabilization at an historically low level.

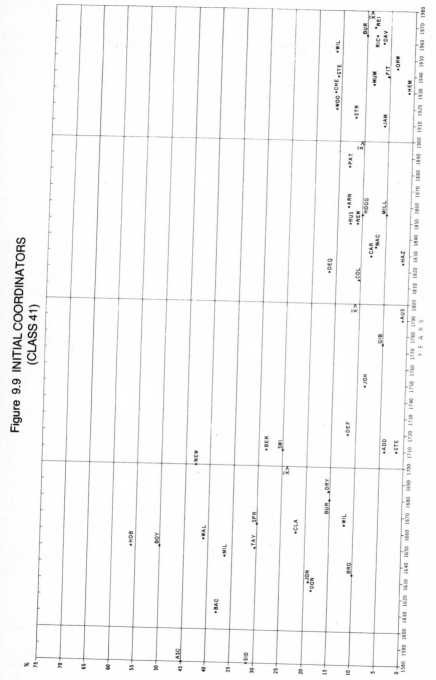

Figure 9.9 INITIAL COORDINATORS
(CLASS 41)

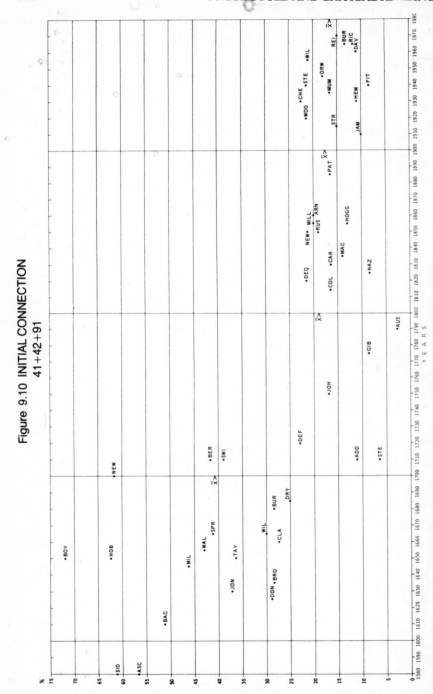

Figure 9.10 INITIAL CONNECTION
41+42+91

And it seems to me . . . There lie now ready . . . There are only therefore . . . *But* I see . . . I shall therefore . . . *Thus* I have . . . I did on purpose omit . . . *But* I shall now add . . . They were, without question . . . *But* they injoy'd not the light long enough, It brake forth . . . *However,* that knowledge . . .

(Sprat, 9068, *History,* 44-45)

There are few men so cramped in their private affairs . . . It is but . . . This is, I think . . . By this Method, . . . Sir Thomas Browne . . . This Passage in Scripture . . . Pursuant to those Passages . . . I cannot recollect . . . What I spent . . . What I possessed . . . What I gave away . . . *Since* I am thus . . . It is the Account . . .

(Addison, 9108, *Spectator,* 177)

At last . . . One evening . . . He was the . . . The Egyptian Governor-General . . . The emissary . . . Mahommed Ahmen . . . "Must!" exclaimed the Mahdi . . . The look was . . . Thereupon, the Governor-General . . . With his handful . . . The news spread . . . *But* it was clear . . . The Mahdi . . . The Retreat . . . The country . . . *And* now . . . The Baggara tribes . . . Their powerful emirs . . . A holy war . . .

(Strachey, 9192, *Victorians,* 262-263)

The per-sentence density of initial connection—50% for Sprat, less than 10% for Addison, and just under 15% for Strachey—is a fair representation of the writers. Before leaving this feature of the language, we should remark on two facts: (1) eighteenth-century writers compensated for the lack of the connecting words in initial position by a variety of devices, notably prepositional phrases and retrospective pronouns and determiners (note the incidence of "This," "those," "It" in the Addison passage); (2) the shortened sentences of the twentieth century bring sentence openings closer to one another, and a writer like Strachey (15.7% connection with a 23 word sentence) is giving us more initial connectors per 1000 words than is a writer like Johnson (17.4% connection with a 44 word sentence).[11]

Surprisingly to me, the verbals do not behave as a group. We have already noted the decline in the use of infinitives. Gerunds over the years fluctuate within a very narrow range,[12] showing no steady trend in one direction or another. At the same time, the participles (class 06) show an increase of roughly a third, beginning about 1800 (Figure 9.11). Once again, we can see the character of the shift in two writers who wrote within less than a century of one another, Swift and Hazlitt, both of whom were relatively "participial" writers for their times.[13]

In this deplorable State of the Clergy, nothing but the Hand of Providence, *working* by its glorious Instrument, the QUEEN, could have

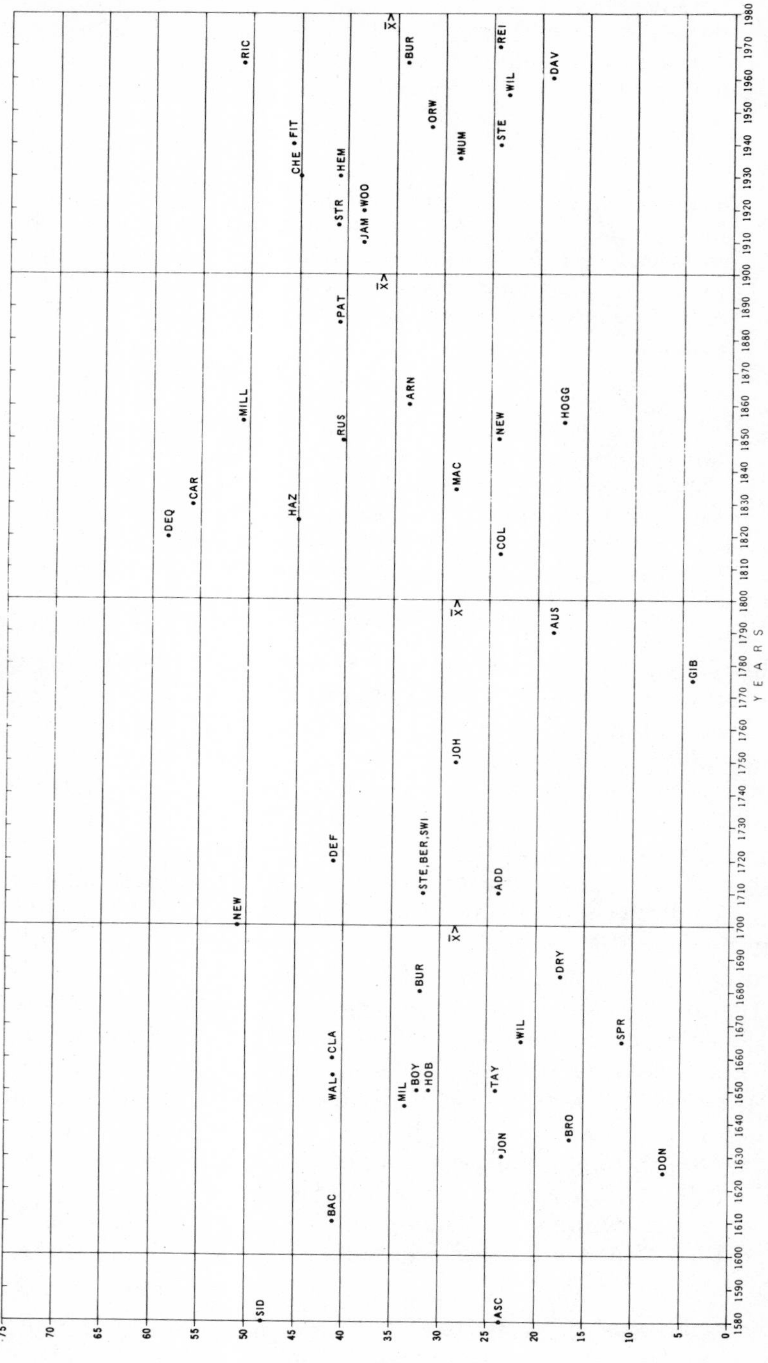

Figure 9.11 PARTICIPLES
(CLASS 06)

been able to turn the Peoples Hearts so surprizingly in their Favour. This Princess, *destined* for the Safety of Europe, and a Blessing to her Subjects, began Her Reign with a noble Benefaction to the Church; and it was hoped, the Nation would have followed such an example; which nothing could have prevented, but the false Politicks of a Set of Men, who form their Maxims upon those of every tottering Commonwealth, which is always struggling for Life, *subsisting* by Expedients, and often at the Mercy of every powerful Neighbour. These Men take it into their Imagination, that Trade can never flourish unless the Country becomes a common Receptacle for all Nations, Religions, and Languages; a System only proper for small popular States, but altogether unworthy; and below the Dignity of an Imperial Crown; which with us is best upheld by a Monarch in Possession of his just Prerogative, a Senate of Nobles and of Commons, and a Clergy *established* in its due Rights with a suitable Maintenance by Law.

(Swift, 9101, *Examiner,* 48)

It is among the miseries of the want of money, not to be able to pay your reckoning at an inn—or, if you have just enough to do that, to have nothing left for the waiter;—to be stopped at a turnpike gate, and forced to turn back;—not to venture to call a hackney-coach in a shower of rain—(when you have only one shilling left yourself, it is a bore to have it taken out of your pocket by a friend, who comes into your house *eating* peaches in a hot summer's-day, and *desiring* you to pay for the coach in which he visits you);—not to be able to purchase a lottery-ticket, by which you might make your fortune, and get out of all your difficulties;—or to find a letter *lying* for you at a country post-office, and not to have money in your pocket to free it, and be obliged to return for it the next day. The letter so unseasonably *withheld* may be supposed to contain money, . . .

(Hazlitt, 9202, *Essays,* 300)

Together with the participles, attributively-placed participial adjectives increased from a pre-1800 average of 15.2 to a post-1800 average of 28.1 per sample (Figure 9.12). Ruskin is a particularly dramatic instance of this shift; in six lines, he can spin off *"flanking* masses," *"decorated* wall," *"projecting* figures," *"living* architecture," *"determined* variation," and *"related* proportion"[14]—a density that neither I nor any of my associates have noticed in a pre-1850 writer, although we have seen several with a similar density since then other than Ruskin: Pater, Davies, Fitzgerald, and James, to name four.

The increase in the usage of participle and participial adjective forms was accompanied by a gradual increase in the use of progressive verb forms, class 023, from an incidence in the seventeenth century of one every 6,000 words to a twentieth-century incidence of one every 350 words. These three phenomena taken together make for a considerable increase, nearly a doubling, of participial forms

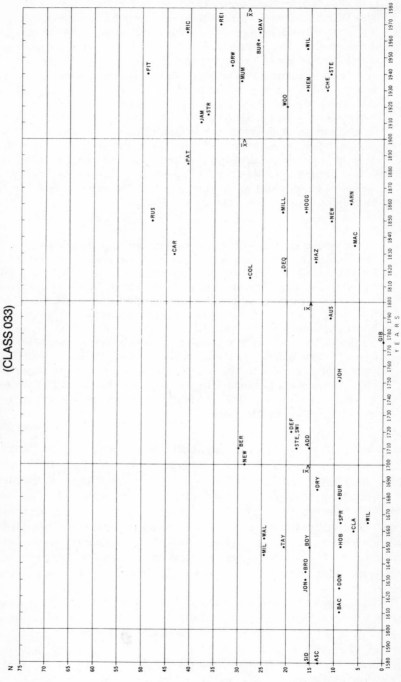

Figure 9.12 PARTICIPIAL ADJECTIVES
(CLASS 033)

between the seventeenth century and today (Figure 9.13). Dryden, who we have been told is a conversational writer (hence, presumably, modern),[15] offers a good contrast with the heavily participial Fitzgerald (participles, participial adjectives, and progressive forms are italicized):

> In each of these, before I undertook them, I considered the genius and *distinguishing* character of my author. I looked on Virgil as a succinct and grave majestic writer; one who weighed not only every thought, but every word and syllable; who was still *aiming* to crowd his sense into as narrow a compass as possibly he could; for which reason he is so very figurative, that he requires (I may almost say) a grammar apart to construe him.
>
> (Dryden, 9096, *Preface to Sylva*, 255)

> We are married. The Sibylline parrots are *protesting* the sway of the first *bobbed* heads in the Biltmore *panelled* luxe. The hotel is *trying* to look older.
>
> The *faded* rose corridors of the Commodore end in subways and subterranean metropolises—a man sold us a *broken* Marmon and a wild burst of friends spend half an hour *revolving* in the *revolving* door.
>
> There were lilacs open to the dawn near the *boarding* house in Westport where we sat up all night to finish a story. We quarreled in the gray morning dew about morals; and made up over a red *bathing* suit.
>
> (Fitzgerald, 9323, *Crack-up*, 41)

Even though they are associated far more with discourse in the social sciences than with literary English, large nominal clusters— sometimes called "noun piles," sometimes "freight trains"—often with a heavy admixture of adjectives, appear markedly more often even among the literates. Two three-class patterns associated with the large nominal cluster increase with each century of our study: adjective-adjective-noun (03-03-01, Figure 9.14) and determiner-noun-noun (31-01-01, Figure 9.15). In the first of these patterns, Pater, a heavy user of modifiers, can show us some of the late Victorian moves in the direction of the kind of clustering present in contemporary English. On one page[16] he gives us "gay, false, adventurous, outer world," "poor, pathetic pleasures," "strange, new, passionate pastoral world," and "best modern fiction," all these clusters ending in 03-03-01. Pater's lushness in this pattern, however, cannot compare with the most fecund of our moderns, whose outburst below took barely a third of a page:

> The *American Corporate State* today can be thought of as a *single vast corporation*, with every person as an involuntary member and employee. It consists primarily of *large industrial organizations*, plus nonprofit institutions such as foundations and the educational system,

Figure 9.13 TOTAL PARTICIPIAL FORMS
06+023+033

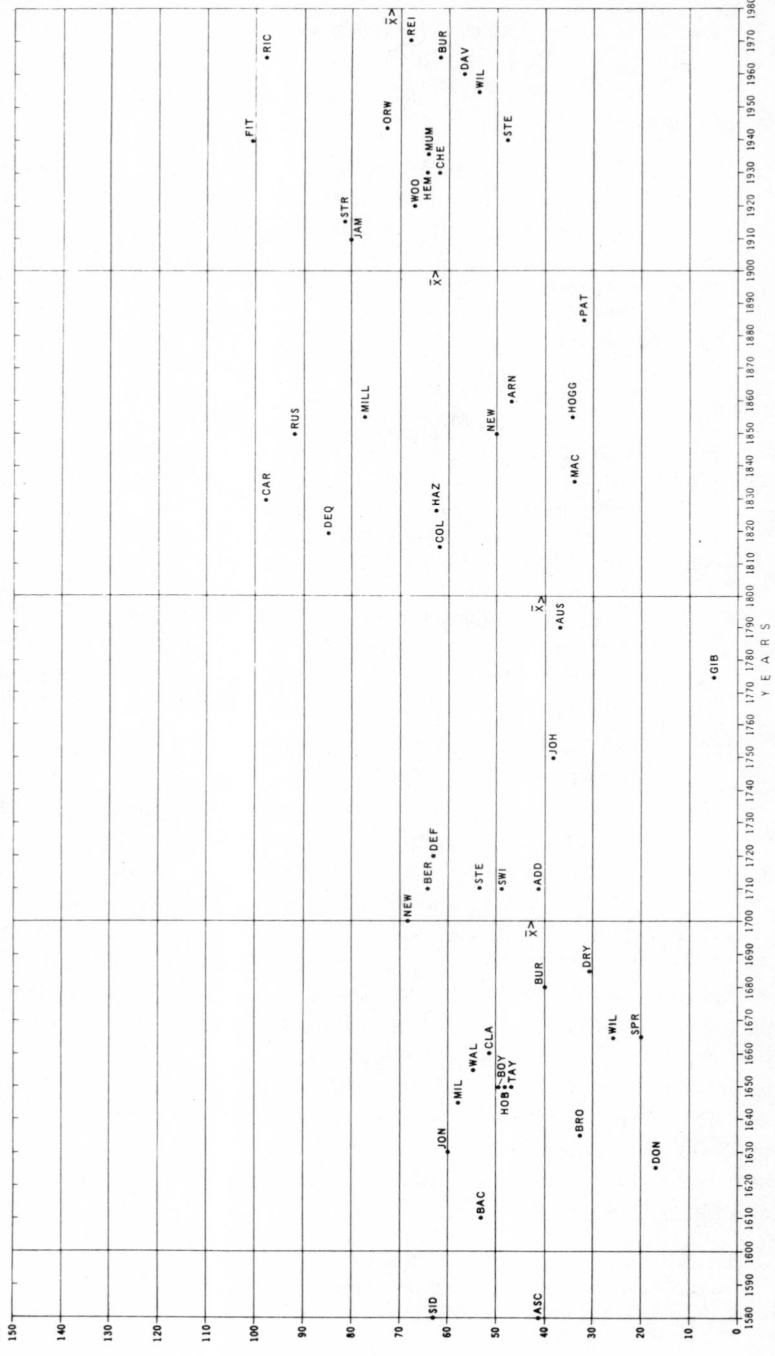

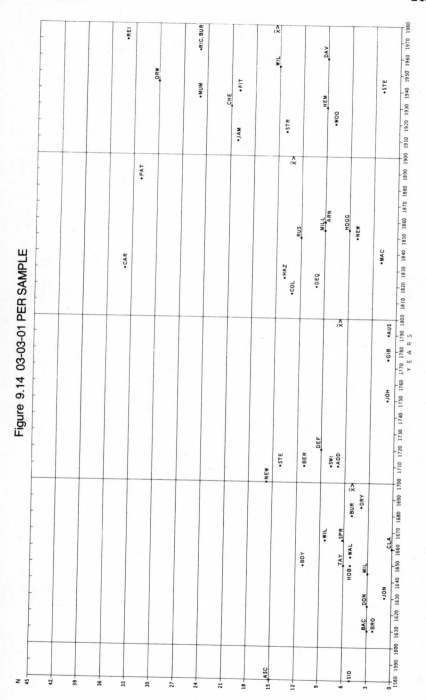

Figure 9.14 03-03-01 PER SAMPLE

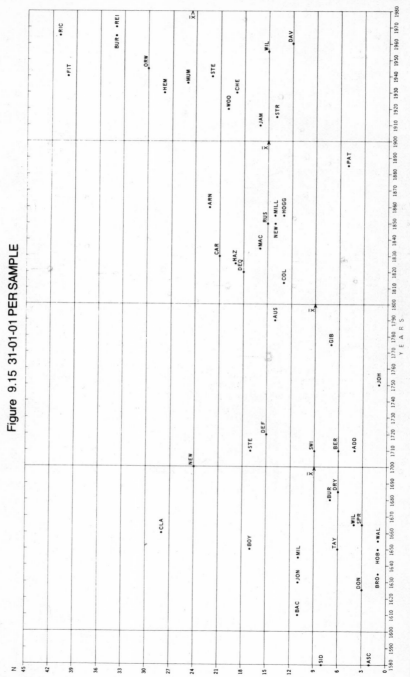

Figure 9.15 31-01-01 PER SAMPLE

all related to the whole as divisions to a business corporation. Government is only a part of the state, but government coordinates it and provides a variety of needed services. The Corporate State is a complete reversal of the *original American ideal* and plan. The State, and not the market or the people or any *abstract economic laws*, determines what shall be produced . . .

(Reich, 9401, Greening, 93)

The second pattern, 31-01-01, is undeniably associated with the rise of the attributive nominal (class 012), from 4.6 per 3,500 words in our seventeenth-century samples to over *nine* times that in our twentieth-century samples (Figure 9.16). That growth has been especially marked since 1900: our twentieth-century samples show an average 42.5 per sample, our nineteenth-century samples 15.0. Once again, a comparison between a Victorian and a modern can be instructive, this time between Cardinal Newman and Mordecai Richler. In Newman's entire sample, we could only find "University Education," "University course," "subject matter," and "self-possession" (all 012-011, several of the items repeated a few times). In the first three pages alone of our Richler sample we uncover "horror comics" (012-011), "rocket-ship" (012-011), "publications vice-president" (012-011), "Superman controversy" (012-011), "self-effacing" (012-033), and "hate-ball" (012-011). And later in the sample, these trains pick up added cars: "art film cliché" (012-012-011), "minority group men" (012-012-011), etc., etc.

The rise of the attributive is part of the rise in the overall use of nouns (Figure 9.17). In the samples prior to 1800, we could expect roughly 20% nouns, or 680 to 700 nouns per sample; that expectation is now, in our later twentieth-century samples, 830 to 860, roughly 24.5% (Figure 9.17). Newman and Mumford can illustrate how dramatic the change has been in the last 100 years, although the trend was set in motion some time in the first quarter of the nineteenth century:

But they must have something to say on every *subject*; *habit, fashion,* the *public* require it of them: and, if so, they can only give *sentence* according to their *knowledge.* You might think this ought to make such a *person* modest in his *enunciations*; not so: too often it happens that, in *proportion* to the *narrowness* of his *knowledge,* is, not his *distrust* of it, but the deep *hold* it has upon him, his absolute *conviction* of his own *conclusions,* and his *positiveness* in maintaining them. He has the *obstinacy* of the *bigot,* whom he scorns, without the *bigot*'s *apology,* that he has been taught, as he thinks, his *doctrine* from *heaven.* Thus he becomes, what is commonly called a *man* of one *idea;* which properly means a *man* of one *science,* and of the *view,* partly true, but subordinate, partly false which is all that can proceed out of any *thing* so partial. Hence it is that we have the *principles* of *utility,* of *combination,* of *progress,* of *philanthropy,* or, in material *sciences,*

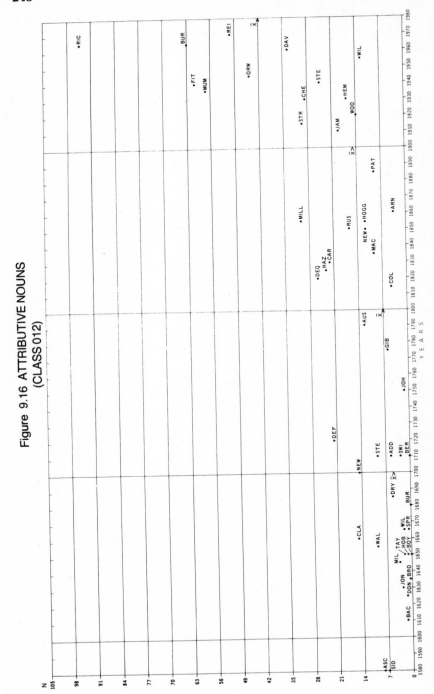

Figure 9.16 ATTRIBUTIVE NOUNS (CLASS 012)

Figure 9.17 NOUNS
(CLASS 01)

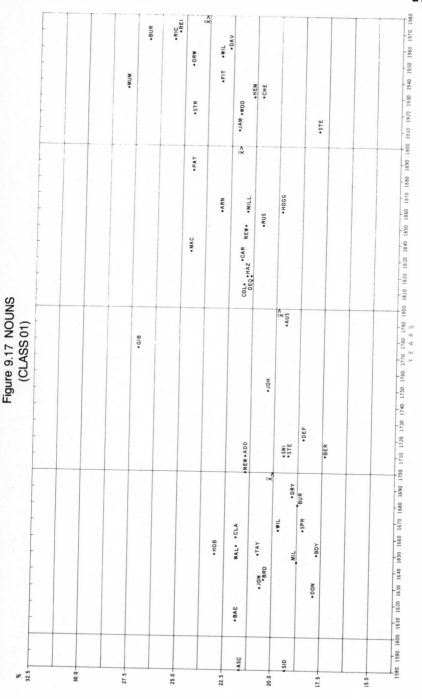

comparative *anatomy, phrenology, electricity,* exalted into leading *ideas,* and *keys,* if not of all *knowledge,* at least of many *things* more than belong to them,—*principles,* all of them true to a certain *point,* yet all degenerating into *error* and *quackery,* because they are carried to *excess,* viz. at the *point* where they require *interpretation* and *restraint* from other *quarters,* and because they are employed to do what is simply too much for them, inasmuch as a little *science* is not deep *philosophy.*

(Newman, 9209, *Idea of a University,* 68)

The *conservation* of the *environment* has still another neotechnic *aspect:* that is the building up in *agriculture* of an appropriate artificial *environment.* Up to the seventeenth *century man's* most important *artifact* was probably the *city* itself; but during this *century* the same *tactics* he had used for his own *domestication* were applied to *agriculture* in the building of *glass hothouses,* and during the nineteenth *century,* with the *increase* of *glass production* and the expanding empirical *knowledge* of the *soils, glass culture* became important in the *supply* of *fruits* and *vegetables.* No longer content with taking *Nature* as it comes, the neotechnic *agriculturist* seeks to determine the exact *conditions* of *soil, temperature, moisture, insolation* that are needed for the specific *crop* he would grow. Within his cold *frames* and his *hothouses* he brings these *conditions* into *existence.*

(Mumford, 9329, *Technics and Civilization,* 258)

Each passage is almost exactly typical of its author in its density of nouns[17]—this, despite the large series in Newman's last sentence. Notice how the careful architecture of subordination evident in the Newman passage has been flattened and macadamized[18] under the steamroller of Mumford's linguistic sensibility. In the Mumford passage, there is only a single adverbial clause ("as it comes" in line 10), and options for adverbial clauses ("as glass production increased") are rejected in favor of nominalizing expressions ("with the increase of glass production").

As usage of nouns grew, other items associated with the noun have also tended to grow: the noun in subject position (015, Figure 9.18), the determiner (31, Figure 9.19)—notably the definite determiner (311, Figure 9.20)—and the adjective (03, Figure 9.21). One nominal usage that has not kept pace with the rise of the noun has been the phrase noun-preposition-noun (01-51-01: "man of God," "lover of sport"); indeed, the cluster has barely held its own since the death of Victoria, as Newman's "modification of habit" has (with the rise of the 012) become contemporary psychology's "habit modification" (Figure 9.22). Similarly, the historical rise of adjectives has subsided in recent years as the "Gothic novel" (031-011) has given way to the "horror film" (012-011).

Of all the major word classes over the last 400 years, despite its re-

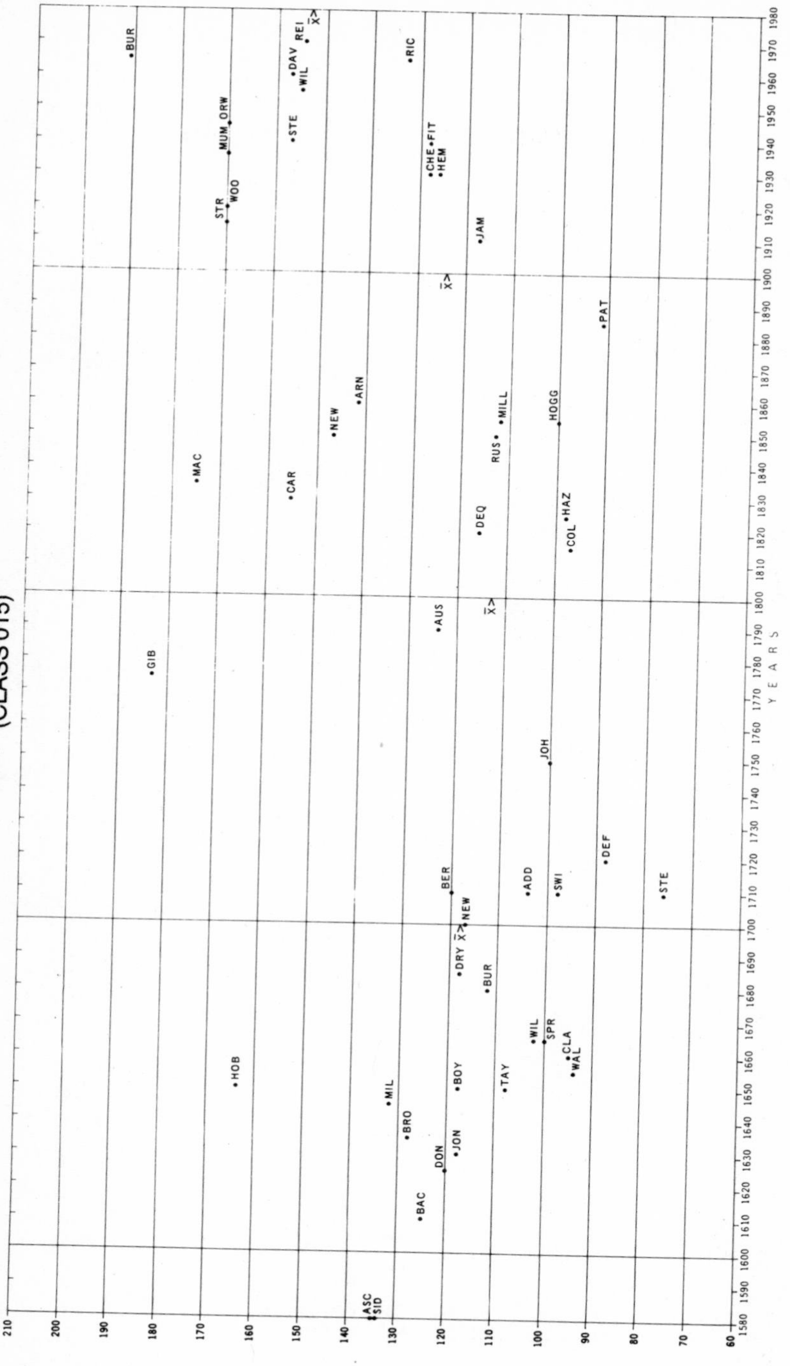

Figure 9.18 NOUN-SUBJECTS
(CLASS 015)

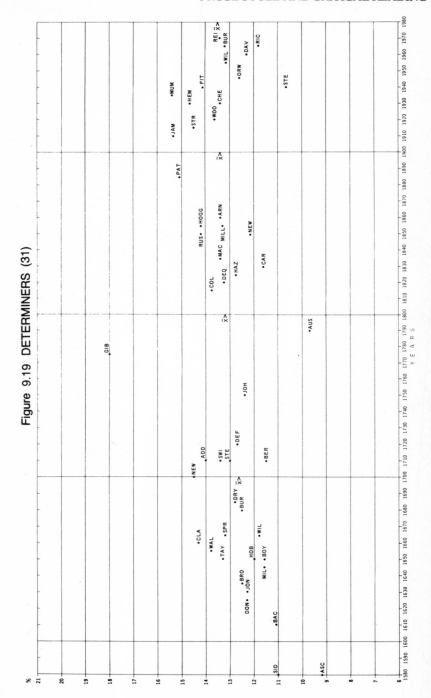

Figure 9.19 DETERMINERS (31)

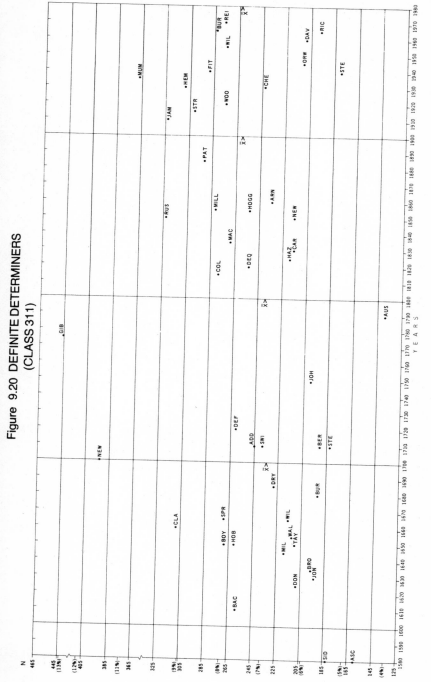

Figure 9.20 DEFINITE DETERMINERS
(CLASS 311)

Figure 9.21 ADJECTIVES
(CLASS 03)

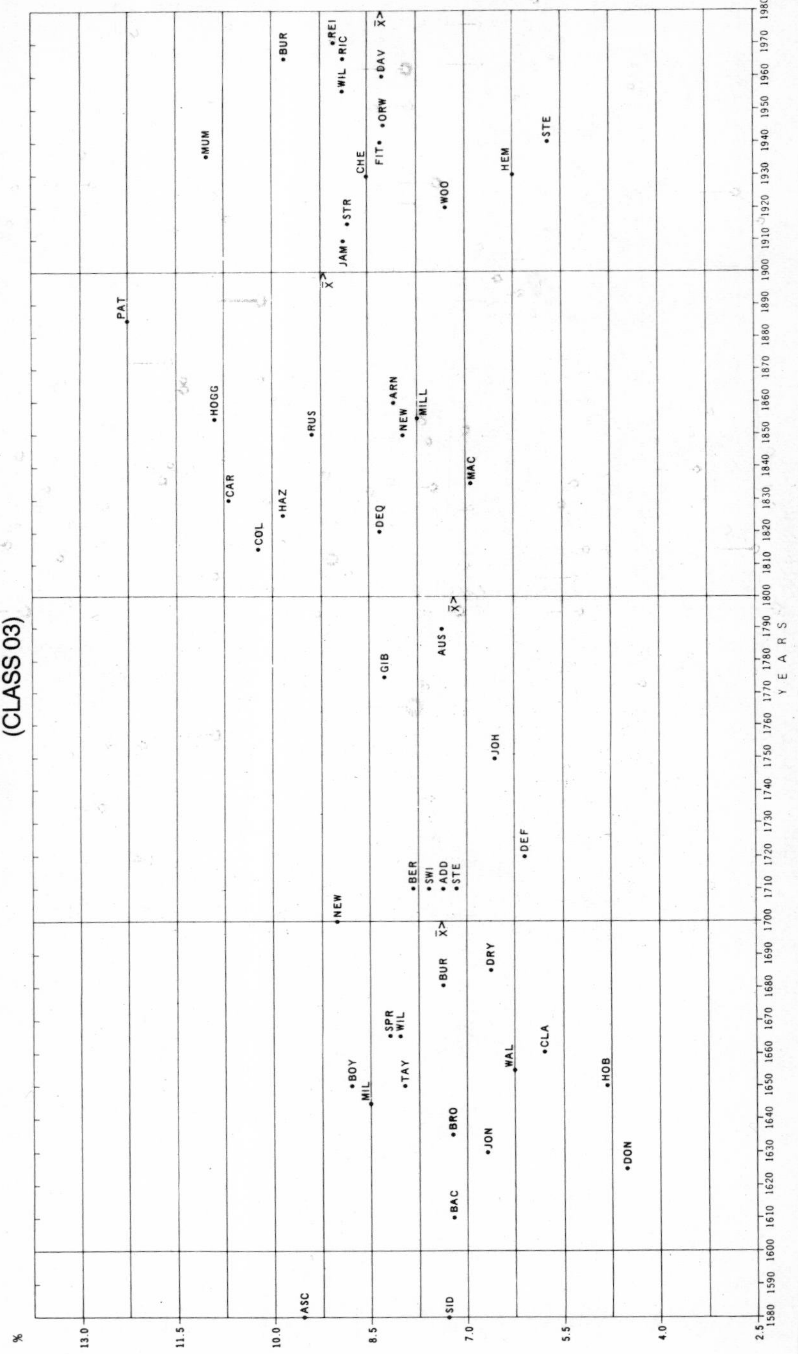

Figure 9.22 01-51-01 PER SAMPLE

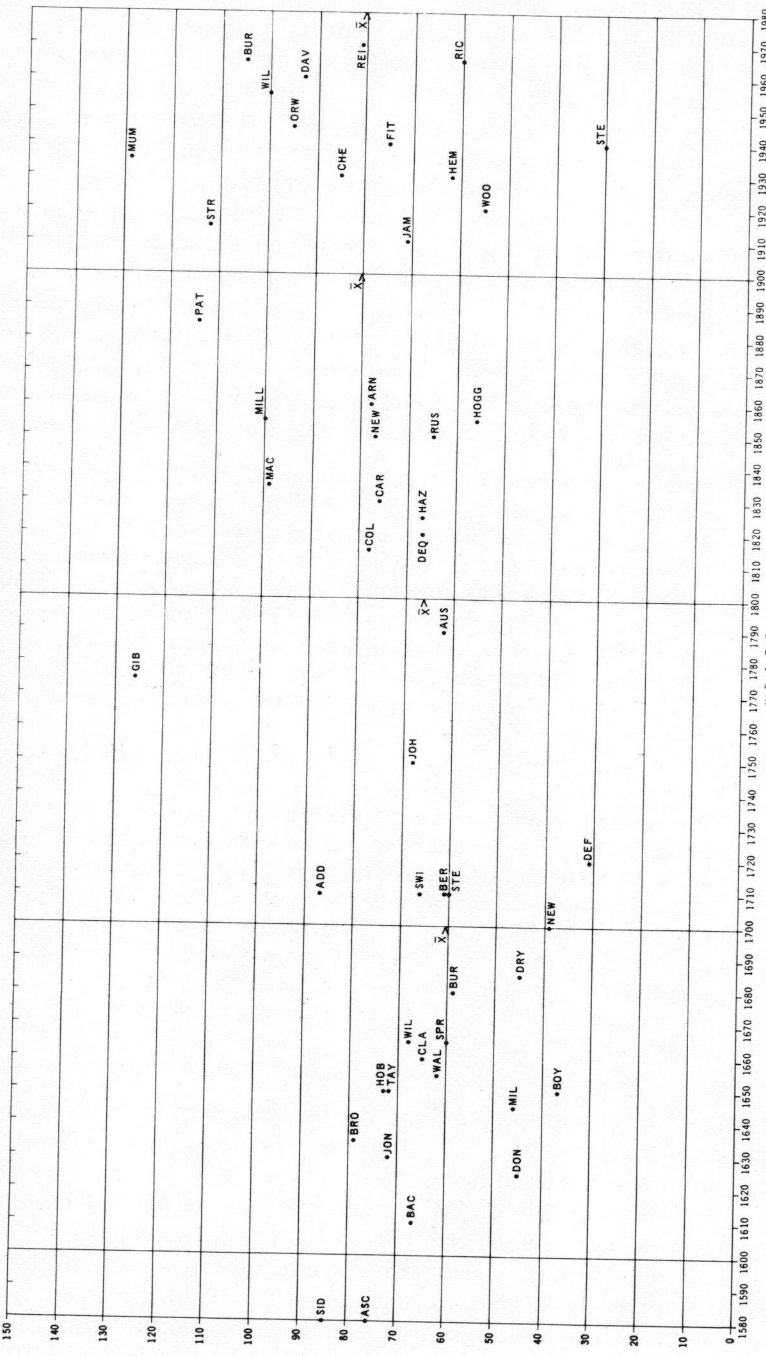

cent shrinkage, the biggest growth item has been the adjective, growing by the late nineteenth century to perhaps 130% of its 1600-1650 base. Interestingly, the growth has been almost entirely in the attributively placed adjectives, as the complement and post-modifying adjectives (032, 034, 035) have either grown very slightly or fluctuated within narrow ranges. The Pater and Reich passages above are illustrative of the adjectival surfeit in which we have come to live in the last 150 years. That surfeit accounts for almost all of the growth of the "M" statistic from 1650 to date (Figure 9.23), the rest being accounted for by a recent slight increase in function adverbs (34, Figure 9.24). We have already noted that narrative forms tend to call forth more adverbs of time and place than do instructive or ex-pository ones,[19] and the rise of the novel—both as a dominant *genre* and as a stylistic model—may have much to do with the kind of shift that we can perceive below in two passages by Pater and James.

> The music of mere metre performs but a limited, yet a very peculiar and subtly ascertained function, in Wordsworth's poetry. With him, metre is but an additional grace, accessory to that deeper music of words and sounds, that moving power, which they exercise in the no-bler prose no less than in formal poetry. It is a sedative to that excite-ment, an excitement sometimes almost painful, under which the lan-guage, alike of poetry and prose, attains a rhythmical power, indepen-dent of metrical combination, and dependent rather on some subtle adjustment of the elementary sounds of words themselves to the image or feeling they convey.
>
> (Pater, 9104, *Appreciations,* 58)

> We can never know what might have become of him with less impor-tunity in his consciousness of the machinery of life, of its furniture and fittings, of all that, right and left, he causes to assail us, sometimes almost to suffocation, under the general rubric of things. Things, in this sense with him, are at once our delight and our despair; we pass from being inordinately beguiled and convinced by them to feeling that his universe fairly smells too much of them, that the larger ether, the diviner air, is in peril of finding among them scarce room to circu-late.
>
> (James, 9179, *Notes on Novelists,* 119)

Notice that in addition to the adverbs of degree, evident in the first passage, the James passage—like the rest of his book—has a tempo-ral emphasis that the other lacks.

The historical tide of "M" reached its crest in the mid-nineteenth century. It has receded a bit in our own age under the influence, among other things, of the generally anti-lush aesthetics of the twen-tieth century. Nevertheless, with an "M" of 388, Hemingway, who would have been in the middle of our seventeenth-century writers, stands chastely alone among our twentieth-century ones. Notice that

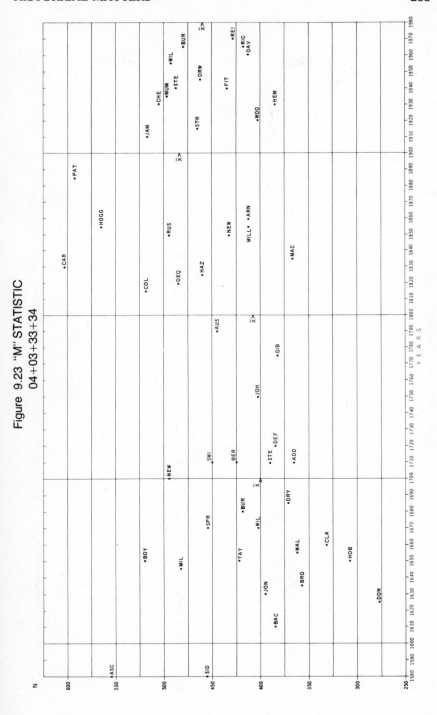

Figure 9.23 "M" STATISTIC
04+03+33+34

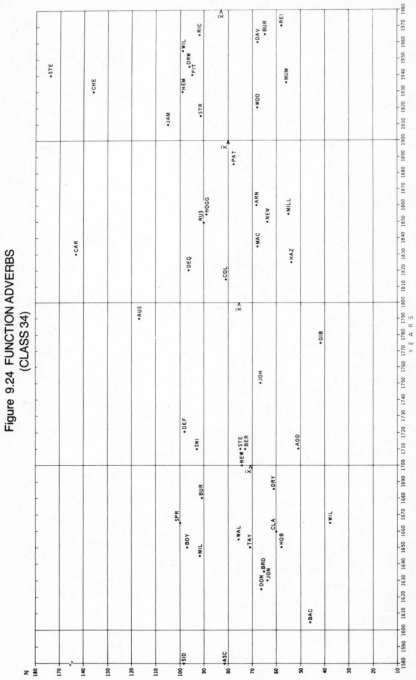

Figure 9.24 FUNCTION ADVERBS
(CLASS 34)

in Figure 9.23 over half of our seventeenth-century writers have "M" statistics under 400; the eighteenth century is split 50-50 above 400 and below; in the nineteenth century a 500 "M" simply makes you one of the boys, along with Carlyle, Coleridge, Ruskin, Hogg, and Pater. Among our twentieth-century samples, only James and Chesterton get over 500, and none of them is close to the 550+ region inhabited by Pater, Carlyle, and Hogg. The general historical movement of "M" can be seen in a comparison among Browne, Ruskin, and Orwell.[20]

> Do *but* extract from the corpulency of bodies, or resolve things beyond their *first* matter, and you discover the habitation of Angels, which if I call the *ubiquitary* and *omnipresent* Essence of God, I hope I shall not offend Divinity: for before the Creation of the World God was *really* all things. For the Angels he created no *new* World, or *determinate* mansion, and therefore they are *everywhere* where is his Essence, and do live at a distance *even* in himself. That God made all things for Man, is in some sense *true*, yet not *so far* as to subordinate the Creation of those *purer* Creatures unto ours, though as *ministring* Spirits they do, and are *willing* to fulfil the will of God in these *lower* and *sublunary* affairs of Man.
>
> (Browne, 9044, *Religio*, 44)

> I cannot *here* enter into the *curious* questions connected with the management of *larger curved* surfaces; into the causes of the difference in proportion *necessary* to be observed between *round* and *square* towers; nor into the reasons why a column or ball may be *richly ornamented*, while surface decoration would be *inexpedient* on masses like the Castle of St. Angelo, the tomb of Cecilia Metalla, or the dome of St. Peter's. But what has been *above* said of the desirableness of serenity in plane surfaces, applies *still more forcibly* to those which are *curved;* and it is to be remembered that we are, *at present*, considering how this serenity and power may be carried into *minor* divisions, not how the *ornamental* character of the *lower* form may, upon occasion, be permitted to fret the calmness of the *higher*.
>
> (Ruskin, 9103, *Seven Lamps*, 122)

> But at that moment I glanced *round* at the crowd that had followed me. It was an *immense* crowd, two thousand *at least* and growing every minute. It blocked the road for a *long* distance on either side. I looked at the sea of *yellow* faces above the *garish* clothes—faces all *happy* and excited over this bit of fun, all *certain* that the elephant was going to be shot.
>
> (Orwell, 9196, *Essays*, 158)

CONCLUSIONS

In offering specific literary examples of some of the linguistic shifts that have taken place over the last 400 years, I have not been attempting to offer a history of prose style. The quotations have been set forth with purely illustrative intent; none of the stylists cited in this chapter is offered as average or typical, for, as we said earlier, there is no such thing as a text written in the mythical linguistic norm. At the same time, what is implied by that norm and by the changes in it suggested by our data is a matter worthy of more than casual attention, and for three reasons: the changes themselves, their rates of movement, and the implications they hold for the study of style.

Many of the historical developments here inferred have been noticed before: the growth in participles and participial forms,[21] the reduction in sentence size and elaboration,[22] the growth in attributive nouns.[23] I have not yet seen much emphasis placed on the reduction in infinitives, in relatives, and in coordinators, and I suspect that the whole phenomenon of the noun freight train, with adjectives included, has been underestimated by all of us except for a few prescriptive grammarians laboring to forestall universal bureaucratic nominalization. History nevertheless moves on in its way, and "Literary English of the Modern Period" is by no means all of a piece. This last is a truism. But when we remark on the fact that Mordecai Richler speaks a very different dialect from that of Sidney or Milton, we usually refer to changes in usage and in the word stock rather than to changes in syntax. The changes in the norms of syntax are as significant as the ones in vocabulary, if not more so, a fact that our profession as a whole tends to slight in its teaching.

It is an important point also that the changes have been by no means uniform or predictable in their development. An historical conception of linguistic change that used the history of the GNP as its model—that saw the language, like the national product, as growing ever bigger, ever better, ever grosser with each passing year— would surely lead us astray. Linguistic changes are not likely to occur at a fixed rate. Some changes, like that in the length of the sentence, are fairly steady and gradual. But others, like the sudden jump in the nineteenth century in the pattern adjective-adjective-noun (03-03-01, Figure 9.14) or the seemingly sudden turning away from dense initial connection in the eighteenth century (Figure 9.10) arrive seemingly unannounced. Of the rise in the 03-03-01 pattern one could say that, with the rise of the novel, descriptive (hence, adjectival) writing became more in demand, and that writers bent the language in the direction where demand led them. Of the decline in initial connection, one could say that the rise of journalism shifted the preponderant rhetorical model from an aural to an intellectual one, so that readers, instead of looking for frontal signposts, began to look for relationships of ideas. One could say the editors and printers did it. One could say not only these things but many others, all of them speculative. Causation, however, is not a primary concern here.

What is primary is that there is no analogic model that properly presents the multiplicity of changes and multiplicity of rates of change that are moving in the language at any given time. Whatever we try—the Gross National Product, vegetative growth and decay, an Hegelian dialectic—it will soon lead us away from the linguistic facts with which we are hoping to come to grips.

The century-by-century fluctuations in various normative parameters of even the literary language should remind us of a central fact: that stylistic studies must be comparative in order to mean much, and that the proper basis of comparison is a group of writers working at the same time and in the same genres as the author(s) under-study—or at least in genres not so obviously different as the personal letter is from the sermon. Macaulay's "M" statistic is an excellent case in point. In the seventeenth century, his 367 would have placed him not far from the mean for the period; among the writers between 1700 and the present, the 367 makes him unique.

I do not think that there can be a history of prose style. Who wrote in the Restoration Style, the Augustan Style, the Renaissance Style, or the Style of the Great War? Nobody, that's who, because such "styles" exist only as textless paradigms in the imaginations of literary critics. There is no more a single "Renaissance Style" than there is an adjectival or a nominal style. *Style* has no life of its own; it has only what emerges as constant form in the utterances of an individual. The history of style, such as it is, is not the history of an abstraction but rather the chronicle of a succession of highly distinct and separate people struggling to express their own individuality against the constraints of a language shaped by their predecessors and their contemporaries.

And what of *our* contemporaries and successors? A speculation on where the language is headed is difficult to resist after spending so much time seeing where it has been. It is my own conviction that the style of Richler rather than that of Davies[24] is the wave of the future, that we will go on enlarging the noun phrase frontally at the expense of postmodifying prepositional phrases and relative clauses and that we will continue to shorten the sentence. It may be that our grand-children will regularly read, without flinching, sentences like "United States language experts study Times Square pool hustler talk," although I must at the same time acknowledge the possibility that the headline writers have dragged us as far in that direction as we are willing to go. Whatever the directions, the literary language will continue to change, will continue to be an instrument shaping and shaped by the writers who use it.

Table 9.2 STATISTICS FOR CHAPTER 9

CATEGORY	Ascham	Sidney	Donne	Bacon	Jonson	Browne	Walton	Hobbes	Milton	Taylor	Clarendon	Newton	Sprat	Wilkins	Dryden	Boyle	Burnet
01	21.4	19.4	17.9	21.9	20.8	20.4	21.9	20.8	18.9	20.7	21.9	21.4	18.3	19.3	18.9	17.6	18.2
015N	136	135	120	126	119	129	93	164	132	109	94	117	100	102	119	118	112
02	6.8	8.2	8.9	6.5	8.3	7.5	7.1	7.4	7.9	7.7	7.0	6.2	6.8	6.0	7.8	6.5	8.2
023N	5	0	1	1	0	0	1	0	0	2	1	0	1	0	0	2	0
03	9.5	7.3	4.5	7.2	6.8	6.3	6.3	4.7	8.5	8.1	5.7	9.1	8.3	8.3	6.7	8.9	7.4
033N	13	15	9	9	16	16	24	8	24	21	6	28	8	3	13	15	8
04	2.7	1.8	1.5	1.5	1.3	1.3	1.0	1.0	1.9	1.3	1.1	2.0	1.1	1.2	1.4	2.3	1.5
05	1.6	1.8	1.8	2.1	1.9	1.8	2.4	1.7	2.1	2.1	2.3	1.0	2.5	1.6	2.0	2.0	1.9
06	.7	1.4	.2	1.2	.7	.5	.9	1.2	1.1	.7	1.2	1.5	.3	.7	.5	.9	.9
07	.6	.8	.8	.5	1.2	.1	.4	.1	1.3	.2	.7	.8	.9	.8	.6	1.1	.8
11	5.1	7.3	10.3	5.1	7.5	8.8	7.3	4.8	5.7	6.6	6.0	5.4	7.9	6.9	9.3	6.7	9.5
21	6.8	8.3	7.0	6.8	6.8	7.8	5.6	7.3	8.3	7.0	7.0	5.9	8.9	9.8	8.2	7.6	6.7
31	9.2	11.0	12.3	11.1	12.2	12.3	13.9	12.0	11.6	13.3	14.2	14.5	13.2	11.9	12.9	11.6	12.5
33	1.1	1.4	.9	.7	1.4	.7	.9	.3	.7	.7	1.0	1.0	.9	1.1	.9	1.0	.8
34	2.8	2.4	1.9	1.3	1.8	1.9	2.2	1.7	2.6	2.1	1.7	2.1	2.9	1.1	1.8	2.8	2.7
41	6.4	4.0	5.8	5.7	5.0	5.5	6.9	5.3	5.7	8.4	6.1	5.6	4.6	4.8	5.6	4.5	5.0
42	2.6	3.6	3.0	2.4	2.2	2.0	2.7	3.2	2.9	2.3	2.2	2.5	2.4	2.8	2.5	2.8	3.2
43	1.4	2.4	2.3	2.3	2.0	2.6	2.2	2.4	2.8	1.7	2.4	1.2	2.1	1.8	2.3	3.2	2.1

45N	91	41	24	45	25	42	22	33	35	18	19	29	19	20	19	51	36
51	11.9	11.1	10.8	11.0	11.4	12.5	12.7	12.4	10.6	11.2	14.0	13.5	12.5	12.7	11.6	12.8	12.4
00N	5	25	5	5	16	23	6	20	10	8	13	6	3	8	13	13	30
D	2940	2965	933	940	1000	909	860	977	3040	832	899	911	875	899	917	3085	926
M	555	455	286	379	396	359	365	312	478	421	339	493	451	402	369	523	418
Sent Length	42.8	38.1	71.2	47.9	34.9	40.6	63.9	40.0	48.7	55	76.4	44.1	38.1	29.7	36.2	72.9	50
Init/41 as %	45	32	19	38	19	10.8	41.8	56.0	36.1	30	22.3	44	30.3	12.5	15.9	50	15
Init/Con as %	57	61	29	51	37	27	43.8	63.3	46.7	36.6	27	62	41.3	30.3	25.5	72	27.5
Strings N	75	58	71	90	63	74	99	91	74	89	144	94	98	86	76	60	86
513101N	84	97	145	119	119	127	172	152	94	145	224	156	128	140	122	141	136
310301N	85	89	48	82	74	74	86	70	113	90	62	98	112	91	90	81	78
310101N	2	8	3	11	11	1	1	1	13	6	28	24	3	4	6	17	7
//ismN	137	68	86	179	131	88	112	81	118	131	117	125	85	104	86	97	88
34(N)	98	82	67	47	64	66	76	58	92	71	60	74	100	38	61	97	91
311(N)	163	189	212	268	202	204	217	265	224	210	322	386	273	220	228	276	194
012(N)	8	7	2	2	3	1	10	1	4	2	16	15	0	2	5	6	0
030301N	15	5	3	3	4	5	5	5	3	6	6	16	6	8	4	9	5
015101N	76	71	45	111	72	79	62	73	96	72	65	39	60	65	45	37	59

Table 9.2 (continued)

CATEGORY	Defoe	Addison	Steele	Berkeley	Swift	Johnson	Gibbon	Austen	Carlyle	Hazlitt	Coleridge	DeQuincey	Macaulay	Mill	Ruskin	Hogg	Arnold
01	18.6	21.6	19.4	17.5	19.2	20.3	27.4	19.2	22.1	21.6	21.9	21.4	24.4	21.5	20.6	19.9	23.0
015N	88	106	76	120	97	110	183	125	156	99	97	116	175	111	122	100	141
02	8.3	8.3	7.6	8.7	8.0	8.9	7.5	9.4	7.6	6.5	6.1	6.5	8.7	6.9	6.2	7.2	7.7
023N	3	2	5	3	0	2	1	8	10	4	5	7	3	6	3	1	6
03	6.2	7.3	7.0	7.7	7.6	6.4	8.4	7.2	10.7	10.0	10.1	8.4	7.0	7.9	9.3	10.9	8.1
033N	19	15	17	30	17	9	0	12	43	14	28	21	6	21	48	16	7
04	1.1	.9	1.4	1.6	1.4	1.4	1.1	1.3	2.1	1.3	1.5	1.9	1.1	1.4	1.6	2.4	1.4
05	2.6	1.0	2.1	1.3	2.1	2.3	1.0	1.6	.6	2.2	1.1	1.3	1.3	1.5	1.1	1.5	1.2
06	1.2	.7	.9	.9	.9	.8	.1	.5	1.6	1.3	.7	1.7	.7	1.5	1.2	.5	1.0
07	.5	.5	.7	.6	.6	.8	.4	.8	.5	.7	.2	.6	.9	.5	.6	.5	.4
11	8.6	8.3	9.2	7.7	6.7	6.5	1.9	12.4	5.4	5.8	5.4	5.9	5.2	5.7	5.6	7.0	7.6
21	7.0	6.7	7.8	10.2	7.9	7.6	5.4	9.0	6.2	6.6	5.6	6.5	6.5	7.7	7.2	6.7	6.4
31	12.7	14.0	13.0	11.5	13.3	12.4	18.0	9.7	11.6	12.8	13.8	13.2	13.4	13.2	14.2	14.2	13.2
33	.9	.9	.6	.7	.7	1.1	.4	1.3	.8	.6	1.2	1.2	.6	1.1	.8	1.2	.7
34	2.9	1.5	2.2	2.1	2.5	2.5	1.2	3.5	4.1	1.6	2.4	2.9	2.0	1.9	2.6	2.7	2.0
41	6.5	3.8	4.2	5.0	4.7	5.0	6.5	4.3	5.1	5.6	5.3	4.3	4.2	4.0	4.8	4.9	4.7
42	2.8	2.3	2.3	3.8	2.3	2.6	1.2	2.2	1.6	1.6	1.9	2.2	2.1	2.8	1.9	1.9	1.9
43	1.5	2.7	2.1	2.4	2.4	2.4	1.6	1.0	1.6	1.7	1.7	1.2	1.6	2.2	1.6	1.5	1.9

45N	17	14	6	28	15	28	6	3	16	0	27	22	.8	13	12	9	8
51	11.2	14.8	13.4	11.4	12.9	12.9	15.3	10.8	12.1	13.2	14.8	14.2	14.6	14.7	14.4	12.8	13.3
00N	12	14	27	28	27	3	0	32	3	9	0	4	0	4	11	2	7
D	3180	796	881	989	923	893	479	912	3401	854	874	906	740	905	921	711	904
M	373	366	389	426	450	402	379	447	601	461	519	487	362	417	498	564	417
Sent Length	62	31.2	36.5	37.1	42.8	44.4	36.6	28.6	31.	31.8	38.5	32.3	20.5	42.5	42.3	32.2	28.2
Init/41 as %	12	4.8	2.1	29.1	25.4	8.7	5.2	1.3	8.2	.9	9	17.5	7	5	13	10.6	13.9
Init/Con as %	23.3	11.8	7.4	42.8	39.8	17.4	9.4	2.6	16.6	8.1	16.8	22.3	14.1	20	19.5	13.4	20
Strings N	8.4	141	128	73	108	110	133	69	88	118	138	109	140	120	138	106	120
513101N	160	168	151	119	158	148	215	99	90	136	135	141	156	126	154	118	146
310301N	65	102	91	83	125	64	158	54	108	99	135	110	106	81	111	144	78
310101N	15	4	17	6	9	1	7	14	21	19	13	18	16	14	15	13	22
//ismN	73	74	62	91	79	67	154	65	111	115	118	49	71	69	77	64	103
34(N)	98	51	75	73	93	87	42	117	143	54	81	97	68	64	90	89	69
311(N)	260	251	186	194	258	211	448	137	218	220	282	250	269	283	327	243	234
012(N)	0	5	10	0	3	2	6	13	34	23	4	26	9	30	17	12	4
030301N	8	7	14	11	7	7	3	8	33	14	13	10	9	9	12	6	9
015101N	25	87	60	61	66	68	126	50	72	67	78	67	99	100	65	56	78

Table 9.2 (continued)

CATEGORY	Newman	Pater	James	Stein	Strachey	Woolf	Fitzgerald	Chesterton	Hemingway	Orwell	Wilson	Davies	Burgess	Richler	Mumford	Reich
01	21.6	24.9	22.2	18.0	24.2	22.4	23.1	21.0	21.8	24.8	23.0	22.6	26.9	25.4	28.4	25.7
015N	147	91	116	169	167	170	174	128	127	165	153	155	190	122	176	160
02	7.4	4.4	5.4	10.4	7.5	8.4	8.1	6.9	8.1	7.3	6.0	8.0	6.0	7.9	5.6	7.6
023N	5	0	4	12	3	10	10	6	8	9	17	7	1	27	4	9
03	8.1	12.2	8.7	5.8	8.9	7.3	8.4	8.5	6.3	8.3	8.8	8.3	9.8	8.8	10.9	9.0
033N	11	41	38	11	37	20	49	32	16	32	16	26	31	14	17	34
04	1.9	1.6	2.4	2.2	1.5	1.5	1.1	1.4	1.4	2.0	2.1	1.7	1.5	1.5	1.4	1.7
05	1.4	.6	.9	.8	1.0	1.9	1.4	.9	1.6	.8	1.7	1.2	1.5	1.6	.8	1.5
06	.7	1.2	1.1	.7	1.2	1.1	1.5	1.3	1.2	.9	.6	.6	1.0	1.5	.9	.7
07	.5	.5	.8	.3	.2	.5	1.4	.7	.6	.6	1.1	.5	.9	.7	1.0	.5
11	7.2	4.7	6.0	10.7	5.8	6.4	7.1	5.9	7.4	5.5	4.9	6.7	4.4	6.4	2.4	5.3
21	8.2	4.2	6.0	9.8	6.8	7.4	5.9	8.4	7.3	7.9	6.8	8.8	6.8	6.0	5.2	7.6
31	12.1	15.1	15.3	10.8	14.7	13.7	14.1	13.2	14.6	12.6	13.1	12.4	13.1	11.0	15.4	13.3
33	.9	1.1	.7	.7	.7	.9	.6	.9	.6	.7	1.0	.3	.9	.4	.5	.2
34	1.6	2.2	3.1	5.1	2.7	2.0	2.8	4.0	2.9	2.8	2.9	2.0	1.9	2.7	1.6	1.6
41	5.4	4.1	3.9	5.9	4.1	4.5	3.3	4.6	5.0	3.7	4.4	4.1	4.4	4.0	4.1	4.4
42	2.0	1.0	1.9	2.9	1.6	2.7	1.8	3.0	2.7	2.3	1.9	2.2	1.5	1.8	1.4	1.7
43	2.5	1.8	1.6	1.5	.9	1.6	1.0	1.4	1.4	1.5	1.8	2.2	1.4	1.1	1.0	1.8

45N	16	10	8	6	12	15	11	17	17	4	13	2	1	18	17	24
51	11.9	15.7	11.0	12.8	12.2	14.1	12.5	11.7	12.5	12.4	11.3	12.9	7.0	15.2	16.6	12.4
00N	14	3	7	11	6	6	10	12	17	20	11	1	20	9	3	10
D	773	659	992	928	846	912	938	918	843	804	918	748	3257	950	766	896
M	428	499	421	478	413	491	463	388	506	436	401	462	476	516	595	435
Sent Length	23.1	33.9	21.3	28.7	25.4	37.4	22.7	28.0	25.5	22.9	22.7	19.8	28.1	37.6	36.2	37.4
Init/41 as %	8	8	7	10.1	7.4	16.6	4.6	.8	17.6	5.4	16	12.3	15.8	6.6	13.5	11.1
Init/Con as %	14.7	18.8	12.5	15.1	11.1	20.9	10.6	11.9	23.9	10	22.7	15.7	22.5	7.7	16.8	21
Strings N	84	153	60	94	83	129	73	87	112	74	85	115	33	149	173	98
513101N	116	143	104	107	121	135	113	167	138	147	158	153	88	177	134	123
310301N	117	150	86	103	103	90	106	66	104	97	90	122	72	113	152	95
310101N	34	25	41	34	12	15	30	6	19	40	20	14	28	16	5	14
//ismN	139	115	88	88	61	83	77	97	78	100	60	63	59	81	100	118
34(N)	55	57	84	65	66	97	93	101	138	98	67	91	176	108	78	55
311(N)	274	379	187	280	207	267	207	309	240	279	275	299	183	324	322	217
012(N)	51	57	95	63	34	13	52	25	29	72	21	30	32	19	9	12
030301N	20	25	25	25	9	15	11	9	21	28	21	15	2	20	39	5
015101N	81	129	93	129	76	80	78	62	69	75	69	90	26	71	114	77

Appendix A
FORMAL STATISTICAL TESTS

THE principal text of this book was written not for mathematicians but for readers of all kinds. Both for that reason and in deference to my own limitations, I have stayed away from formal statistical manipulations in the main body of the text. Nevertheless, it is useful even for the specialized humanist to be familiar with a few elementary statistical procedures, and I offer this appendix to entertain the possibility of such a familiarity. To be dealt with here are some of the most elementary kinds of statistics: mean and standard deviation, Pearson's r, and Chi-square. These were selected because they are relatively easily calculated, the numbers they produce are susceptible of being readily related to the texts of the samples, and they can be used in statistical significance testing by those who desire a completely rigorous treatment.

MEAN AND STANDARD DEVIATION

The mean is simply the average of a group of numbers. The standard deviation is a measure of the degree of dispersion of those numbers around the mean. For example, the following two groups of numbers each have a mean of 5: A (3, 4, 5, 6, 7) and B (1, 1, 5, 8, 10). The standard deviation of the first group, however, is 1.6, and the standard deviation of the second group is 4.1.

Standard deviation is computed by the following steps: (1) take the mean of the group; (2) find the difference between each member of the group and the mean; (3) square each difference; (4) take the sum of the squares; (5) divide that sum by $n-1$ (one less than the number of members in the group); and (6) compute the square root of the quotient of step 5. Thus in our two examples A and B above, the mean would be taken by simple averaging; steps 2 through 6 would go as follows:

(2) Differences between mean and members—
      A: 2, 1, 0, 1, 2   B: 4, 4, 0, 3, 5

(3) Squares of the differences—
    A: 4, 1, 0, 1, 4   B: 16, 16, 0, 9, 25

(4) Sums of the squares—
    A: 10   B: 66

(5) Sums of the squares divided by $n-1$—
    A: 2.5   B: 16.25

(6) Square root of the quotients—
    A: $\sqrt{2.5} = 1.6$ B: $\sqrt{16.25} = 4.1$

Mean and standard deviation have been used in stylistics to indicate the homogeneity and diversity, within individual word classes, of various groups of samples. Under the "authorship" hypothesis,[1] there should be less dispersion around the mean for any given word class in a group of samples from the same author than there would be in a group of samples of different authors. Milic used the technique in his study of Swift, and with a slightly different end in view I used it in my previous study of Sprat.[2] Because both Swift and Sprat were consistent writers, even when moving from genre to genre, the use of the standard deviation was virtually foreordained to demonstrate their consistency. What would the result be for a writer like Carlyle, the changes in whose style, repeatedly and specifically chronicled, are visible to the naked eye?

It is a very interesting question. Table A.1, in its way, gives us a surprising answer to it. Table A.1 is derived from the data displayed in Chapter 8, Table 8.5. It shows the mean and standard deviation for each substantial (1.0% +) word class for the following groups of samples: all five Carlyle samples (*Schiller, Sartor, Past and Present, French Revolution, Frederick*); four "late" Carlyle (all except *Schiller*); the 13 control samples. In addition for the same samples, it shows as n (number) figures for correlatives (class 45), pattern markers (61), terminal punctuation (99), and intra-sentence full stops (98).

In a Carlyle-Carlyle comparison (columns 1 and 2), we can note with some surprise that of the 20 categories displayed, 11 show greater homogeneity (lower SD) over the five works than over the four late works. Those categories in which the standard deviations grow with the addition of the *Schiller* figures are the categories in which demonstrated changes in his style took place: participles and gerunds (06 and 07), determiners (31), function adverbs (34), and subordination, in which his [subordinator-relative] (42-43) ratio changed from 1:2 in *Schiller* (abnormally low) to roughly 1:1 in his remaining works. Other categories in which the dispersion is greater for the five Carlyle works than for the four are the intrasentence full stop (98) and the very small (less than 1%) class of pattern marker

Table A.1 MEAN AND STANDARD DEVIATION FOR SUBSTAN-
TIAL WORD CLASSES, CARLYLE VS. CONTROLS

	CARLYLE ALL 5		CARLYLE LATE 4		CONTROLS	
	$\bar{X}$	SD	$\bar{X}$	SD	$\bar{X}$	SD
01	23.52	1.27	23.48	1.47	22.16	1.53
02	6.96	.56	7.07	.06	6.99	1.09
21	6.16	.15	6.18	.17	6.60	1.14
05	1.16	.27	1.13	.31	1.34	.53
06	1.80	.42	1.95	.30	1.84	.49
07	.58	.13	.63	.09	.55	.16
31	12.18	1.14	11.70	.47	14.64	1.07
33	.74	.13	.73	.15	.89	.23
34	3.30	.92	3.63	.65	2.26	.45
03	9.94	.75	9.80	.79	9.15	1.47
04	1.51	.44	1.53	.51	1.63	.33
51	12.56	1.17	12.21	.99	13.98	1.20
11	5.72	.88	5.73	1.01	6.00	1.21
41	4.98	.48	4.95	.55	4.54	.64
42	1.28	.30	1.40	.16	1.96	.41
43	1.34	.32	1.25	.29	1.71	.37
45	11.8	4.71	11.75	5.43	15.5	7.8
99	123.0	16.59	122.75	19.15	111.61	27.24
98	48.2	14.87	44.5	14.27	41.15	16.56
61	24.8	6.46	25.5	7.23	20.38	4.98

(The last four rows 45, 99, 98, 61 are braced together with the label n.)

(61). These greater dispersions can be accounted for. The dispersion in class 98 derives from the fact that Carlyle was more various in the ways in which he cut up his sentences than was any writer in the inventory after Bacon. The dispersion in class 61 is probably a feature of the size of the class; it is one of the smallest, and small word classes can vary greatly from work to work in one author.

In a Carlyle-controls comparison (column 1 vs. column 3), Carlyle's samples are more homogeneous than are those of the controls. His standard deviations are lower in 17 of the 20 categories. The three exceptions to the general rule are the determiners (31), the function adverbs (34), and the pattern markers (61). As we have already noted, the determiners and the function adverbs are two classes in which Carlyle made radical and visible changes in his style. The greater dispersion in class 61 is probably once again a feature of the size of the class.

I must say that I find this comparison surprising, for I had expected a greater number of classes to be more widely dispersed in Carlyle. I suppose that the statistics merely reflect a fact of the process of style formation: whatever visible changes a writer is able to make in his style, he is likely, on balance, to write more like himself than like any 13 contemporaries. Perhaps this is a useful piece of knowledge, and the standard deviation, although it cannot provide us with fingerprint information or exact criteria of identification, is a solid indicator of dispersion and homogeneity in any class over a number of samples.

Another use for this test arose in Chapter 4, "The Sentence," when we used mean and standard deviation to measure the degree of variation in sentence length in Macaulay and in the Psalms. The comparison can be found on page 33.[3]

PEARSON'S r

Pearson's product-moment correlation coefficient, r, is one of the most commonly used correlation coefficients; it shows the degree of (linear) correspondence or fit of one set of numbers with another. The set of numbers can be the distribution of word classes in one sample of prose (compared with the distribution in another sample); it can also be one word class or phrase in each of 50 or 100 samples compared with a different word class or phrase in each of the same 50 or 100. We shall offer both kinds of computation.

The formula for Pearson's r is as follows:

$$r = \frac{n(\Sigma xy) - (\Sigma x)(\Sigma y)}{[\sqrt{n(\Sigma x^2) - (\Sigma x)^2}][\sqrt{n(\Sigma y^2) - (\Sigma y)^2}]}$$

Σ means sum

To illustrate the use of Pearson's formula, we can take a hypothetical test of physical coordination, scored on a scale of 7, given to five pairs of brothers. We would like to determine the correlation between the performances of older brothers and those of their younger siblings. We call the older brothers group X and the younger brothers group Y. The results are as follows:

| | Group X (Older) | | Group Y (Younger) | | |
Name	X	X²	Y	Y²	XY
Doe	3	9	5	25	15
Jones	3	9	3	9	9
Smith	3	9	4	16	12
Cluett	6	36	5	25	30
Brown	5	25	5	25	25
Sums	20	88	22	100	91

In this case, n (the number of pairs of observations) is 5. Having all the necessary numbers, we can substitute and work out the formula:

$$r = \frac{455-440}{\sqrt{440-400} \sqrt{500-484}} = \frac{15}{4\sqrt{40}} = \frac{15}{25.2} \doteq 0.6$$

The correlation, in short, is about .6. This working out of the formula is merely illustrative; one should have as many observations as possible, since sampling error is inversely related to n. Indeed, many of the results that we got from using Pearson's formula to compare one sample with another in the two-digit coding system (29 classes) were inconclusive because the standard error for this size of sample is so large.

In actual application, we set up five correlation matrices (Tables A.2, A.3, A.4, A.5, and A.10) to see how different groups of numbers were interrelated. The first three and the fifth matrices are correlations between word-class distributions of various writers; the fourth matrix compares the relationship among nouns, adjectives, prepositions, and prepositional phrases.

In the first matrix, we took five 720-token (30-card) cuts from three samples:

Cut A: Sample 9001   Lodge *Rosalind* Cards 90010001-90010030
Cut B: Sample 9005   Sidney Old *Arcadia* Cds. 90050001-90050030
Cut C: Sample 9002   Lyly *Euphues A/W* Cds. 90020001-90020030
Cut D: Sample 9002   Lyly *Euphues A/W* Cds. 90020031-90020060
Cut E: Sample 9002   Lyly *Euphues A/W* Cds. 90020061-90020090

The matrix is given in Table A.2. It shows what one might expect from reading: that the Sidney cut is more different from the Lodge and Lyly cuts than the latter two are from one another; and that the Lyly cuts are substantially more like one another than they are like either the cut from Lodge or the cut from Sidney.[4]

When we enlarge sample size from 700 to 3500 words, Pearson's r is likely to increase both between writers and within writers. The correlation matrix in Table A.3 is derived from four samples from the same three authors. As we might expect, inter-author correlations are lower than intra-author correlations, although far less dra-

Table A.2 CORRELATION MATRIX FOR FIVE 700-WORD SAMPLES

	Lodge A	Sidney B	Lyly C	Lyly D	Lyly E
Lodge A	—	.79	.82	.81	.80
Sidney B		—	.75	.77	.73
Lyly C			—	.94	.95
Lyly D				—	.97
Lyly E					—

Table A.3 CORRELATION MATRIX FOR FOUR 3,500 WORD SAMPLES

	Lodge	Lyly	Sidney OA	Sidney NA
Lodge	—	.9794	.9849	.9791
Lyly		—	.9841	.9836
Sidney (Old Arcadia)			—	.9947
Sidney (New Arcadia)				—

matically than when we are working with cuts of 700 tokens. More-over, such a result cannot be expected all the time. Correlations like those in Table A.4 have turned up.

These results, which seem to fly in the face of both common sense and our own experience as literary readers, can be explained. Especially anomalous is the correlation of .9313 between Bacon's letters and the *Advancement of Learning*. Bacon's style does have distinctive markings, in its techniques of cohesion, in phrasing, and in its "D" Value, which is extremely stable in our six samples. At the same time, Bacon sought—with evident conscious effort—to trim his style to his occasions,[5] and in many respects he was successful. We have already noted the wide dispersions from one Bacon work to another in such categories as period length or percentage of nouns. To some extent the weak correlations within Bacon's corpus are evidence of the wide range of word-class distributions available to him. To a greater extent, they reflect the varying demands of genre, subject matter, and audience. For example, Bacon's letters correlate with Sidney's letters more strongly than with any other sample of the first 100; generic factors—the suppression of nouns, the increased use of personal pronouns, the extent of unsignalled subordinations, and the shortening of period—overrode factors that derive from the dis-

Table A.4 CORRELATION MATRIX FOR SEVEN
3,500-WORD SAMPLES

		9009 Sid/Ltr	9015 Don/Ser	9018 Bac/Ltr	9021 Bac/Adv	9023 Bac/H7	9044 Bro/Rel	9046 Bro/Hyd
Sidney Letters	(09)	—	.9661	.9913	.9229	.9385	.9764	.8882
Donne Sermons	(15)		—	.9800	.9465	.9417	.9670	.9000
Bacon Letters	(18)			—	.9313	.9460	.9791	.8942
Bacon Adv't	(21)				—	.9797	.9731	.9792
Bacon Henry VII	(23)					—	.9791	.9803
Browne Religio	(44)						—	.9502
Browne Hydriotaphia	(46)							—

tinctiveness of each man's voice. Similarly, in a 27-sample matrix (Table A.10), the strongest correlation between *The Defence of Poesie* and any other work was not between it and another Sidney but between it and *Areopagitica,* which happens to be the only other work of the 27 cast as a public oration. And there are strong correlations among the hortatory pamphlets—between, say, Milton's early tracts and his late tracts (.9936), Sprat's *History of the Royal Society* (.9935), and the tract of Stillingfleet (.9956).

This is not to say that an *r* of .99 or better will give us infallible generic identification. After all, there is a .99+ correlation between our "New" *Arcadia* sample and Raleigh's *History of the World.* Nevertheless, two facts about Table A.10 are worth noting: (1) a high number of the correlations of .99 or better are generically related; and (2) certain unique works—Donne's *Devotions,* Bacon's *Essays,* and Browne's *Hydriotaphia*—show no .99 correlation with any other sample in the matrix, although this can also be said of *The Advancement of Learning* and others. Further probing revealed that although intra-author correlations are often weaker than intra-genre ones, *intra-work* correlations are the strongest of all that we turned up. In reference to this last point, we took three *pairs* of equally random samples from Bacon's *Advancement*, Sprat's *History*, and Hemingway's *Death in the Afternoon*,[6] and calculated correlation coefficients between the first and the second sample in each work. The coefficients were .9964, .9981, and .9957, respectively. It would seem, therefore, that an *r* in excess of .995 between two 3,500 word random samples would be strong *prima facie* evidence that they are from the same work, although we should be chastened by the .9956 correlation between early Milton and Stillingfleet in this regard.

Sample-to-sample comparisons of *r* suffer from a double limitation. First, the 29 classes of our two-digit code are too few for the reason previously mentioned; a 50-class code would be better suited for the computation of *r*. Second, things not especially relevant to the critical apprehension of an author's true voice tend to throw the results off, not only in correlation coefficients but, as we presently see, in other tests of fit between two samples. For example (Tables A.4, A.7, and A.8), the style of *The Advancement of Learning* is very close to that of *Henry VII*, far closer than the relatively weak .9797 *r* would suggest. *Henry VII*, however, has a considerable amount of quoted material in it (class 09), of which almost none appears in *The Advancement*, and the latter work has many Latin snippets (class 08), which do not appear in *Henry VII*; without these two classes, there would be a correlation of .994 between the two samples.

Applying Pearson's formula to the question of relationships between individual word classes in the language at large has been more fruitful. Using the 50 samples of Chapter 9, we considered a cluster of word classes and one phrase (51-31-01) to ascertain the degree of correlation between each word class and each of the others as well as between each word class and the prepositional phrase. In this test, the results were more gratifying. Table A.5 gives the correlation coefficients among noun (01), adjective (03), determiner (31), preposition (51), and prepositional phrase (51-31-01) for the 50 samples. We can note that, in contrast to the sample-to-sample coefficients, the range in this group is large, from −.26 to .75. There is a strong correlation between determiners and prepositions, as well as between determiners and prepositional phrases; there is a positive but moderate correlation between prepositions (51) and the standard prepositional phrase (51-31-01);[7] there is a positive but slightly weak correlation between adjectives and nouns and between prepositions and nouns. These results accord with those reported to me from the research in progress of other scholars in the field;[8] all reports that I have had thus far say that the two strongest mathematical relationships in the language are that between determiners and prepositional phrases (51-31-01) and that between determiners and prepositions.

The reasons Pearson's *r* works better on this type of test than on a

Table A.5 CORRELATION MATRIX FOR FIVE WORD CLASSES

	Noun	Adj	Det	Prep	Prep Phr
Noun (01)	—	.39	.06	.36	−.01
Adjective (03)		—	.18	.46	−.26
Determiner (31)			—	.68	.75
Preposition (51)				—	.53
Prep. Phrase (51-31-01)					—

sample-to-sample comparison are easy to see. First, it is possible in dealing with correlations between word classes to gather enough samples to reduce the standard error to manageable size. Second, there are no writers who throw the results off by using, say, no prepositions or no determiners.

To sum up, Pearson's formula may be a useful but by no means conclusive instrument for establishing an hypothesis about the identity or genre of a particular sample, provided the sample is random in character and of sufficient length. And, given a sufficient sample base, it can describe consistently and accurately the mathematical relationships among phenomena in the language at large—not only among word classes but between them and various phrase groups.

THE CHI-SQUARE TEST

The Chi-square test provides an indication of the covariance of two categorical variables; as such, it gives a test of the independence of the variables. Applied to samples of language, it can give us a very good idea of the goodness of fit between the word-class distributions of two different samples.[9] For this purpose it is a more sensitive test than is Pearson's r. The Chi-square formula can be stated thus:

$$\chi^2 = \sum \frac{(f_o - f_e)^2}{f_c},$$

where f_o is the observed frequency, and f_e is the frequency "expected" under some hypothesis. In applying the test to two different word-class distributions, we would execute the formula for each word class for each author being compared and add all these results together to arrive at a total χ^2 for the two samples. For illustrative purposes, we can take four word classes from two different samples; these word classes are the noun (01), all classes of verb (02, 21, 05, 06, 07), the adjective (03), and the adverb (04). Their totals are given

Table A.6 FREQUENCY DISTRIBUTION OF FOUR WORD CLASSES FOR TWO SAMPLES

	Nouns	Verbs	Adjectives	Adverbs	Total
Sample A	160 (159.90)	47 (50.95)	32 (26.02)	6 (8.13)	245
Sample B	135 (135.10)	47 (43.05)	16 (21.98)	9 (6.87)	207
Total	295	94	48	15	452

in Table A.6. A "null" hypothesis in this case would be that sample identity is unrelated to part-of-speech distribution. The expected cell frequencies (f_e), derived from the "Total" row,[10] are in parentheses in Table A.6. Notice that the totals of f_e expected frequency, are the same as those for f_0, observed frequency. The x^2 values and totals for Table A.6 are as follows:

Sample A	0.000	0.313	1.384	0.558	2.255
Sample B	0.000	0.372	1.636	0.660	2.668
Total	0.000	0.685	3.020	1.218	4.923

To decide whether a x^2 value is surprising, one must compare it, using commonly available tables, with its number of "degrees of freedom." A contingency table having R rows and C columns has $(R-1)(C-1)$ degrees of freedom. Therefore the above table has $(2-1)(4-1)$ or 3 degrees of freedom. Consultation with a x^2 table reveals that a total x^2 of 4.923 is surprising. On the basis of this evidence, we would reject the null hypothesis and would conclude, pending further verification, that sample identity and part of speech distribution are related to each other, in other words, that an individual sample has a distinctive distribution rather than one determined by the characteristics of the language at large.

We applied the test to two-digit word-class distributions from seven samples as follows:

9000 Ascham *Scholemaster*
9021 Bacon *Advancement of Learning*
9022 Bacon *Advancement of Learning*
9023 Bacon *Henry VII*
9044 Browne *Religio Medici*

Table A.7 CHI-SQUARE MATRIX FOR SEVEN SAMPLES

		ADV'T 9021	ADV'T 9022	HEN 7 9023	REL. M. 9044	adv't 9551	smstr 9548
SCHOLEMASTER	9000	193	176	222	296	108	59
ADVANCEMENT	9021		79	219	218	108	113
ADVANCEMENT	9022			115	139	100	108
HENRY VII	9023				194	73	165
RELIGIO	9044					162	143
advancement	9551						62

We also added translations of the 750-word selections from Ascham and Bacon that appear in Louis Milic's *Stylists on Style.* These partial samples we designated 9648 (scholemaster) and 9551 (advancement). The Chi-square matrix is given in Table A.7. There were 30 degrees of freedom in each comparison.

All of the results are "surprising" because with 30 degrees of freedom a x^2 of 60 or larger has a very small probability. Therefore we must reject the null hypothesis and conclude that sample identity *is* related to word usage, even for different samples by the same author. Remembering that the smaller the x^2 the better the fit, we can rank the degrees of fit as follows:

1. SCHOLEMASTER—scholemaster   59
2. advancement—scholemaster   62
3. ADVANCEMENT—ADVANCEMENT   79
4. ADVANCEMENT—advancement   100
5. SCHOLEMASTER—advancement   108
6. ADVANCEMENT—advancement   108

Except for the anomalies of #2 and #5, the Chi-square test confirms what we intuitively know: that samples from the same work tend to be more alike than samples from different works. The Chi-square test, however, like Pearson's *r,* is thrown off by the presence of small and volatile classes that appear in some samples but not in others. For example, the comparison among the three *Advancement* samples is badly thrown off by class 08, which occurs 102 times in the first full-size sample, 27 times in the second full-size sample, but not at all in the 750-word sample. Similar distortion is introduced by classes 09, 44, 71, and 97. By eliminating these five classes and refiguring the x^2 values, we arrive at the results given in Table A.8. There are now 25 degrees of freedom. Values of x^2 of 37 or less are "unsurprising."[11] We may conclude, therefore, that the *Scholemas-*

Table A.8 CHI-SQUARE MATRIX FOR SEVEN SAMPLES WITH SOME WORD CLASSES DELETED

	ADVT	ADVT	HEN 7	REL. M	advt	schol
SCHOLEMASTER	167	148	196	281	91	31
ADVANCEMENT		43	55	201	44	101
ADVANCEMENT			58	111	47	95
HENRY VII				166	48	138
RELIGIO					141	126
advancement						56

ter samples are not dissimilar to a degree that one could call statistically significant. The rank order of fit for this table is as follows:

1. SCHOLEMASTER—scholemaster
2. ADVANCEMENT—ADVANCEMENT
3. ADVANCEMENT—advancement
4. ADVANCEMENT—advancement
5. HENRY 7—advancement
6. ADVANCEMENT—HENRY 7

The removal of the volatile classes gives us a representation that accords with what we already know. Once again (as in Table A.7), there is a mild anomaly in the Chi-square between the two short samples, and once again *Religio Medici* shows as the most idiosyncratic of all the works used in the table.

Generally speaking, for the comparison of one sample with others, the Chi-square test is likely to be more meaningful than a correlation coefficient, at least with this grammar, in which the number of variables (i.e., of word classes) is not sufficient for heavy reliance on Pearson's formula.

A NOTE ON SAMPLE SIZE

It seems to me that any sample of 700 or more words of continuous discourse is likely to reveal major stylistic features of its author. The extent to which this is true within the conventions of the York Inventory will be examined in due course. First, however, it should be noted that for different purposes different sample sizes will be appropriate. A study of sentence length or complexity would seem to require a minimum of 500 sentences, which means in the twentieth century roughly 10,000 words, in earlier periods even more. A full study of initial connection probably should cover 500 to 1,000 sentences. Word-class distributions within the Fries-Milic grammar seem to be reliably represented by a single 3,500-word sample, provided that the sample is truly random: only in one case—that of George Orwell (samples 9401 and 9196)—have we seen substantial differences in the major word classes between one 3,500-word sample of a work and another sample of the same size.[12] The difference in Orwell's case is easy to account for: sample 9196 was a truly random sample of the whole of the Secker and Warburg edition of Orwell's *Essays*; Sample 9401 was a sample taken from only four of those essays. Even so, there were certain similarities between the two samples in phrasing, "D" value, sentence length, and some word classes. All our other sample pairs (equally random) have tended to behave like the paired samples of *Death in the Afternoon, The Advancement of Learning,* and Sprat's *History of the Royal Society;* i.e., they have tended to yield extremely similar information about the author.

Table A.9 compares four samples from the Chi-square matrices given in Tables A.7 and A.8. How valid are the two 750-word samples as indices of the styles of the works whence they are taken? One difficulty presented by the data is that these 750-word passages were selected by an editor for a book that had a specific purpose: to present important statements about style by eminent stylists. Each of the authors in the collection had thought a lot about style and knew what he was doing when he took up pen to write about it. Hence, many of the passages—these two in particular—bear clear linguistic markings of emphasis and/or grand style: higher M statistic, lower subordination (42+43), more formal parallelism (class 45).[13]

The factor above, plus the small size of the samples, introduces distortions into the partial samples, notably in strings, in compounding (class 41), and in use of the verb system (classes 21 and 02). Nevertheless, the 750-word samples give some interesting clues about author-to-author differences: Ascham's greater syntactic variety ("D"), his greater reliance on the modifiers ("M"), his extreme use of formal parallelism (45), his unique avoidance of determiners (31), his extreme penchant for the function adverbs (34)—all these plus Bacon's tendency to compound things (41). Nevertheless, we have no guarantee that these particular aspects of the respective author's styles would appear in other 750-word cuts. I am convinced that an unusually high or low "D" statistic will infallibly appear in 750 words of an author's prose; for example, I doubt that any 750-word selection in *Stylists on Style* has a "D" statistic as high as Ascham's 338. Other habits that are truly extreme for their time (like Ascham's "M" statistic or his avoidance of determiners) may well be likely to appear. It nevertheless seems risky to speak conclusively—at least within this grammatical convention—about the style of an author or work without having in hand at least one and preferably two 3,500-word random samples.

Table A.9 CHI-SQUARE FOR TWO FULL SAMPLES AND TWO PARTIAL SAMPLES

	SCHOLEMASTER 9000 Ascham (full sample)	scholemaster 9551 (SOS sample)	advancement 9548 Bacon (SOS sample)	ADVANCEMENT 9021 (full sample)
01	21.4	20.2	25.0	21.9
02	6.8	6.7	4.9	6.6
03	9.5	13.1	8.6	7.2
04	2.7	1.8	.8	1.5
05	1.6	1.8	2.3	2.0
06	.7	.4	.9	1.2
07	.6	.8	1.2	.5
08	.9	—	—	2.8
09	.1	—	1.5	.1
11	5.1	5.4	3.0	5.1
21	6.9	5.4	5.6	6.8
31	9.2	7.5	12.0	11.1
32	.8	.4	.3	.3
33	1.1	1.2	.9	.7
34	2.9	2.8	2.1	1.3
35	.8	1.0	.3	.6
41	6.4	5.4	8.2	7.5
42	2.6	1.8	1.3	2.4
43	1.4	1.8	2.1	2.3
44	.1	.1	.1	.7
45	2.6	3.8	2.0	1.3
51	11.9	11.0	13.0	12.0
61	.2	—	.7	1.0
62	2.1	1.7	2.3	2.1
71	.3	—	—	—
81	.9	.9	.7	1.1
91	.5	.7	.5	1.1
98	.3 (n = 10)	1.3 (n = 10)	1.1 (n = 8)	1.2 (n = 40)
99	2.3 (n = 81)	2.3 (n = 18)	1.6 (n = 12)	2.1 (n = 70)
00	.1	.1	.1	.7
"D"	1000/2885	388	339	940
"M"[a]	545	659	427	379
Strings[a]	75	41	104	93
Parallelisms[a]	137	189	184	187

[a]Normalized to 3,500-word sample size.

Whether the same stricture should apply to all grammatical conventions is moot. Some grammars reveal a lot more than others do about what is underneath the surface of a text. Stratificational analysis, for example, can treat cohesion with such exhaustiveness that perhaps no more than a 1,000-word sample is necessary for an exploration of an author's most characteristic techniques. Gutwinski's stratificational study of Hemingway, based on a sample of roughly 1,000 words, is fully compatible with the results of our surface study of a sample seven times that size. Clearly, proper sample size depends on what is being sought from the text and how the text is being analyzed. It also depends on the detachment and disinterestedness with which the sample is selected.

CONCLUSIONS

The purpose of this appendix has been to illustrate for humanists a few—and only a few—of the statistical manipulations that it is possible to perform on materials like those produced by the York Inventory. The interest of this book has been first descriptive and second interpretive. Although the material has been given quantitative expression, *statistical* techniques have been tangential to the book's main areas of concern. Scholars interested in the possibility of author-identification in literary works or in the use of literary materials for statistical ends should go to the work of Brainerd[14] and of Wachal,[15] each of whom in his own style presents an interesting range of possibilities in the relationship between literature and numbers.

Variables for Table A.10

1. 9001 Lodge, Rosalind
2. 9002 Lyly, Euphues, Anatomy of Wit
3. **9004 Sidney, Defence of Poesie**
4. 9005 Sidney, Old Arcadia
5. 9007 Sidney, New Arcadia
6. 9009 Sidney, Letters
7. 9014 Donne, Devotions
8. 9015 Donne, Sermons
9. 9018 Bacon, Letters
10. 9020 Bacon, Essays (1625)
11. 9021 Bacon, Advancement of Learning
12. 9023 Bacon, Henry VII
13. 9026 Hobbes, Leviathan
14. 9029 Burton, Anatomy of Melancholy
15. 9036 Taylor, Holy Dying
16. 9038 Taylor, Sermons
17. 9041 Raleigh, History of the World
18. 9044 Browne, Religio Medici
19. 9046 Browne, Hydriotaphia
20. 9049 Milton, early tracts
21. 9051 Milton, late tracts
22. 9060 Milton, Areopagitica
23. 9069 Sprat, History of the Royal Society
24. 9070 Sprat, Sermons
25. 9092 Stillingfleet, Sermons
26. 9093 Stillingfleet, tract
27. 9099 Dryden, Essays

Table A.10 CORRELATION MATRIX FOR 27 SAMPLES

	1	2	3	4	5	6	7	8	9	10	11	12	13
1	--	.979	.985	.984	.979	.963	.973	.958	.971	.977	.970	.984	.987
2		—	.982	.984	.983	.981	.976	.956	.987	.963	.933	.950	.968
3			—	.977	.979	.972	.969	.958	.976	.988	.971	.973	.988
4				—	.994	:987	.982	.961	.985	.958	.936	.963	.972
5					—	.991	.984	.964	.989	.959	.937	.960	.970
6						—	.985	.966	.991	.954	.922	.938	.957
7							—	.974	.989	.963	.938	.956	.975
8								—	.980	.955	.946	.941	.959
9									—	.960	.931	.946	.967
10										—	.982	.968	.982
11											—	.979	.980
12												—	.992
13													—
14													
15													
16													
17													
18													
19													
20													
21													
22													
23													
24													
25													
26													
27													

14	15	16	17	18	19	20	21	22	23	24	25	26	27
.984	.982	.985	.987	.986	.962	.991	.985	.979	.983	.976	.980	.989	.989
.966	.956	.952	.978	.975	.904	.965	.965	.969	.970	.958	.976	.958	.983
.985	.975	.975	.988	.988	.947	.985	.987	.990	.985	.975	.986	.982	.990
.963	.959	.959	.987	.979	.923	.975	.976	.963	.976	.967	.973	.969	.986
.963	.958	.955	.990	.978	.913	.967	.977	.962	.972	.956	.971	.964	.985
.954	.944	.938	.978	.976	.888	.954	.965	.953	.964	.951	.969	.950	.981
.958	.964	.962	.978	.983	.908	.963	.971	.957	.968	.958	.980	.965	.987
.970	.950	.952	.963	.967	.900	.947	.951	.942	.945	.930	.955	.949	.971
.965	.954	.951	.979	.979	.894	.957	.963	.957	.963	.948	.972	.955	.987
.986	.984	.983	.972	.987	.951	.982	.980	.989	.983	.975	.986	.981	.983
.980	.983	.986	.963	.973	.979	.981	.979	.977	.970	.962	.969	.984	.964
.965	.978	.986	.983	.979	.980	.990	.990	.972	.976	.970	.970	.992	.975
.977	.984	.988	.987	.989	.966	.990	.992	.984	.982	.975	.986	.993	.988
—	.977	.976	.974	.980	.950	.979	.974	.979	.972	.961	.972	.975	.981
	—	.995	.968	.982	.965	.987	.981	.987	.985	.978	.988	.985	.979
		—	.971	.982	.976	.990	.983	.984	.981	.975	.983	.991	.979
			—	.987	.947	.984	.991	.973	.981	.966	.975	.983	.991
				—	.950	.986	.989	.982	.985	.977	.989	.986	.995
					—	.980	.969	.957	.961	.965	.947	.982	.944
						—	.993	.988	.993	.989	.985	.995	.985
							—	.984	.990	.982	.985	.992	.987
								—	.989	.980	.989	.982	.981
									—	.992	.990	.988	.988
										—	.986	.984	.977
											—	.984	.988
												—	.985
													—

Appendix B

THE HOLDINGS OF THE YORK INVENTORY

9000 ASCHAM, Roger, *The Scholemaster,* Lawrence V. Ryan, ed. (New York, 1967): 34, 72, 108, 152, 146, 36.

9001 LODGE, Thomas, *Rosalynde* (London, 1962): 2, 7, 23, 33, 42, 52.

9002 LYLY, John, *Euphues: The Anatomy of Wit,* Morris W. Croll and Harry Clemons, eds. (London, 1916): 14, 44, 68, 106, 156, 174.

9003 LYLY, John, *Euphues and His England,* Morris W. Croll and Harry Clemons, eds. (London, 1916): 262, 290, 296, 304, 348, 394, 403.

9004 SIDNEY, Sir Philip, *The Defence of Poesie* (Meuston, England, 1968): C3, H3, G3, J, G, E2, N, B3.

9005 SIDNEY, Sir Philip, "Old" *Arcadia,* in *The Prose Works of Sir Philip Sidney,* Albert Feuillerat, ed. (Cambridge U. Press, 1912), 4 Volumes. Volume IV: 184, 254, 20, 116, 268, 330.

9006 SIDNEY, Sir Philip, "Old" *Arcadia, Ibid.:* 4, 64, 92, 190, 280, 378.

9007 SIDNEY, Sir Philip, "New" *Arcadia,* in *The Prose Works of Sir Philip Sidney,* 4 Volumes. Volume I: 48, 188, 256, 278, 298, 356, 390.

9008 SIDNEY, Sir Philip, "New" *Arcadia, Ibid.:* 6, 170, 292, 304, 336, 422, 432.

9009 SIDNEY, Sir Philip, *Letters,* in *The Works,* Volume III: 76, 176, 78, 122, 124, 126, 152, 154.

9010 NASHE, Thomas, *Peirce Penniless,* in *Selected Writings of Thomas Nashe,* Stanley Wells, ed. (Cambridge, Mass., 1965): 56, 64, 74, 78.

9011 NASHE, Thomas, "The Unfortunate Traveler," in *Shorter Elizabethan Novels,* George Saintsbury, ed. (London, 1972), 2 Volumes. Volume I: 272, 278, 284, 286, 294, 314, 328.

9012 PSALMS, in the *Bible,* King James Version (Cambridge U. Press, N.D.): 692, 696, 700, 704, 742, 744, 760, 766.

9013 THE ACTS, in the *Bible,* King James Version, (Cambridge U. Press, N.D.): 2:19-47, 3:1-18, 6:4-15, 7:1-60, 8:1-21, 9:28-43, 10:1-30, 12:1-25, 13:1-14, 14:9-28, 15:1-22, 16:28-40, 17:1-30, 19:13-41, 20:1-14.

9014 DONNE, John, *Devotions Upon Emergent Occasions* (Ann Arbor, 1959): 30, 32, 34, 77, 78, 80, 82, 102, 104, 106.

9015 DONNE, John, *The Sermons of John Donne,* George R. Potter and Evelyn M. Simpson, eds. (Berkeley and Los Angeles, 1962), 12 Volumes. Volume IV: 308, 384, 100, 202, 206, 278.

9016 DONNE, John, *Ibid.*, Volume VII: 240, 424, 54, 142, 174, 230.

9017 DONNE, John, *Ibid.,* Volume III: 74, 114, 164, 166, 184, 304.

9018 BACON, Francis, *Letters,* in *The Works of Francis Bacon,* Basil Montagu, ed. (London, 1825), 16 Volumes. Volume XII: 84, 90, 82, 86, 88, 90, 44, 50, 54, 58, 64, 66, 70, 82.

9019 BACON, Francis, *Novum Organum,* in *The Works,* 16 Volumes. Volume XIV: 34, 42, 50, 70, 82.

9020 BACON, Francis, "1625" Essays, in *The Works,* Volume I: 72, 168, 18, 140, 114, 100, 30, 46, 66.

9021 BACON, Francis, *The Advancement of Learning,* in *The Works,* Volume II: 52, 60, 130, 132, 178, 214, 220, 264, 300.

9022 BACON, Francis, *Ibid.:* 68, 80, 226, 94, 124, 242, 168, 240, 34.

9023 BACON, Francis, *The History of Henry VII,* in *The Works,* Volume III: 116, 195, 207, 228, 324, 338, 362, 390, 406.

9024 JONSON, Ben, *Timber,* R.S. Walker, ed. (Syracuse, 1953): 32, 90, 99, 58, 54, 42.

9025 HOBBES, Thomas, *Leviathan,* John Plamenatz, ed. (New York, 1963): 92, 178, 194, 340, 440, 468.

9026 HOBBES, Thomas, *Ibid.:* 22, 24, 148, 156, 320, 322.

9027 HOBBES, Thomas, *Ibid.,* Part III only: 294, 296, 316, 332, 424.

9028 BURTON, Robert, *Anatomy of Melancholy* (London, 1932), Volume I: 68, 100, 102, 34, 40, 58, 60, 66.

9029 BURTON, Robert, *Ibid.,* Volume III: 288, 324, 338, 378, 14, 40, 202, 190.

9030 BURTON, Robert, *Ibid.,* Volume II: 90, 228, 260, 276, 338, 348, 428, 62.

9031 CLARENDON, Edward Hyde, Earl of, *History of the Rebellion* (Oxford, 1702), 3 Volumes. Volume I: 40, 56, 95, 157, 267, 332, 423, 521.

9032 CLARENDON, Edward Hyde, Earl of, *History of the Rebellion* (Oxford, 1703), 3 Volumes. Volume II: 72, 155, 204, 311, 393, 459, 520, 554.

9033 CLARENDON, Edward Hyde, Earl of, *History of the Rebellion* (Oxford, 1704), 3 Volumes. Volume III: 503, 576, x, y, 296, z, 458.

9034 TAYLOR, Jeremy, *The Great Exemplar of Sanctity and Holy Life* (London, 1657): 485, 21, 126, 191, 208, 285, 333, 424.

9035 TAYLOR, Jeremy, *Ibid.:* 1, 40, 68, 198, 294, 338, 383, 8.

9036 TAYLOR, Jeremy, *The Rule and Exercise of Holy Dying* (London, 1857): 10, 56, 62, 84, 118, 130, 174, 176, 300.

9037 TAYLOR, Jeremy, *Ibid.:* 2, 8, 48, 92, 128, 234, 242, 244, 262.

9038 TAYLOR, Jeremy, *Sermons Preached at Golden Grove* (London, 1654): 174, 244, 310, 316, 36, 126, 50.

9039 TAYLOR, Jeremy, *Ibid.* (London, 1655): 46, 62, 72, 78, 94, 96, 140, 168, 186, 196, 240.

9040 RALEIGH, Sir Walter, "Voyages," in *The Tercentenary Edition of Hakluyt's Voyages* (London, 1897): 35, 36, 101, 100, 37, 86, 68, 67, 49, 48, 21, 20.

9041 RALEIGH, Sir Walter, *The Works of Sir Walter Raleigh* (Oxford, 1829), 1 Volume: 592, 618, 660, 710, 790, 876, 848.

9042 WALTON, Izaak, *The Compleat Angler,* R. LeGalliene, ed. (London, 1904): 24, 59, 83, 88, 167, 67, 52, 172.

9043 WALTON, Izaak, *The Lives of John Donne, Sir Henry Wotton, Richard*

Hooker, George Herbert, Robert Sanderson (London, 1927): 24, 52, 70, 106, 178, 296, 300, 400.

9044 BROWNE, Thomas, Religio Medici, in Religio Medici and Other Writings, Frank L. Huntley, ed. (London, 1951): 4, 14, 26, 32, 48, 72, 86.

9045 BROWNE, Thomas, Hydriotaphia, in Religio Medici and Other Writings, Frank L. Huntley, ed. (London, 1951): 134, 136, 98, 104, 110, 118, 122, 126.

9046 BROWNE, Thomas, Garden of Cyrus, in Religio Medici and Other Writings, Frank L. Huntley, ed. (London, 1951): 172, 182, 184, 196, 202, 216, 220, 228.

9047 BROWNE, Thomas, Christian Morals, in Religio Medici and Other Writings, Frank L. Huntley, ed. (London, 1951): 248, 256, 270, 278, 284, 286, 236, 240.

9048 MILTON, John, "Doctrine and Discipline of Divorce," in The Columbia Edition of the Works of John Milton, Frank Allen Patterson, ed. (New York, 1940), 18 Volumes. Volume III, Part II: 382, 390, 394, 400, 490, 496, 408, 468.

9049 MILTON, John, "Early Tracts," in The Columbia Edition of the Works of John Milton, 18 Volumes. Volume III. Part I: 42, 88, 144, 156, 176, 190, 204, 296.

9050 MILTON, John, "Readie and Easie Way," in The Columbia Edition of the Works of John Milton, 18 Volumes. Volume VI: 132, 136, 138, 142, 118, 120, 124, 128.

9051 MILTON, John, "Late Tracts," in The Columbia Edition of the Works of John Milton, 18 Volumes. Volume VI: 4, 14, 38, 88, 98, 158, 168, 176.

9052 LOCKE, John, An Essay Concerning Human Understanding, John W. Yolton, ed. (London, 1961): 180, 118, 210, 222, 276, 44, 78.

9053 LOCKE, John, Ibid.: 26, 48, 100, 114, 188, 204, 246.

9054 LOCKE, John, Treatise of Civil Government (II), Charles L. Sherman, ed. (London and New York, 1937): 20, 36, 48, 78, 92, 100.

9055 RHYMER, Thomas, Essays, Curt A. Zimansky, ed. (New Haven, 1956): 68, 74, 76, 8, 18, 30, 36, 56.

9056 RHYMER, Thomas, Ibid.: 172, 82, 98, 112, 118, 130, 158, 170.

9057 COLLIER, Jeremy, A Short View of the Immorality and Profaneness of the English Stage (London, 1698): 20, 38, 40, 66, 68, 84, 92, 108, 112.

9058 COWLEY, Abraham, The Works of Mr. Abraham Cowley (London, 1711), 3 Volumes: 183, LII, LVIII, LXII, 624, 620, 616, 610, 612, A2.

9059 L'ESTRANGE, Sir Roger, The Mystery of the Death of Sir E. B. Godfrey Unfolded (London, 1682): 112, 1, 2, 8, 52, 56, 64, 106, 83.

9060 MILTON, John, "Areopagetica," in John Milton Complete Poems and Major Prose, Merritt Y. Hughes, ed. (New York, 1957): 742, 736, 746, 718, 720, 726, 732.

9061 ANDREWES, Lancelot, Lancelot Andrewes Sermons, G. M. Story, ed. (Oxford, 1967): 26, 32, 72, 126, 134, 244.

9062 HALIFAX, George Savile, Marquis of, "Advice to a Daughter," in The Lady's New Year's Gift (London, 1927): 4, 23, 14, 17, 43, 20.

9063 HALIFAX, George Savile, Marquis of, "Character of a Trimmer," in The Lady's New Year's Gift (London, 1927): 85, 57, 87, 99, 83, 66.

9064 BUNYAN, John, "Pilgrim's Progress," in *Grace Abounding and Pilgrim's Progress,* Roger Sharrock, ed. (London, 1966): 146, 254, 288, 360, 356, 222, 258.

9065 BUNYAN, John, "Grace Abounding," in *Grace Abounding and Pilgrim's Progress,* Roger Sharrock, ed. (London, 1966): 8, 29, 91, 15, 73, 100.

9066 COXERE, Edward, *Adventures by Sea,* E.M.W. Meyerstein, ed. (London, 1946): 4, 6, 8, 10, 48, 60, 62, 70.

9067 SPRAT, Thomas, "Life and Writings of Cowley," in *Critical Essays of the Seventeenth Century,* J.E. Spingarn, ed. (Bloomington, 1963), 3 Volumes. Volume II: 120, 124, 126, 130, 134, 140, 144.

9068 SPRAT, Thomas, *History of the Royal Society,* Jackson Cope and H. W. Jones, eds. (St. Louis, 1958): 20, 80, 130, 368, 428, 44, 324

9069 SPRAT, Thomas, *Ibid.:* 408, 102, 364, 118, 84, 56, 10.

9070 SPRAT, Thomas, *Sermons Preached on Several Occasions* (London, 1722): 402, 26, 28, 42, 114, 158, 178, 180, 216, 276, 330.

9071 SPRAT, Thomas, *A Relation of the Late Wicked Contrivance of Stephen Blackhead & Robert Young* (London, 1692): 20, 34, 36, 6, 8, 18, 20, 30, 32, 34, 72, 74.

9072 SPRAT, Thomas, *The Bishop of Rochester's Discourse to his Clergy at his Visitation in the Year 1695* (London, 1696): 6, 8, 14, 18, 30, 34, 38, 40, 50, 52, 60.

9073 GLANVILL, Joseph, *The Vanity of Dogmatizing* (London, 1661): 10, 12, 32, 34, 76, 78, 112, 114, 142, 144, 162, 164, 208, 210, 238, 240.

9074 GLANVILL, Joseph, *Essay Concerning Preaching* (London, 1678): 4, 6, 8, 10, 24, 26, 28, 36, 38, 40, 64, 66, 68, 70, 72, 74, 76, 78, 86, 88, 90.

9075 BOYLE, Robert, *Some Considerations Touching the Style of Holy Scriptures* (London, 1663): 4, 6, 34, 36, 38, 116, 118, 120, 130, 132, 174, 176.

9076 BOYLE, Robert, *Some Considerations Touching the Usefullness of Natural Philosophy,* R. Sharrock, ed. (Oxford, 1663): 42, 5, 64, 144, 152, 154, 278, 292.

9077 BOYLE, Robert, *Origine of Forms and Qualities* (London, 1667): 64, 108, 128, 150, 168, 184, 188, 216, 138.

9078 NEWTON, Isaac, *Opticks* (London, 1948): 184, 222, 262, 62, 88, 104, 123, 124, 174, 180.

9079 MARVELL, Andrew, *The Rehearsal Transposed* (London, 1673): 64, 84, 232, 144, 146, 188, 190, 224, 226, 394, 396, 4, 6.

9080 MARVELL, Andrew, *Ibid.:* 26, 112, 132, 178, 214, 276, 310, 156, 14, 170.

9081 MARVELL, Andrew, *The Poems and Letters of Andrew Marvell,* H.M. Margoliouth, ed. (Oxford, 1927), 2 Volumes. Volume II: 294, 318, 68, 120, 36, 316, 240, 272, 76, 168, 264, 216.

9082 BURNET, Gilbert, Three Sermons (1) A Sermon Preached Before the Prince of Orange (London, 1689): 22, 26. (2) The Bishop of Salisbury's Sermon . . . On the Fast-Day (London, 1690): 4, 8, 12, 22. (3) The Bishop of Salisbury's Sermon . . . for the Protestants of Orange (London, 1704): 6, 26, 12, 16.

9083 BURNET, Gilbert, *Bishop Burnet's History of his Time* (London, 1724), Volume I: 665, 765, 92, 165, 218, 320, 505, 532, 595.

9084 BURNET, Gilbert, *Ibid.,* Volume II: 15, 141, 174, 215, 340, 378, 473, 515, 524, 575, 643.

9085 BURNET, Gilbert, *Passages of the Life and Death of the Right Honourable John Earl of Rochester* (London, 1680): 4, 6, 8, 12, 14, 16, 38, 40, 42, 50, 52, 54, 78, 80, 82, 128, 130, 132.

9086 BURNET, Gilbert, *The Bishop of Sarum's Vindication* (London, 1696): 18, 16, 22, 24, 30, 32, 52, 54, 60, 62, 64, 66, 84, 86, 94, 96, 128, 130.

9087 TILLOTSON, John, "Sermons," in *The Works of Dr. John Tillotson,* Thomas Birch, ed. (London, 1820), 10 Volumes. Volume II: 80, 152, 298, 344, 352, 366, 424.

9088 TILLOTSON, John, *Ibid.*, Volume IV: 228, 396, 310, 454, 466, 500, 464, 188.

9089 TILLOTSON, John, "Tract," in *The Works,* Volume X: 312, 324, 342, 364, 372, 410, 428.

9090 WILKINS, John, Bishop of Chester, *Sermons Preached upon Several Occasions Before the King at White-Hall* (London, 1677): 104, 116, 156, 158, 60, 68, 144, 10, 8, 12, 24, 28, 44, 88.

9091 STILLINGFLEET, Edward, "Sermons," in *The Works of Bishop Edward Stillingfleet* (London, 1710), 6 Volumes. Volume I: 459, 78, 205, 620, 346, 388, 364.

9092 STILLINGFLEET, Edward, *Ibid.:* 35, 204, 252, 427, 485, 732, 655.

9093 STILLINGFLEET, Edward, "Tract," in *The Works,* Volume VI: 16, 24, 74, 188, 206, 248, 266, 344, 390.

9094 HOWARD, Sir Robert, *The Life and Reign of King Richard II* (London, 1681): 2, 64, 12, 86, 106, 140, 154, 170, 176.

9095 HOWARD, Sir Robert, "Misc. Prefaces," in *Critical Essays of the Seventeenth Century,* J.E. Spingarn, ed. (Bloomington, 1963), 3 Volumes. Volume II: 96, 98, 4, 6, 8, 10, 93, 94.

9096 DRYDEN, John, *Essays of John Dryden,* W.P. Ker, ed. (New York, 1961), 2 Volumes. Volume I: 150, 182, 192, 222, 254, 266, 278.

9097 DRYDEN, John, *Essay of Dramatick Poesie,* in *Essays,* Volume I: 28, 40, 54, 60, 78, 80, 96.

9098 DRYDEN, John, *Original and Progress of Satire,* in *Essays,* Volume II: 86, 104, 112, 28, 34, 50, 68, 72.

9099 DRYDEN, John, *Prefaces and Essays,* in *Essays,* Volume II: 6, 148, 198, 204, 246, 234, 268.

9100 DAVIS, John, "Voyages," in *Richard Hakluyt Voyages and Documents,* Janet Hampden, ed. (London, 1958): 304, 306, 310, 312, 314, 316.

9101 SWIFT, Jonathan, "The Examiner," in *The Prose Writings of Jonathan Swift,* Herbert Davis, ed. (Oxford, 1939), 14 Volumes. Volume III: 48, 50, 60, 164, 124, 114, 38, 24, 150, 152, 148, 138, 140.

9102 GIBBON, Edward, *Decline and Fall of the Roman Empire,* William Smith, ed. (New York, N.D.), 6 Volumes. Volume IV: 92, Volume V: 416, Volume II: 466, Volume III: 576, Volume V: 344, Volume VI, 700.

9103 RUSKIN, John, *Seven Lamps of Architecture,* E.T. Cook and A. Wedderburn, eds. (London, 1903): 174, 175, 204, 264, 27, 82, 92.

9104 PATER, Walter, *Appreciations* (London, 1901): 36, 44, 52, 58, 60, 68, 78.

9105 ARNOLD, Matthew, *Essays in Criticism* (London, 1896): 86, 128, 232, 376, 54, 128, 246, 300, 196.

9106 JOHNSON, Samuel, *The Rambler*, W.J. Bate and A.B. Strauss, eds. (New Haven, 1969): 6, 40, 54, 28, 92, 22, 90.

9107 BERKELEY, George, *The Principles of Human Knowledge*, Simon Collyns, ed. (London, 1893): 156, 158, 14, 160, 146, 64, 76, 100, 52.

9108 ADDISON, Joseph, *The Spectator*, Donald F. Bond, ed. (Oxford, 1965), 5 Volumes. Volume I: 388, 230; Volume IV: 88, 212, 410; Volume V: 28, 44.

9109 STEELE, Richard, *The Spectator*, Donald F. Bond, ed. (Oxford, 1965), 5 Volumes. Volume V: 148, 462, 218, 356, 416, 110, 244.

9110 CARLYLE, Thomas, *Sartor Resartus* (London, 1896): 90, 140, 228, 232.

9111 MACAULAY, Thomas, *Critical and Historical Essays* (London, 1865), 3 Volumes. Volume I: 110–111, 378–379; Volume II: 328–329, 136–137; Volume III: 448–449, 244–245.

9121 DEFOE, Daniel, *A Journal of the Plague Year* (London, 1966): 80, 58, 120, 132, 212.

9130 JOHNSON, Samuel, "The Rambler," *The British Essayists*, Alexander Chalmers, ed. (London, 1802), Volume XII: 264, 88, 114, 60, 36, 18.

9135 MACAULAY, Lord Thomas B., *The History of England From The Accession of James II* (Philadelphia, 1880), 5 Volumes. Volume I: 318, Volume II: 476, Volume III: 134, Volume IV: 228, Volume V: 70.

9136 MACAULAY, Lord Thomas B., *The Miscellaneous Writings of Lord Macaulay* (London, 1860), 2 Volumes. Volume I: 80, 130, 179, 234, 273, 320, 374.

9138 DARWIN, Charles, *The Voyage of the Beagle* (New York, 1961): 74, 140, 204, 316, 484.

9139 FROUDE, James Anthony, *Thomas Carlyle* (London, 1911): 250, 292, 6, 92, 72, 504, 284.

9140 CARLYLE, Thomas, *History of Frederick the Great* (Boston, N.D.): 364, 502, 354, 304, 248, 158.

9141 SPENCER, Herbert, *The Principles of Sociology* (London, 1877), 3 Volumes. Volume I. 2nd Edition: 92, 78, 228, 389, 452, 172, 570.

9149 AUSTEN, Jane, *Letters to her Sister Cassandra and Others*, R.W. Chapman, ed. (London, 1952): 72, 196, 40, 352, 228, 242, 152.

9161 TROLLOPE, Anthony, *The New Zealander*, N. John Hall, ed. (Oxford, 1972): 104, 56, 178, 10, 120, 22, 188.

9164 STEVENSON, Robert Louis, *Sketches and Criticisms* (New York, 1905): 204, 206, 208, 24, 72, 116, 130, 186, 210, 284.

9166 CHESTERTON, G.K., *All I Survey—A Book of Essays* (New York, 1967): 60, 24, 48, 124, 130, 182, 258, 216, 248, 70.

9168 NICOLSON, Harold, *The English Sense of Humour* (London, 1956): 12, 46, 188, 138, 136, 152, 176, 94.

9172 HUXLEY, Aldous, *Point Counter Point* (London, 1933): 108, 76, 32, 290, 338, 252, 156, 458, 534, 471.

9179 JAMES, Henry, *Notes on Novelists* (New York, 1916): 20, 44, 118, 110, 280, 258, 350.

9182 WAUGH, Evelyn, *Brideshead Revisited* (London, 1945): 84, 142, 154, 262, 276, 344, 282, 342, 100.

9187 WOOLF, Virginia, *The Common Reader,* First Series (New York, 1925): 176, 138, 132, 204, 262, 246, 94, 62, 46.

9192 STRACHEY, Lytton, *Eminent Victorians* (New York, 1963): 66, 86, 110, 148, 184, 252, 262, 208, 12.

9194 BURGESS, Anthony, *The Novel Now* (London, 1967): 16, 88, 114, 40, 54, 178, 124.

9196 ORWELL, George, *The Critical Essays of George Orwell* (London, 1960): 168, 30, 56, 20, 190.

9198 STEINER, George, *Language and Silence* (New York, 1967): 166, 46, 56, 250, 122.

9201 DEQUINCEY, Thomas, *The Confessions of an English Opium Eater* (London, 1948): 51, 53, 60, 57, 58, 26.

9202 HAZLITT, William, "Selected Essays," in *Prose of The Romantic Period,* Carl Ray Woodring, ed. (Boston, 1961): 51, 52, 53, 125, 768, 299.

9203 DEQUINCEY, Thomas, *The Confessions of an English Opium Eater* (London, 1948): 28, 190, 192, 169, 170.

9204 HAZLITT, William, "Selected Essays," in *Prose of The Romantic Period,* Carl Ray Woodring, ed. (Boston, 1961): 300, 325, 326, 176, 178, 91.

9205 COLERIDGE, Samuel Taylor, *Biographia Literaria,* W.L. Allison, ed. (New York, 1882): 250, 253, 261, 333, 169, 256, 308, 163, 191, 338.

9206 COLERIDGE, Samuel Taylor, *Ibid.*: 221, 199, 160, 145, 154, 654, 542, 555, 500, 448.

9207 MILL, John Stuart and Harriet Taylor Mill, *The Subjection of Women,* in *Essays on Sex Equality,* Alice S. Rossi, ed. (Chicago, 1970): 124, 126, 128, 130, 132, 134, 136.

9208 MILL, John Stuart, *On Liberty,* in *A Selection of the Works of John Stuart Mill,* John M. Robson, ed. (Toronto, 1966): 2, 4, 6, 8, 10, 12.

9209 NEWMAN, John Henry, *The Idea of a University,* Charles F. Harold, ed. (New York, 1947): 195, 68, 90, 198, 4, 146.

9210 NEWMAN, John Henry, *Ibid.*: 326, 286, 376, 268, 394, 310.

9211 HOGG, Thomas Jefferson, *The Life of Percy Bysshe Shelley,* Edward Moxon, ed. (London, 1858), 4 Volumes. Volume I. Part I: 48, 50, 76, 106, 108, 110, 201, 203.

9212 HOGG, Thomas Jefferson, *Ibid.*: 138, 140, 2, 88, 90, 220, 222, 224, 183, 184, 186.

9213 MILL, John Stuart and Harriet Taylor Mill, *The Enfranchisement of Women,* in *Essays on Sex Equality,* Alice S. Rossi, ed. (Chicago, 1970): 93, 94, 96, 98, 102, 104, 106, 108, 110, 112, 114, 116, 118, 120.

9214 MILL, John Stuart, *Utilitarianism,* in *A Selection of the Works of John Stuart Mill,* John M. Robson, ed. (Toronto, 1966): 150, 152, 154, 156, 158, 160, 162.

9215 MILL, John Stuart, "Marriage and Divorce," in *A Selection of the Works of John Stuart Mill,* John M. Robson, ed. (Toronto, 1966): 86, 84, 67, 68, 70, 72, 74, 76, 78, 80, 82.

9216 CARLYLE, Thomas, *The Life of Friedrich Schiller,* in *The Collected Works of Thomas Carlyle* (London, 1869), 34 Volumes. Volume XXXIV: 200, 78, 62, 40, 154, 174.

9301 HEMINGWAY, Ernest, *Death in the Afternoon* (New York, 1932): 7, 48, 58, 79, 99, 119, 155, 189, 213, 235, 237.

9302 FRANKLIN, Benjamin, *Autobiography* (New York, 1940): 28, 30, 66, 78, 110, 204.

9313 TWAIN, Mark, *Humorous Sketches,* Charles Neider, ed. (New York, 1961): 64, 128, 264, 490, 558, 316.

9316 MENCKEN, H.L., *A Mencken Crestomathy* (New York, 1962): 226, 486, 52, 298, 558, 164, 434.

9318 STEIN, Gertrude, *Paris France* (New York, 1970): 4, 60, 66, 32, 94, 54, 34, 86, 52.

9319 HEMINGWAY, Ernest, *Death in the Afternoon* (New York, 1932): 38, 48, 128, 194, 222, 246.

9323 FITZGERALD, F. Scott, *The Crack-up,* Edmund Wilson, ed. (New York, 1946): 78, 40, 50, 226, 56, 34.

9324 FITZGERALD, F. Scott, *Tender is the Night* (New York, 1931): 24, 14, 180, 272, 76, 120, 232, 248, 296.

9327 WILSON, Edmund, *Axel's Castle* (New York, 1931): 24, 14, 180, 272, 76, 120, 232, 248, 296.

9329 MUMFORD, Lewis, *Technics and Civilization* (New York, 1934): 422, 258, 190, 28, 384, 108.

9336 NABOKOV, Vladimir, *Lolita* (New York, 1957): 38, 214, 40, 160, 58.

9345 ADAMS, Henry, *The Education of Henry Adams* (New York, 1918): 32, 486, 132, 274, 16, 220.

9346 POUND, Ezra, *Literary Essays of Ezra Pound,* T.S. Eliot, ed. (New York, 1968): 224, 306, 10, 102, 420, 394, 286.

9401 ORWELL, George, *A Collection of Essays* (Garden City, 1954): 44, 208, 52, 268, 140, 158, 170.

9402 REICH, Charles, *The Greening of America* (New York, 1971): 276, 60, 236, 144, 348, 14, 188.

9611 CALLAGHAN, Morley, *A Native Argosy* (New York, 1929): 32, 136, 222, 306. *Strange Fugitive* (Edmonton, 1970): 10, 118, 212.

9614 DAVIES, Robertson, *A Voice From the Attic* (Toronto, 1960): 38, 10, 24, 140, 106, 192, 280, 292.

9617 RICHLER, Mordecai, *Hunting Tigers Under Glass* (New York, 1968): 78, 82, 108, 116, 138, 52.

9622 BERTON, Pierre, *The Smug Minority* (Toronto, 1968): 36, 46, 56, 84, 98, 116, 138.

9625 FRYE, Northrop, *Anatomy of Criticism* (New York, 1969): 122, 52, 220, 60, 18.

9627 McLUHAN, H. Marshall, *Understanding Media* (New York, 1964): 40, 26, 268, 242, 138, 110.

9701 CARLYLE, Thomas, *Past and Present,* Richard Altick, ed. (Boston, 1965): 146, 192, 8, 74, 260, 60, 110.

9703 CARLYLE, Thomas, *The French Revolution* (New York, 1947): 478, 158, 372, 668, 574, 30.

NOTES

Chapter 1

[1] L.T. Milic, *Style & Stylistics* (New York, 1967).

[2]Frederick Mosteller and David L. Wallace, *Inference and Disputed Authorship: The Federalist* (Reading, Mass., 1964).

[3]W. Fucks, "Possibilities of Exact Style Analysis," in J. Strelka, ed., *Patterns of Literary Style* (New York, 1971), p. 83.

[4]Barron Brainerd, "Semi-lattices and Taxonomic Systems," *NOUS,* IV (1970), 189–199; "An Exploratory Study of Pronouns and Articles as Indices of Genre in English," *LANGUAGE & STYLE,* 5 (1972), 239–259; "On the Distinction between a Novel and a Romance," *Computers & the Humanities,* 7 (1973), 259–270; "On the Number of Words a Character Speaks in the Plays of Shakespeare," *Computer Studies in the Humanities & Verbal Behavior,* IV (1973), 57–63.

[5]Mosteller and Wallace, "Inference"; R. Wachal, "Linguistic Evidence, Statistical Inference, and Disputed Authorship" (unpub. Wisconsin dissertation, 1966).

[6]Louis T. Milic, "Metaphysical Criticism of Style," in Martin Steinmann, ed., *New Rhetorics* (New York, 1967), pp. 161–175.

[7]Cf. "Computer Content Analysis for Measuring Attitudes . . .," by Ole R. Holsti, *Computer Studies in the Humanities & Verbal Behavior,* 1 (1968), 200–216.

[8]B. Vickers, *Francis Bacon and Renaissance Prose* (Cambridge, England, 1968), pp. 27–33.

Chapter 2

[1]For detailed accounts, see E.P.J. Corbett, *Classical Rhetoric for the Modern Student* (New York, 1965), pp. 549–566, and George Williamson, *The Senecan Amble* (Chicago, 1952), pp. 93–102.

[2]M. Steinmann, editorial note in *New Rhetorics,* M. Steinmann, ed. (New York, 1967), p. 176.

[3]*Ibid., passim.*

[4]James Sledd, "Some Notes on English Prose Style," in J.V. Cunningham, ed., *The Problem of Style* (New York, 1966), pp. 185–204.

[5]L.T. Milic, *Stylists on Style* (New York, 1969), pp. 2–8.

[6]*Viz* The enormous number of HOWTOTHINK books that had such a

vogue in freshman English courses in the decade 1945–1954: *Think Before You Write, Better Prose through Better Thinking,* and so forth. Interestingly, the only survivor of this great heyday of organic form in the teaching of college composition is James McCrimmon's *Writing With a Purpose* (Boston, 1952), which was based on the actual problems confronting the student.

[7]B. Croce, "Indivisibility of Expression," in Cunningham, *Problem of Style,* p. 206.

[8]*Ibid.,* p. 208.

[9]E.g., Montaigne, Hemingway, Buffon, Voltaire, Maugham, and others.

[10]L.T. Milic, *A Quantitative Approach to the Style of Jonathan Swift* (The Hague, 1967), pp. 44–48.

[11]W.K. Wimsatt, "Style as Meaning," in Seymour Chatman and S.R. Levin, eds., *Essays on the Language of Literature* (New York, 1967), pp. 369–372.

[12]See above, notes 2–5.

[13]R. Ohmann, "Prolegomena to the Analysis of Style," in Chatman and Levin, *Essays,* p. 403 ff.

[14]R. Ohmann, "Literature as Sentences," in Chatman and Levin, *Essays,* p. 238.

[15]L. Milic, *Swift,* pp. 74–75.

[16]M. Schapiro, "Style," in Cunningham, *Problem of Style,* pp. 19–56.

[17]J. Spencer and Michael Gregory, "An Approach to the Study of Style," in Donald C. Freeman, ed., *Linguistics and Literary Style* (New York, 1970), p. 83.

[18]The selection of such significant aspects begins with a literate and knowledgeable reader. Cf. M.A.K. Halliday, "Descriptive Linguistics and Literary Studies," in Freeman, *Linguistics and Literary Style.*

[19]Single idiosyncrasies are, no doubt, of considerable importance to any attributive study, such as that of Swift by Milic and those of the *Federalist Papers* by Mosteller and Wallace.

[20]For a look at the process in detail, see Roald Dahl's story, "Taste," in *Someone Like You* (New York, 1953).

[21]For studies of stable generic properties, see the articles by Brainerd cited in Chapter 1, footnote 4. See also Jean Starobinski, "The Style of Autobiography," in Seymour Chatman, ed., *Literary Style: A Symposium* (New York, 1971).

[22]J. Suter, ed., *A Book of English Collects* (New York, 1925), pp. 3–6.

[23]Isocolon—syllabic equality among the members of a period, a common device in liturgical prose. "Have mercy upon us; have mercy upon us, Most merciful Father," is an instance of isocolon, three successive six-syllable members.

[24]See Suter's introductory essay to *Collects.* See also M. Croll, "The Cadence of English Oratorical Prose," in *Style, Rhetoric, Rhythm* (Princeton, 1966), pp. 303–360.

[25]Spencer and Gregory, "Approach to the Study of Style," p. 75.

[26]See Chatman, *Literary Style,* pp. 55, 63. See also Alphonse Juilland in Chatman and Levin, *Essays,* p. 380: "The conception of stylistics as a 'Science of deviations' . . . can cloud irremediably one's perspective on the set of literary features. . . ."

[27]I. Watt, "The First Paragraph of the Ambassadors: An Explication," in H.S. Babb, ed., *Essays in Stylistic Analysis* (New York, 1972).

[28]W. Nelson Francis, "Syntax and Literary Interpretation," in Chatman and Levin, *Essays,* pp. 209–216.

[29]See Curtis W. Hayes, "A Study in Prose Styles," in Freeman, *Linguistics and Literary Style,* pp. 279–296.

[30]The contrast here would be between cuts of the length of Gutwinski's and Milic's (350 to 700 words per cut), which can be read as coherent pieces of discourse of interest to the literary critic, and those of Brainerd (50 to 100 words per cut), which are of interest largely as mathematical artifacts.

[31]Sample-to-sample reliability for various sample sizes is discussed in Appendix A. Split samples showed internal reliabilities ranging from .90 (1,400 words) to .99 (3,500 word samples). Milic's statistical work in Chapter VI of his *Swift* pointed to such an outcome.

[32]C.C. Fries, *The Structure of English* (New York, 1952).

[33]E.g., its conflation of the pattern markers *there* and *it* with the infinitive signal *to,* its inclusion of *not* as an intensifier.

Chapter 3

[1]Full listing in Appendix B.

[2]Such cases would include works like Milton's *Areopagitica,* for which we used the Hughes edition, in which the page size is too large and the work too short for random sampling.

[3]See Chapter 1, note 4.

[4]See "Against the Typology of Styles," in Chatman and Levin, *Essays.*

[5]Internal reliability, along with other statistical concepts, is discussed in Appendix A.

[6]C.C. Fries, *The Structure of English,* pp. 92–94.

[7]*Ibid.,* p. 93.

[8]The limit of 1,000 is imposed by the amount of core originally available to us on the York Computer. A "D" statistic above 1,000 is measured by the word of text at which 1,000 was reached and is expressed 1000/2984 (the "D" statistic reached 1,000 at the 2984th word of text). The higher an author's "D," the sooner he will reach 1,000.

[9]A single-sample ranking of Milic's authors in the York Inventory in terms of "D" had Johnson highest, then Swift, then Addison's *Spectator* essays, Macaulay's literary and historical essays, and Gibbon. Milic's ranking had Swift highest, then Johnson, Macaulay, Addison, and Gibbon; Johnson's "D" range overlapped with Swift's. The reason for the minor differences in rank order are two: (1) we sampled only Addison's *Spectator* essays, which in Milic's studies had a higher "D" value than Addison's mean; (2) we took our Johnson sample from *Rambler,* in which the sentences are nearly double the length of the sentences in Milic's two samples, *Lives* and *Rasselas;* longer sentences tend to produce higher "D" values.

[10]Mean and standard deviation are discussed in Appendix A.

[11]The rise of the noun (its increase from roughly 20% of an "average" literary text in 1800 to nearly 25% today) is dealt with in Chapter 9. There has been a particularly dramatic increase in the number of nouns used attribu-

tively, and (partly in view of this evidence) it is our hypothesis that noun clusters in the twentieth century are far larger than they were 150 years ago.

[12]The addition of some dozen classes to the code, after the first 100 samples, demonstrated the utility of this procedure.

Chapter 4

[1]Robert S. Wachal in "Linguistic Evidence" gives an excellent summary of the research. Throughout this book, "period length" and "sentence length" are used interchangeably.

[2]In Milic's study of Swift and in my study of Sprat, "Style, Precept, Personality," *Computers & the Humanities*, 5 (1971), 257–274.

[3]See W.F. Gutwinski, "Cohesion in Literary Texts" (unpub. U. of Connecticut dissertation, 1969), to be published in a revised and updated form by Mouton in 1976.

[4]The mean is the average of a group of numbers. Standard deviation is the dispersion around that average. For example, the groups (2, 3, 10, 17, 18) and (8, 9, 10, 11, 12) both have a mean of 10.0. The standard deviations, however, are 5.0 and 1.1, the lower standard deviation reflecting the greater homogeneity of the second group. In sentence groups, mean length in words tends to be roughly double the standard deviation (e.g., the Sprat and Clarendon samples in Table 4.2), although the tendency is by no means a uniform law, as the Macaulay-*Psalms* contrast later on (Table 4.4) indicates. Appendix A deals with this and other statistical matters.

[5]Lucius Sherman, "On Certain Facts and Principles in the Development of Form in Literature," *University of Nebraska Studies*, I (1892), 337–366, and "Some Observations Upon the Sentence Lengths in English Prose," *University of Nebraska Studies*, I (1888), 119–130. Wachal, "Linguistic Evidence," p. 313, concludes that "the most useful variable in discriminating full-length essays . . . is the variance of period-length measured, not in words, but in units smaller than the word. . . ." The syntactic encoding of the York Inventory prevents our taking counts of vowels and/or syllables at this point, although we may later put the natural-language texts into machine-readable form.

[6]Bacon's *Novum Organum* sample had sentences averaging 35.6 words; his *Henry VII* sample averaged nearly 60 words per sentence. Similarly, Thomas Browne's *Christian Morals* sample had sentences averaging 26.8 words; the sample from *Hydriotaphia* averaged 43.7.

[7]Among the Inventory's pre-1660 writers, Sidney's mean sentence length (49.8 words) is exceeded only by two preachers, John Donne and Jeremy Taylor.

[8]The observation about Macaulay has been made several times before. In his examination of Macaulay's entire corpus, Sherman found the average period to be 23+ words long, a figure stunningly close to Milic's average for two samples of 21.7 and to the York average for one sample of 20.5.

[9]E.g., Milic on Swift, Cluett on Sprat, Gutwinski on Hemingway.

[10]The "biblicality" of Hemingway's style is discussed more fully in Chapter 7 below.

[11]The Pearson product-moment correlation is .706 for 97 of the first 100

York Inventory samples. In layman's terms, the relationship between the two is fairly strong.

[12]No doubt there are various ways that anaphora could be "counted." For example, the Macaulay sequence ABAAACAA might easily be counted six rather than nine anaphoric sentences (AAAA + AA). The count of six does not reflect the degree of anaphora in the passage, however. The technique of counting described in the text is the one that we have used since 1968, when we began with a pilot study of Sprat, Glanvill, Burnet, Tillotson, Dryden, and Hobbes. It seemed then and still seems to me the best way of counting under these conventions of syntactic coding. Ultimately the judgment of what technique is best is an intuitive one.

[13]The sentence openings are from Gibbon, Ch. XXXV, pp. 576–577.

[14]See the discussion of syntactic variety in Chapters 4 and 6.

[15]Figures 4.3, 4.4a.

[16]See R. Adolph, *Rise of Modern Prose Style* (Cambridge, Mass., 1968), and Cluett, "Style, Precept, Personality: A Test Case."

[17]Sprat, *History of the Royal Society,* Jones and Cope ed. (St. Louis, 1958), p. 112.

[18]The averages were 79 subordinators, 64 relatives.

[19]Chapter 6 of Milic's *Swift* suggests how the "D" statistic can be used both singly and in a cluster with other variables.

[20]The "D" program of the York Inventory stops when it comes to an intra-sentence full stop, then moves on past the stop. It would not matter, for example, if the Orwell statement on page 50 ended in a colon (code 98), the "D" program would still interrupt itself at that point.

[21]Entities like Gibbon (450), the King James Bible (550/710), Macaulay (740), and Sidney (six samples all over 1,000) are among the exceptions.

[22]Bacon had the largest range of any of our multi-sample authors in the following categories: (1) number of periods per 3,500 words; (2) noun subjects; (3) class 21 (auxiliaries plus the "be" system); (4) initial syndeton; (5) main verbs; and (6) nouns, verbs, and auxiliaries combined. Some of the wide dispersion can be attributed to the fact that Bacon wrote in a variety of genres; much or perhaps most of it can be attributed to the fact that by both philosophic predisposition and temperament Bacon was one of the most self-conscious writers in the Inventory.

[23]W.F. Mitchell, *English Pulpit Oratory* (London, 1932), pp. 305–306.

[24]The doublet was a source of stylistic differentiation for Wimsatt, Lannering, and Milic in their studies respectively of Johnson, Addison, and Swift.

[25] See W.K. Wimsatt, *The Prose Style of Samuel Johnson* (New Haven, 1941).

[26]This finding, tentatively put forward by Milic in Chapter VI of *Swift* (p. 230, fn. 169), has been revalidated again and again in the York Inventory.

[27]The two theoretical poles in a 3,500 word sample might be, say, three sentences vs. 220. In three sentences it is easy to achieve 100% variety (three different beginnings); in 200 sentences it is almost impossible. Clearly, as each additional sentence is written, a further possibility for variety is exhausted; or, alternatively, a previous pattern is duplicated. The greater the number of sentences, the likelier the possibility of duplication.

Chapter 5

[1]G. Williamson, *The Senecan Amble* (Chicago, 1952).

[2]Cf. Milic, "Against the Typology of Styles," in Chatman and Levin, *Essays,*

[3]This average increases markedly after World War I, to the point where today a "normal" style might be expected to have 24% nouns. This and other historical developments are discussed in Chapter 9.

[4]Burton does not come above the 23% line if all words of his samples are counted; he does come above that line if we count only the English words. The large number of Latin snippets in Burton (coded as 08) reduces his percentages for all classes of English words. His mean percentage of 08's per sample was 4.64.

[5]The reader should consult Rulon Wells's piece, "Nominal and Verbal Style," in Thomas Sebeok, ed., *Style in Language* (Cambridge, Mass., 1960), pp. 213–220.

[6]Cf. Milic, *Swift*, p. 196.

[7]The Pearson product-moment correlation is .42 for the 33 samples in this chapter, .36 for the 50 samples of Chapter 9. In layman's terms, there is a positive but not strong relationship between the respective phenomena.

[8]See Chapter 4 above.

[9]The correlation (Pearson's *r*) between determiners and nouns for the 50 samples of Chapter 9 is .06 (very weak). The correlation between determiners and the phrase 51-31-01 is .75 (strong).

[10]The correlation for the Chapter 9 samples, adjective/noun, is .39, a stronger index of nouns than any other, for those samples. But even this "strongest" index is relatively weak, a fact that supports our contention that there are many "nominal" styles.

[11]Carlyle meets our expectations *re* adjectives, but in no other respect does he do so.

[12]See the concluding chapter of James D. Koerner's *The Miseducation of American Teachers* (Boston, 1964): "L'Envoi—English or Psychemanto?"

[13]Milic's findings, based on two Johnson samples well removed from the one in the York Inventory, are parallel. See *Swift*, p. 164.

[14]Carlyle is treated extensively in Chapter 8.

[15]The selection seems arbitrary, and perhaps arbitrarily low for this particular group of 33 samples. Viewed in an historical perspective, however, 18.5% is not low: of the six writers in this chapter writing after 1700, Johnson is the only one to clear the 18.5% barrier.

[16]In the three-digit version of the code, "be" as a main verb (class 213) can be extruded from the other class 21's.

[17]Our researchers have run no verb-noun correlations. Barron Brainerd, working on our first 97 samples, found a large negative correlation.

[18]For a full discussion of Sidney's unique use of the verb system in his two *Arcadias,* see Chapter 6.

[19]The term is from Adolph's *Rise of Modern Prose Style*, p. 224.

[20]Newman's propensity for the modals doubtless derives from an affection for *should* situations, Mill's for *might.* In Fitzgerald's case, the high density

of "be" form tense auxiliaries (class 214) is related to his predisposition for -*ing* verb forms.

[21]See Figures 5.11 and 5.12.

[22]It seems clear to me that over the last 400 years the verbals have not behaved as a group. The decline of the infinitive, especially in subject position, combined with the rise of -*ing* forms, would seem to justify the separation. See Chapter 9, Figures 9.8 and 9.13.

[23]See the works of Sherman and Curme listed in the Bibliography. Sidney's total verbal percentages are all between 6.0% and 6.9%, Jonson's is 5.9%, both substantially higher than later writers. Cf. Chapter 9, Figures 9.8, 9.11, 9.12, and 9.13.

[24]See Milic, *Swift*, p. 181.

[25]We have not considered such things as participial adjectives (033), progressive tense forms (023), and absolute participles (068, 069).

[26]Cf. L.J. Becker and Clair Gustafson, *Encounter with Sociology: The Term Paper* (Berkeley, 1965).

[27]Orwell, "Politics and the English Language"; White, *The Elements of Style*; Koerner, *The Miseducation of American Teachers.*

[28]1,000-word sample of *The Protestant Ethic.*

[29]See Figure 5.11.

[30]Paul Roberts, *English Sentences* (New York, 1962), was the first venture into the field. By 1965, it was selling at an annual rate of 20,000 copies and had been joined by several competing entries in the field from other publishers.

[31]Louis Milic's 1972 paper at Bologna (Eleventh Congress of Linguistics) raises the question of how "transformed" the passive voice is.

[32]One would expect Reich, in view of his interests, to be the most passive of recent writers. He would not rank high on the scale in Figure 5.11, however; his passive main verb total is only 1.1%. Much of the Psychomantoid feeling that readers seem to get from his prose probably comes from repetitiousness, the unliterary devices such as mixed metaphors, and the awkward collocations that derive from his use of attributive nouns.

[33]The passage, with 0.7% passives, illustrates his normal avoidance of the passive voice. His entire sample showed 1.0% passive verbs.

[34]In Milic's study of Swift, intensifiers (class 33) usually were part of a normal distribution, for two reasons: (1) they included the class D adverbs that we have moved to class 34, and (2) they included *not.*

[35]See Chapter 3 above.

[36]Milic, *Swift*, p. 165.

[37]In "These Seeming Mysteries" (Columbia University dissertation, 1969), I encoded stratified samples of Sprat's early sermons, his late sermons, and his Visitation Discourse of 1695 (his last published homily). The "M" statistics per 3,500 words were all above 500, the top one being 720.

[38]Compared with Tillotson, South, and Burnet, Sprat was extraordinarily fecund in rhetorical question and exclamation ("These Seeming Mysteries," p. 240); his average, per 3,500 words, was 17 rhetorical questions and exclamations. Carlyle's figure for our *Sartor Resartus* sample was 17, far in excess of any other nineteenth-century sample we have at present writing.

[39]If, that is, by "biblical" we mean low in the modifying words.

[40]The Strachey sample, which was processed after the research for this chapter was completed, yielded over 24% nouns, as did many other of the post-1870 samples.

Chapter 6

[1]Croll, *Style, Rhetoric, Rhythm,* pp. 94–111.

[2]H.C. White, R.C. Wallerstein, and R. Quintana, eds., *Seventeenth Century Verse and Prose,* 2 Vols. (New York, 1950), Vol. I, introduction.

[3]Cf. E.S. Donno, *Elizabethan Minor Epics* (New York, 1963); Kenneth Myrick, *Philip Sidney as a Literary Craftsman* (Cambridge, Mass., 1935).

[4]An internal full stop is nearly always a colon or a semi-colon, although sometimes it is an exclamation point or question mark. It marks a place where, in the opinion of both translators, the author could have broken his single sentence into two sentences.

[5]We have been asked if "*by and for* the people" would count as 1, 2, or 3 parallelisms. The translation would be 512-411-512; the count would be of two parallelisms (the two 512's); 51-41-51 is not included in our series counts. As regards Sidney, Lyly, Nashe, and Lodge, the question is almost academic, since the construction is almost nonexistent among them. Indeed, the only place where I have seen it widely used is in documents written in legalese.

[6]See Chapter 9, Figure 9.1 and Figure 9.5. The history of the decline in English sentence length is almost exactly parallel to that of the decline in use of the coordinator.

[7]Gertrude Stein, as distinctive in her time as Sidney was in his, is a similar kind of anomaly in reverse: relatively short sentences combined with uniquely copious use of *and.* See Table 7.3 for Miss Stein's statistics.

[8]The number of adjectives per 3,500 words in Stillingfleet's sermons ranged up to 290, in Tillotson's to 278, in Sprat's to 403. In four samples of Donne the average was 187, the range 182 to 191. In three samples of Clarendon the average was 192, the range 182 to 202.

[9]Of the 80-odd writers processed to the present writing, only seven have failed to produce a 3,500 word-sample with 20.0% or more nouns.

[10]Lyly, 9003, *Euphues and his England,* p. 394.

[11]See Figures 6.12a and 6.12b.

Chapter 7

[1]D.S.R. Welland, "Hemingway's English Reputation," in Roger Asselineau, ed., *The Literary Reputation of Hemingway in Europe* (New York, 1965), pp. 20–21.

[2]Richard Bridgman, *The Colloquial Style in America* (New York, 1966), pp. 195–229.

[3]George Steiner, *Language and Silence* (New York, 1967), p. 30.

[4]A number of the pitfalls of stylistic typology are dealt with in Chapter 5.

[5]Earl Rovit, *Ernest Hemingway* (New York, 1963), p. 48.

[6]William Barrett, *Time of Need* (New York, 1972), pp. 73ff.

[7]N. Forster and R. Falk, *American Poetry and Prose* (New York, 1960), p. 1081.

[8]Hemingway received upwards of $250,000 for the film rights to *For Whom the Bell Tolls,* not only a record to that time but staggering in the light of the value of the dollar, the level of taxation, and the extent of unemployment (12%).

[9]Compare the Rovit citation above with the passages he himself selected as epitomizing Hemingway's critical thought. An interesting corollary to this contradiction is that when an author sets down his innermost essential thoughts about his craft he does so in a style other than his own or at least other than the one he habitually uses. A concept worth pursuing, had we but world enough and time.

[10]Rovit, *Ernest Hemingway,* p. 34.

[11]All *Death in the Afternoon* citations are by page number in the Scribner paperback edition: The Scribner Library, Lyceum Editions.

[12]Arthur Waldhorn, *A Reader's Guide to Ernest Hemingway* (New York, 1972), p. 133.

[13]Richard K. Peterson, *Hemingway Direct and Oblique* (The Hague, 1969), p. 56.

[14]For an extensive treatment of initial connection, see Chapter 4.

[15]Peterson, *Hemingway, passim,* but especially pp. 135–139, 197–199; Gutwinski, "Cohesion," pp. 101–117.

[16]The judgment that James and Wilson are "old-fashioned" is based mainly on three facts: (1) their sentences are longer; (2) there are fewer unsubordinated sentences in their prose; and (3) there is more subordination per sentence—all these comparisons being made against the other controls of this chapter.

[17]See Chapter 4.

[18]The passage begins, "I was always embarrassed by the words sacred, glorious, and sacrifice. . . ." It appears on pages 184–185 of *A Farewell to Arms,* Scribner Library edition (New York, n.d.).

[19]The case is similar to that of the legendary Victorian nobleman who, roughly once a year, at somebody else's dinner party, would swallow his spoon. The gesture was so startling that in the minds of his friends it came to constitute the entirety of his dining style, and nobody ever noticed that he ate left-handed and frequently with the wrong fork.

[20]Further possible patterns for a general test would be adjective-noun-auxiliary (03-01-21) and adjective-noun-verb (03-01-02), but of our control samples only Mumford, James, and Nabokov showed more than 8 per sample of either of these patterns.

[21]See Chapter 4.

[22]The un-nominal *Bible,* with a mere 17% or so nouns, produced a mean of 161 51-31-01 phrases. Cf. Chapter 4.

[23]The *very* un-nominal Bunyan, with roughly 15.6% nouns, produced almost as many 51-31-01 phrases as did the nominal Strachey (147 to 153). Strachey's noun percentage was 24.2.

[24]The obvious historical phenomenon of noun upcreep is dealt with in Chapter 9.

[25]The first substantive section of Chapter 4, "Nominal Styles," may shed some light on the Hemingway-James relationship.

[26]Cf. Peterson, *Hemingway*, pp. 119–132. *Death in the Afternoon*, it should be noted, is the high point of Hemingway's foreignism prior to *For Whom the Bell Tolls*. This much can be said on the basis of the obvious. As to which of Hemingway's most foreignized books (the two mentioned plus *The Old Man and the Sea*) is pre-eminent, no judgment can be made without some rigorous concordancing of a sort that picks up clusters as well as single words.

[27]See Appendix A,

[28]*Lolita*, Berkeley Medallion Books (New York, 1966), p. 176.

[29]In Peterson, *Hemingway*, pp. 122–132, there is a lengthy discussion of certain lexical and abstract features of Hemingway's noun clusters.

[30]Hemingway, with 3.1% main verb *be*'s (class 213) in both samples, ranked sixth of our 17 writers. Mean for the control samples was 2.5%. The difference may seem inconsequential, but expressed as a raw number (104 vs. 80) it is substantial.

[31]Cf. Chapter 4, treatment of the "D" statistic, and Chapter 5, "Nominal Styles."

[32]The cluster 42-11-21 (subordinator-pronoun-auxiliary) was, with five occurrences in 131 sentences, the second most frequent opening in our second *Death in the Afternoon* sample; at four occurrences in 121 sentences, it ranked fourth in the first sample.

[33]Gutwinski, "Cohesion," p. 114.

[34]The hypothesis here receives oblique support from the findings of Chapter 8, on Thomas Carlyle. The question raised by Mansell as to the "real" date of *The Old Man and the Sea*, although interesting, is peripheral to the hypothesis. See D. Mansell, "The Old Man and the Sea and the Computer," *Computers & the Humanities*, 8 (1974), 195–206.

Chapter 8

[1]Henry James, "The Correspondence of Carlyle and Emerson," *The Century*, XXVI (1883), 272.

[2]John Holloway, *The Victorian Sage* (London, 1953), p. 26.

[3]George Levine, "Use and Abuse of Carlylese," in G.L. Levine and W.A. Madden, eds., *The Art of Victorian Prose* (London, 1968), p. 103.

[4]G.B. Tennyson, *Sartor Called Resartus* (Princeton, 1965).

[5]Grace J. Calder, *The Writing of "Past and Present," Yale Studies in English*, Vol. I, CXVII (New Haven, 1949).

[6]Rene Wellek, "Carlyle and German Romanticism" (1929), in *Confrontations* (Princeton, 1965).

[7]Francis X. Roellinger, Jr., "The Early Development of Carlyle's Style," *PMLA*, LXXII (1957), 950.

[8]Levine, "Use and Abuse," pp. 124–125.

[9]Frederick L. Burwick, "Stylistic Continuity and Change in the Prose of Thomas Carlyle," in L. Dolezel and R. Bailey, eds., *Statistics and Style* (Amsterdam, 1969), p. 184.

[10]*Ibid.,* p. 189.

[11]*Ibid.,* p. 186.

[12]*Ibid.,* p. 187.

[13]Robert Lee Oakman, "Syntax in the Prose Style of Thomas Carlyle," unpublished doctoral dissertation, Indiana University, 1971, p. 82.

[14]*Ibid.,* p. 82.

[15]*Ibid.,* p. 89.

[16]*Ibid.,* p. 91.

[17]*Ibid.,* p. 92.

[18]*Ibid.,* pp. 146–147.

[19]J.W. Smeed, "Thomas Carlyle and Jean Paul Richter," *Comparative Literature,* XVI (1964), 230–253.

[20]Oakman discusses introductory sentence elements on page 88 of "Syntax in the Prose Style," with a somewhat different emphasis.

[21]*Ibid.,* p. 88.

[22]In a range of 22.1% to 25.5%.

[23]The strings are fully catalogued in Chapter 3 above.

[24]Carlyle, *Life of Friedrich Schiller* (London, 1899), p. 40.

[25]*Ibid.,* p. 124.

[26]Carlyle, *Life of Frederick the Great,* 4 Vols. (Boston, 1903), Vol. IV, p. 304.

[27]See Miss Calder's work, cited in note 5 above.

[28] *Past and Present,* p. 47.

[29]A manual count would probably reveal an even greater disparity in seriation between Carlyle and the other Victorians, mainly because so many of Carlyle's series are asymmetrical and interrupted.

[30]From Wellek, "Carlyle and German Romanticism."

[31]Table 8.5, at the end of the chapter, gives a full account of the incidence of classes 982 and 992, and 983 and 993 in our samples. Interestingly, as the exotic punctuation increases, so does the incidence of nominatives of address and exclamations.

[32]Oakman, "Syntax in the Prose Style," p. 82.

[33]*Ibid.*

[34]Burwick, "Stylistic Continuity," p. 185.

[35]*Ibid.*

[36]W. Fucks, "Possibilities of Exact Style Analysis," in J. Strelka, ed., *Patterns of Literary Style* (New York, 1971).

Chapter 9

[1]And, in earlier periods, George Philip Krapp and R.W. Chambers.

[2]L .T. Milic, "Against the Typology of Styles," in Chatman and Levin, eds., *Essays,* p. 448.

[3]See Appendix A for statistical treatment of several aspects of the findings of the Inventory.

[4]"Rank shifting" here is used, as it has been throughout, to denominate a subordinate element containing a verb *or* a verbal; the total number of such rank shifts for any sample can be ascertained by adding together the subordinators, the relatives, and the three kinds of verbals.

[5]Correlative conjunctions (either/or, both/and, not only/but also, etc.) are easy to discern in our time; they were less so before 1800, when several balanced constructions were common (as/so, though/yet). Our inclination in these latter cases was to code the pair as a subordinator (42) and an adverb (04 or 34).

[6]The amount of clausal subordination present in the two passages is, respectively, 7 clauses in 203 words for Ruskin, 3 clauses in 97 words for Strachey—a reduction of 10%, which, when combined with the reduction in sentence length, makes for a major simplification of sentence.

[7]Sprat, like Hemingway, was only a plain talker *about* style. See Mitchell, *Pulpit Oratory*, and Cluett, "Style, Precept."

[8]Both passages are more subordinated than are the total samples from which they are taken. The decline in subordination, as well as in length, however, is illustrated by both the passages and the figures (Table 9.2) for the samples.

[9]The overall decline in density of coordinators suggests that the English sentence might have been reduced in size over the years more through loss of compounding than through loss of complexity.

[10]See pp. 243ff.

[11]Table 9.2. Each man is almost exactly on the mean for his era.

[12]The mean for any era in Table 9.2 is roughly 0.6% of text. Each age seems to produce a Browne or a Strachey (at 0.1% or 0.2%), and each age produces someone relatively high, although the eighteenth and nineteenth centuries did not give us anyone so gerund-prone as either Milton (1.1%) or Fitzgerald (1.4%).

[13]In our study, only Defoe has more participles than Swift. This accords with what Milic noted in *Swift*, an unusual dependence on the verbals. Hazlitt, like Swift, is well above the median for his century in participles.

[14]Ruskin, 9103, *Seven Lamps,* 204.

[15]James R. Sutherland identifies the "conversational" properties of Restoration prose as modernizing. *On English Prose* (Toronto, 1956), *passim.*

[16]Pater, 9104, *Appreciations,* 53.

[17]Newman's has 52 nouns in 244 words (21.3% vs. a total of 21.6% for his entire sample); Mumford's has 36 nouns in 135 words (26.7% vs. a total of 28.4% in his entire sample). A further interesting and, it seems to me, typical, feature of comparison is the length of individual words: Mumford's are perceptibly longer than Newman's.

[18]The term is from H.M. McLuhan, "The Effect of the Printed Book on Language in the Sixteenth Century," in M. McLuhan and E.S. Carpenter, eds., *Explorations in Communication* (Boston, 1960), p. 128.

[19]See "Modifying Styles," Chapter 5, especially Figure 5.13b.

[20]The "M" statistics of the three passages, normalized to 3,500 words, are as follows: for Browne, 350; for Ruskin, 497; for Orwell, 478. Each of these is almost exactly representative of the author, and each in its turn is not far from being representative of its period.

[21]T.R. Lounsbury, *History of the English Language* (College Park, 1970, reissue), p. 448; also Albert C. Baugh, *A History of the English Language* (New York, 1957), p. 221.

[22]Robert A. Peters, in *A Linguistic History of English* (New York, 1968),

notes the tendency of the Modern English sentence to be both shorter and less compounded (pages 233–243, "Comparative Historical Syntax").

[23]R. Cluett and L. Ahlborn, *Effective English Prose* (New York, 1965), pp. 3–14.

[24]Of the 50 writers used for our historical survey, only Davies, Burgess, Mumford, Richler, and Reich are still alive. Of these, Davies is the most conservative in syntax: he is below twentieth-century means for elements that are growing in the language ("M" statistic, 31-01-01, density of unsubordinated sentences, nouns, attributive nouns), and he tends to be above twentieth-century means for elements that are shrinking (rank shifts, subordinators, relatives, correlatives). Richler on the contrary, by and large, especially in the following areas: nouns, relatives, subordinators, density of unsubordinated sentences, and attributive nouns. In these last two areas, he is distinctive in the degree to which he seems to have distanced his contemporaries in the headlong rush to 2001.

Appendix A

[1]The "authorship" hypothesis postulates that the style of a piece of writing is more strongly influenced by the stylistic propensities of its author than it is by the conventions of its genre. The "genre" hypothesis postulates the opposite.

[2]Cluett, "Style, Precept." The different end that I originally had in view was to weaken the "authorship" hypothesis by demonstrating wider dispersions in samples from Sprat than among samples from controls. The numbers did not bear me out.

[3]As a final note to this section, it should be acknowledged that we have not exhausted the possibilities for this kind of test, having used it only as a test of the homogeneity of word-class percentages over different samples. It should also be pointed out that greater homogeneity is not always an earnest of identity; the reader can see by recurring to Figures 8.10b (exclamation points and question marks per sample), 8.13b (attributive nouns), and 8.15a (postmodifying adjectives). In the first two Figures, the four late Carlyle samples show greater dispersion and range than the controls (i.e., *less* homogeneity), but in both cases, Carlyle's style after *Schiller* is markedly deviant; the distortions that reduce homogeneity are in the direction of Carlyle's unique peculiarity. Similarly in Figure 8.15a, where all five Carlyle samples show greater dispersion and range than the controls: Carlyle's lifelong use of postmodifying adjectives was highly idiosyncratic and grew more so with time.

[4]Notice that the statement is confined to the matter of *relative* similarity. In order to assess how "high" or how "good" an r is in some absolute sense, one must perform significance tests. Although in some circumstances with some kinds of data an r of .7 to .8 would be high—as in the correlation between the occurrence of two different word classes in the language at large—such correlations as those between different authors in Table A.2 are low, considering similarity as measured by r (Table A.4). Questions of significance are too complex to deal with here and in any case should be explained by a statistician.

[5]See Karl R. Wallace, *Francis Bacon on Rhetoric* (Chapel Hill, 1943).

[6]Samples 9021 and 9022, 9068 and 9069, 9301 and 9319, respectively.

[7]The fact that determiners correlate more strongly with 51-31-01 than do prepositions seems a mystery. They have done so in every test of this type known to me at present writing, however.

[8]Milic had similar results with the data of his *Swift*. Barron Brainerd, working on 97 of the first 100 samples (1580 to 1700) of the York Inventory, had similar results to these, with the exception of a stronger correlation between determiners and nouns. Further research will be required to ascertain whether this difference is accidental or derives from a genuine difference between the period 1580 to 1700 and the modern period as a whole (i.e., 1580 to 1970).

[9]"Goodness of fit" refers to the degree of match between lines and/or curves on a graph. In Figure A.1, the data of which are drawn from Chapter 6, there is a good fit between the representation of the two Sidney samples, a less good fit between Sidney and Nashe. But, one hastens to add, not nearly so poor a fit as one encounters between Sidney or Nashe and Richler. Figure A.1 represents the following data:

	Nouns	Verbs	Adjectives	Adverbs
Sidney 1	18.4	8.1	6.8	1.6
Sidney 2	18.1	8.9	6.4	1.7
Nashe 2	21.2	8.8	6.9	1.2
Richler	25.4	7.9	8.8	1.5

Figure A.1 GOODNESS OF FIT

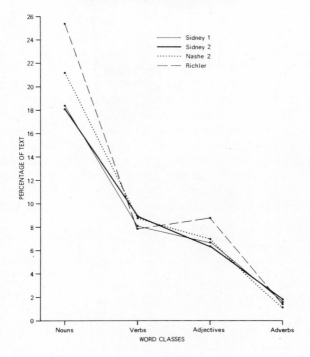

[10]The f_e for nouns is 295/452, for verbs is 94/452, for adjectives is 48/452 and for adverbs is 15/452. For simplicity's sake we have omitted the verbals and the function words; the formula's operation is similar for a 29-class system to what it is for a four-class system.

[11]Once again, derived from a χ^2 table.

[12]Samples 9401 and 9196.

[13]These markings of the Grand Style are discussed in my Sprat article, cited in footnote 2 above.

[14]Barron Brainerd, "Semi-lattices and Taxonomic Systems," *NOUS*, IV (1970), 189–199; "An Exploratory Study of Pronouns and Articles as Indices of Genre in English," *LANGUAGE & STYLE*, 5 (1972), 239–259; "On the Distinction between a Novel and a Romance," *Computers & the Humanities, 7* (1973), 259–270; "On the Number of Words a Character Speaks in the Plays of Shakespeare," *Computer Studies in the Humanities & Verbal Behavior*, IV (1973), 57–63; *Mathematical Linguistics in Automatic Language Processing* (Amsterdam, 1974); *Weighing Evidence in Language and Literature* (Toronto, 1974).

[15]Robert S. Wachal, "Linguistic Evidence."

BIBLIOGRAPHY

This is a list of works that bear *directly* on the research for this book; it does not include a considerable number of works the relevance of which is indirect or in the nature of background.

Adolph, R. *The Rise of Modern Prose Style* (Cambridge, Mass., 1968).

Asselineau, R. *The Literary Reputation of Hemingway in Europe* (New York, 1965).

Babb, H.S., ed. *Essays in Stylistic Analysis* (New York, 1972).

Barrett, William. *Time of Need* (New York, 1972).

Baugh, A.C. *A History of the English Language* (New York, 1957).

Becker, L.J. and Clair Gustafson. *Encounter with Sociology: The Term Paper* (Berkeley, 1965).

Brainerd, Barron. "Semi-lattices and Taxonomic Systems," *NOUS,* IV (1970), 189–199.

———. *Mathematical Linguistics in Automatic Language Processing* (Amsterdam, 1974).

———. *Weighing Evidence in Language and Literature* (Toronto, 1974).

———. "On the Number of Words a Character Speaks in the Plays of Shakespeare," *Computer Studies in the Humanities & Verbal Behavior,* IV (1973), 57–63.

———. "An Exploratory Study of Pronouns and Articles as Indices of Genre in English," *Language & Style,* V (1973), 239–259.

———. "On the Distinction between a Novel and a Romance," *Computers & the Humanities,* VII (1973), 259–269.

Bridgman, Richard W. *The Colloquial Style in America* (New York, 1966).

Calder, Grace J. *The Writing of "Past & Present," Yale Studies in English,* Vol. I, CXII (New Haven, 1949).

Chatman, Seymour, ed. *Literary Style: A Symposium* (New York, 1971).

Chatman, Seymour and S.R. Levin, eds. *Essays on the Language of Literature* (New York, 1967).

Cluett, R. and L. Ahlborn. *Effective English Prose* (New York, 1965).

Cluett, R. "Style, Precept, Personality: A Test Case," *Computers & the Humanities,* V (1971), 257–274.

———. "These Seeming Mysteries . . ." (Columbia University dissertation, 1969).

Corbett, Edward P.J. *Classical Rhetoric for the Modern Student* (New York, 1965).

Croll, Morris W. *Style, Rhetoric, Rhythm* (Princeton, 1966).

Cunningham, J.V. *Problem of Style* (New York, 1966).

Curme, George O. *English Grammar* (New York, 1947).

_____. *Syntax* (Boston, 1931).

Dahl, Roald. *Someone Like You* (New York, 1953).

De Laura, David J., ed. *Victorian Prose: A Guide to Research* (New York, 1973).

Dolezel, L. and R. Bailey, eds. *Statistics and Style* (Amsterdam, 1969).

Donno, Elizabeth S. *Elizabethan Minor Epics* (New York, 1963).

Forster, N. and R. Falk, *American Poetry and Prose* (New York, 1960).

Freeman, Donald C., ed. *Linguistics and Literary Style* (New York, 1970).

Fries, C.C. *The Structure of English* (New York, 1952).

Gutwinski, W.F. "Cohesion in Literary Texts" (University of Connecticut dissertation, 1969).

Holloway, John. *The Victorian Sage* (London, 1953).

Holsti, Ole R. "Computer Content Analysis for Measuring Attitudes," *Computer Studies in the Humanities & Verbal Behavior,* I (1968), 200–216.

James, Henry. "The Correspondence of Carlyle and Emerson," *The Century,* XXVI (1883).

Koerner, James D. *The Miseducation of American Teachers* (Boston, 1964).

Lannering, J. *Studies in the Prose Style of Joseph Addison* (Uppsala, 1951).

Levin, Harry. "Observations on the Style of Hemingway," *Kenyon Review,* XII (1951), 581–609.

Levine, George L. and W.A. Madden, eds. *The Art of Victorian Prose* (London, 1968).

Lounsbury, T.R. *History of the English Language* (College Park, 1970).

Mansell, Darrel. "The Old Man and the Sea and the Computer," *Computers and the Humanities,* VIII (1974), 195–206.

McCrimmon, James M. *Writing with a Purpose: a first course in college composition* (Boston, 1951).

McLuhan, H.M. and E.S. Carpenter, eds. *Explorations in Communication* (Boston, 1960).

Miles, Josephine. *Renaissance, Eighteenth-Century, and Modern Language in English Poetry,* (Berkeley and Los Angeles, 1960).

Milic, L.T. *Style and Stylistics* (New York, 1967).

_____. *Stylists on Style* (New York, 1969).

_____. *A Quantitative Approach to the Style of Jonathan Swift* (The Hague, 1967).

Mitchell, W.F. *English Pulpit Oratory* (London, 1932).

Mosteller, Frederick and David L. Wallace. "Inference in an Authorship Problem," *Journal of the American Statistical Association,* LVIII (1963), 275–309.

Myrick, Kenneth O. *Philip Sidney as a Literary Craftsman* (Cambridge, Mass., 1935).

Oakman, Robert Lee, "Syntax in the Prose Style of Thomas Carlyle" (Indiana University dissertation, 1971).

Orwell, George. "Politics and the English Language," in *The Collected Es-*

says, Journalism and Letters of George Orwell, Sonia Orwell and Ian Argus, eds. (London, 1968).

Peters, Robert A. *A Linguistic History of English* (New York, 1968).

Peterson, Richard K. *Hemingway Direct and Oblique* (The Hague, 1969).

Pyles, T. *Origins and Development of the English Language* (New York, 1964).

Roberts, Paul. *English Sentences* (New York, 1962).

Roellinger, Francis Jr. "The Early Development of Carlyle's Style," *PMLA,* LXXII (1957), 950.

Rovit, Earl. *Ernest Hemingway* (New York, 1963).

Sebeok, Thomas, ed. *Style in Language* (Cambridge, Mass., 1960).

Sherman, Lucius A. *Analytics of Literature* (Boston, 1893).

_____. "On Certain Facts and Principles in the Development of Form in Literature," *University of Nebraska Studies,* I (1892), 337–366.

_____."Some Observations Upon the Sentence Lengths in English Prose," *University of Nebraska Studies,* I (1888), 119–130.

Smeed, J.W. "Thomas Carlyle and Jean Paul Richter," *Comparative Literature,* XVI (1964), 230–253.

Steiner, George. *Language and Silence* (New York, 1967).

Steinmann, Martin, ed. *New Rhetorics* (New York, 1967).

Strelka, J., ed. *Patterns of Literary Style* (New York, 1971).

Suter, J., ed. *A Book of English Collects* (New York, 1925).

Sutherland, J.R. *On English Prose* (Toronto, 1957).

Tennyson, G.B. *Sartor Called Resartus* (Princeton, 1965).

Vickers, B. *Francis Bacon and Renaissance Prose* (Cambridge, 1968).

Wachal, R.S. "Linguistic Evidence, Statistical Inference and Disputed Authorship" (University of Wisconsin dissertation, 1966).

Waldhorn, Arthur, ed. *A Reader's Guide to Ernest Hemingway* (New York, 1972).

Wallace, Karl R. *Francis Bacon on Communication and Rhetoric* (Chapel Hill, 1943).

Wellek, Rene. "Carlyle and German Romanticism" (1929), in *Confrontations* (Princeton, 1965).

White, E.B. and William Strunk. *The Elements of Style* (New York, 1972).

White, H.C., R.C. Wallerstein, and R. Quintana. *Seventeenth Century Verse and Prose* (Madison, 1950).

Williamson, G. *The Senecan Amble* (Chicago, 1952).

Wimsatt, W.K., Jr. *The Prose Style of Samuel Johnson* (New Haven, 1941).

INDEX

311